D1553841

TAJIKISTAN: THE TRIALS OF INDEPENDENCE

TAJIKISTAN:
THE TRIALS OF
INDEPENDENCE

Edited by

Mohammad-Reza Djalili, Frédéric Grare
and
Shirin Akiner

St. Martin's Press
New York

First published as *Le Tadjikistan à l'épreuve de l'indépendance*
by the Graduate Institute of International Studies, Geneva, 1995

St. Martin's Press, Scholarly and Reference Division,
175 Fifth Avenue, New York, N.Y. 10010

First published in the United States of America in 1997
Printed in Great Britain

ISBN 0–312–16143–3

Library of Congress Cataloging in Publication Data

Tadjikistan à l'épreuve de l'indépendance. English
Tajikistan: the trials of independence/edited by Mohammad-Reza
Djalili, Frédéric Grare and Shirin Akiner.
p. cm.
Includes bibliographical references and index.
ISBN 0–312–16143–3 (cloth)
1. Tajikistan–History. I. Djalili, Mohammad-Reza. II. Grare,
Frédéric. III. Akiner, Shirin. IV. Title.
DK928.85.T3313 1997
958.608'6–dc21   97-17189
                               CIP

Thanks to the astonishing ease with which they undertake to change the world, the Russians, once established in Central Asia, that bastion of Sunni Islam, managed to create a secular society in a matter of decades. They made town-dwellers of the chiefly rural and nomadic Turks; the metropolitan and bookish Tajiks they turned into peasants and mountain herders.

Charif and Roustam Choukourov, *Peuples d'Asie centrale*,
Syros, Paris, 1994

Contents

Contents

Acknowledgements

The editors of this book would like to thank the Graduate Institute of International Studies, the Modern Asia Research Centre, the Institute of Development Studies and the Aga Khan Foundation, whose financial support has made this book possible. They would like to express their profound gratitude to Mrs Mariejo Duc, whose work enabled this book to appear, and to Miss Lene Madsen, who did the translations for the first edition. The second edition was translated from French and Russian by Cybele Hay.

M.-R. Djalili is particularly grateful to the Fritz Thyssen Foundation, Cologne, whose support enabled him to carry out a series of studies in Central Asia and the Caucasus.

Note on Transliteration

The approximate and conventional nature of transliteration always makes it a difficult exercise. Central Asia's diversity of languages and frequent alphabet changes give rise to further complications. For the first edition, the editors adopted a policy of non-intervention, leaving the authors free to use whichever method they chose. For the second edition, standard spellings have been used for the principal geographical and personal names. Other transliterations have been changed to make them conform with English, rather than French, spelling conventions, but otherwise left unaltered.

Introduction

Wedged in between Uzbekistan, Kyrgyzstan, China and Afghanistan, Tajikistan is, at 143,000 km², the smallest of the ex-Soviet Central Asian republics and, with some 5.5 million inhabitants, the third most populous. Its peripheral position and mountainous terrain have also made it the least developed country in the CIS, with the lowest rate of urbanisation and the highest demographic growth. Since it achieved independence in September 1991, Tajikistan has been going through a very painful period of transition, punctuated by a series of political crises, which have resulted in the division of its people into rival and antagonistic clans; foreign intervention, chiefly by Russians and Uzbeks; and a civil war spilling over its borders into Afghanistan and Uzbekistan, where thousands of Tajiks have fled for refuge.

This work, which brings together thirteen essays about Tajikistan, takes as its central theme the conflict which erupted in the Republic in 1992.[1] This focus has been chosen not only because the conflict is an important event in the history of this young nation, but also because it highlights the complexities of Tajikistan's situation. The war reveals the deep contradictions eroding Tajik society and at the same time foreshadows events that an 'independent' Tajikistan may undergo in the future. Rooted in the social and historical conditions of Tajikistan, the conflict above all raises questions about the country's identity and its organisation as a separate state.

The Tajiks are the Persian-speakers of former-Soviet Central Asia, and the issue of language lies at the heart of the foundation of the Tajik state. The Republic of Tajikistan, an enclave of Iranian language in a Turcophone area, is defined essentially by this linguistic characteristic, the more so since Stalin's doctrine of nationality, which lay behind the Soviet nation-building project, takes language and territory as the chief defining factors. The language question guided the creation of Tajikistan, fuelled the political debate at times of upheaval, created tensions in the relationship with Uzbekistan, where significant Tajik communities live, and prompted overtures towards the Persian-speaking world outside the former Soviet Union. But the pre-eminence of the Persian language in the Republic does not by itself explain the identity of Tajikistan. The first part of this work, 'Construction of a National Identity', addresses the question of what constitutes Tajik identity. Pierre Centlivres and Micheline Centlivres-Demont examine the ethnic composition of the region and the dynamics which govern relations between ethnic groups. Guissou Jahangiri attempts to trace the political processes through which Tajik identity was formed in the early years of the Soviet period, and evaluates the extent to which its construction has been completed.

The second part of the book, 'Division and Conflict', deals with the tensions and contradictions within contemporary Tajik society, and their escalation into conflict after the break-up of the Soviet Union. Michel Hammer analyses the transition of perestroika, which was not welcomed by the Tajik élite, while Stéphane Dudoignon focuses on the power struggles between the old oligarchy and the new élites which have attempted to emerge since independence. Bess Brown gives a succinct history of the war from the first riots to the stalemate which was achieved after Imomali Rakhmonov took power in Dushanbe.

In the third section, 'The Tajik Conflict and the Wider World', three essays investigate the repercussions of the civil war for other states in the region. Catherine Poujol clarifies Russia's attitudes towards Tajikistan and the other Central Asian states. How far can Russia tolerate the political changes taking place in these countries? How can the will to democratise touted by Moscow be reconciled with its unfailing support for the conservative faction in Dushanbe? How much respect does President Yeltsin's entourage really have for the sovereignty of the fledgling Central Asian states? What is the Russian army's role on the border between Tajikistan and Afghanistan? Is it protecting the neo-Communist Tajik regime against the incursions of the Islamic-democratic opposition? Is its mission to prevent any extension of the Afghan conflict into Tajikistan? Or does Russia merely consider that maintaining stability on this border, separating two theoretically sovereign states, is in its own vital interests, and hence, must be in those of the CIS? The situation in Tajikistan is also of interest to neighbouring countries such as Afghanistan, Pakistan and Iran, argue Mohammad-Reza Djalili and

Introduction

Frédéric Grare. Geographical proximity means that any Afghan government (and a large number of the factions fighting for power in Kabul today) cannot be indifferent to what is happening in Tajikistan. Pakistan, which is seeking to develop an extensive Central Asian policy, cannot conceive of a strategy which would exclude Tajikistan. As for Iran, it is particularly sensitive to anything concerning the only Persian-speaking state of the former USSR. Olivier Roy discusses the usefulness of seeing the crisis as a model of conflicts elsewhere in Central Asia. The Tajik crisis has revealed a tendency in the new power dynamics of Central Asia which has been latent for several years, namely Uzbekistan's desire to 'exteriorise' its power and influence regional relationships in its own favour.

External bodies, national and international, have tried to promote peace and stability in Tajikistan. Their efforts are assessed in the fourth part of this work, 'Peace-Making and Peace-Keeping'. Michael Orr, an authority on military issues, examines the role of the Russian army in the Tajik war. The arduous progress of the Inter-Tajik peace talks is documented and analysed by Irina Zviagelskaya, while Olivier Brenninkmeijer discusses the contribution of the UN and OSCE to peace-building and democratisation in the country.

The situation in Tajikistan is characteristic of the crisis all societies encounter when the downfall of a totalitarian system generates hopes of a radical improvement in individual lives, but is in fact succeeded by economic collapse and gross violations of human rights. The last section, 'Humanitarian Dimensions', deals with the concerns of humanitarian organisations such as the International Committee of the Red Cross (Jean-Marc Bornet) and Amnesty International (Ian Gorvin).

We have included a Bibliography at the end of the book, as a useful aid to readers who wish to continue studying the Tajik situation in the broader context of Central Asia as a whole.

Mohammad-Reza Djalili, Frédéric Grare and Shirin Akiner

Note

1 Most of the papers collected in this book were presented in preliminary form at a colloquium organised in December 1993 in Geneva.

CONSTRUCTION
OF A
NATIONAL IDENTITY

Chapter 1

Tajikistan and Afghanistan: The Ethnic Groups on Either Side of the Border

Pierre Centlivres
Micheline Centlivres-Demont

Tajikistan

The Republic of Tajikistan, established in 1929 on the territory of the former Autonomous Republic of the same name, partially corresponds to the eastern part of the old Emirate of Bukhara; the Emirate also included parts of Turkestan and Badakhshan which are today in Afghanistan (Becker 1968). It was barely 100 years ago, in 1895, that the borders were firmly established between the Emirate, which had become a Russian protectorate, and the Afghanistan of Abdur Rahman, which was under the supervision of British India. The populations of the north-east of Afghanistan and the south of Tajikistan can therefore be considered as one large group which has evolved differently on either side of the border because of different ethnic policies and socio-economic development.

In presenting this study of the peoples of Tajikistan, we have concentrated on the works of Soviet ethnographers, especially B. Kh. Karmysheva; on the *Atlas of the Peoples of the World* of 1964, and on the ethnographic maps in the *Atlas of the Tajik SSR* (1968). It should be noted, however, that ethnographic maps can only give a flat representation of very heterogeneous and complicated realities, and reveal nothing of the dynamism of the various ethnic communities (Centlivres 1979). Ethnic groups are not natural objects but elaborate constructions modelled by the course of history, to which intellectuals, ethnologists, linguists and others occasionally contribute.

In 1895 Abdur Rahman, the Emir of Kabul, had to concede the right bank of the River Panj, which was to become the province of Gorny ('Mountain') Badakhshan, to the Emir of Bukhara, keeping the left bank as part of Afghanistan. The Darya-ye Panj thus became a state border for the first time.[1] Had the balance of power between the regional players been different, the border could have been the River Kokcha, as it was more than 2,000 years ago between Sogdiana and Bactria.

The ethnic distribution in southern Tajikistan is affected by the area's division into several valleys, running from the north-east to the south-west, which carry the tributaries of the Panj and later the Amu.

1. The Soviet *Atlas of Tajikistan* (1968) contains an ethnic map which shows twelve groups, as follows:
   - five groups speaking Turkic languages: Uzbeks, Kyrgyz, Kazakhs, Turkmen and Tatars;
   - six groups speaking Indo-European languages: Tajiks, Russians, Ukrainians, Germans, Gypsies and the so-called Central Asian Jews;
   - a group formed by several non-Arabic-speaking Arab communities which live in the villages along the Afghan border, in the south-west of the country, in an area which is otherwise Turcophone.

As might be expected, their geo-ecological distribution is to some extent similar to that in north-eastern Afghanistan. The Tajiks, a common term for Persian-speaking populations of diverse origin, live partly in villages in the high valleys and partly in towns; the people called by cartographers and ethnologists Pamiris or Mountain Tajiks, the Galchas of ancient times, inhabit the mountainous Autonomous Province of Gorny Badakhshan in the south-east, where there are also encampments of Kyrgyz. The Uzbeks, according to the 1968 *Atlas*, live along the lower reaches of the valleys in the south-west of Tajikistan and close to the border with Uzbekistan. Still in the southern half of the country, the Uzbeks are predominant around Shaartuz, Regar, Kurgan-Tyube, Panj and Kulyab, and to the south of Dushanbe. German settlers are mentioned in Dushanbe and around Vakhsh, along the lower reaches of the river of that name. Russians figure on the map as isolated points, particularly in the towns – except to the east of Khojent, where their presence is given as massive – and in the Vakhsh Valley and Kulyab. Kazakhs can be found along the border with Afghanistan in the south-west; Turkmen in lower Kafirnigan.

2. The ethnic map in the *Atlas of the Peoples of the World* (*Atlas Narodov Mira*), which appeared a few years earlier in 1964, enumerates nineteen ethnic groups for Tajikistan. This is because it

4

lists as separate entities six populations which are, often disputably, known as Mountain Tajiks. This purely geographic title corresponds neither to a real ethnic unit, nor to an indigenous appellation. The six groups are Ismaili Muslims who live in Gorny Badakhshan and speak East Iranian languages. They call themselves by names derived from their places of origin. Four of them, the Rushanis, Shughnanis, Ishkashimis and Wakhis, are also to be found in north-eastern Afghanistan. A residual group from the Hissar region, the Yagnobis, now displaced and assimilated, is also mentioned in this map.

In any case, these twelve or nineteen ethnic groups seem few in comparison to the 57 ethnic groups of Afghanistan which figure in the Tübingen *Atlas* (Orywal 1983). Limiting ourselves to the Afghan north, there appears to be far greater ethnic splintering to the south than to the north of the Amu Darya. This is because Soviet ethnographers, in conformity with the theory and ideology of the nation-building process, gathered several groups together under the names of Tajik and Uzbek, and treated them as homogeneous entities. The Communist conception of nations and nationalities rested on the hypothesis that ethnic minorities and marginal groups would move closer to, and eventually merge with, the ethnic groups chosen to form the Uzbek and Tajik nations. Soviet cartographers and ethnographers thus reduced and integrated Persian- or Iranian-speaking groups into the bosom of the Tajik whole, and Turkic-speakers into the Uzbek whole. But the works of these ethnographers still contain traces and descriptions of numerous groups of Turkic-speakers who are distinct from the ethnic Uzbeks of Uzbekistan and Tajikistan. They have been described and explained in greater detail than those of Afghanistan, but the same Turkic-speaking groups, often assimilated with Uzbeks by outsiders but distinguished by the populations themselves, can be found on both sides of the border.

Let us consider the Turcophone population. Soviet ethnologists see two main components in the Uzbek whole (Karmysheva 1960 and 1964):

a) The first is composed of Turcophones who have over a long period of time adopted an agricultural and urban way of life; a sedentary people without tribal divisions. In the old Emirate they were called Sarts, Tats or even Tajiks, regardless of the language they spoke.

b) The second consists of groups who have kept the name and sometimes the subdivisions of their tribe. At the beginning of this

5

century, they were still cattle-breeders and often semi-nomadic; others pursued a pastoral agricultural lifestyle similar to that of the Persian-speakers of the mountain regions.

The classification of the second component is still relevant today.

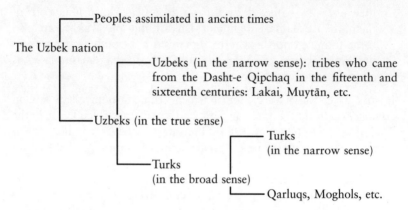

The Uzbek nation

— Peoples assimilated in ancient times

— Uzbeks (in the true sense)

— Uzbeks (in the narrow sense): tribes who came from the Dasht-e Qipchaq in the fifteenth and sixteenth centuries: Lakai, Muytān, etc.

— Turks (in the broad sense)

— Turks (in the narrow sense)

— Qarluqs, Moghols, etc.

The first category in this second component consists of the Uzbeks in the narrow sense, who emerged in the *Dasht-e Qipchaq*[2] in about the fourteenth century and migrated to Transoxiana in the sixteenth century under the leadership of Mohammad Shaybani Khan (1500–10). These Uzbeks assert membership of a particular tribe (e.g., the Ming, Kungrad, Lakai, Muytān, Mangit or Qataghan), sometimes even of a tribal subdivision. The Qataghan, in particular, gave its name to an erstwhile province of Afghanistan (Centlivres 1975). Since the eighteenth century at least, forced migrations have accelerated the dispersion of the Uzbek tribes on both banks of the Amu Darya. The last but one major migration on both sides of the Panj-Amu took place after the *Basmachi* uprising in the 1920s and the forced collectivisations of the early 1930s.[3] A significant number of the *Muhajir* at that time were Turkmen and Uzbeks, among the latter thousands of Kungrad and Lakai from Transoxiana (Centlivres and Centlivres-Demont 1988b).[4] Some of their descendants are currently (1994) living in Pakistani Baluchistan, some of them at least waiting to return to northern Afghanistan.

The second category comprises the Turcophone peoples who were already living in Tajikistan, Uzbekistan and Afghanistan before the arrival of Shaybani's Uzbek tribes. They have preserved their own identity, the names of their groups, their habitat and their dialects.

They are to be found on both sides of the border. Their neighbours often call them Turks; however, the ethnonym Turk is only adopted by some of these people; the others call themselves names which evoke the Turco-Mongol invasions of the thirteenth to fifteenth centuries. The best-known groups are the Qarluqs, who live near the River Kokcha in Afghanistan – where we studied them around Rustaq in the 1970s – as well as in the Zarafshan Valley in the north of Tajikistan, and in the southern part of the Republic. Some Afghan Qarluqs fled Afghanistan at the time of Abdur Rahman to establish themselves around Kulyab. Another group, the Moghols, live around Taliqan and to the south of Faizabad in Afghanistan, and around Hissar and on the right bank of the Panj in Tajikistan. Established in Transoxiana during the time of Timur/Tamerlane (1336–1405), some of them removed to Afghanistan under pressure from Russia and Bukhara in the nineteenth century; they returned at the end of the century, but they or their children emigrated to Afghanistan again during the period of enforced collectivisation. This centuries-long, often tragic to-ing and fro-ing shows no sign of coming to an end. One could mention other groups here, too, such as the Barlas, who bear the name of a Mongol tribe.

The distinct identities of these Turks, in the broad sense, were and still are based on minor linguistic differences within the East Turkic group and on their geographical distribution at different levels in the landscape. They were displaced by the Shaibanid Uzbeks onto higher land: upstream and into the foothills, between the high mountain areas of the Tajiks and the plains where the Uzbeks raised cattle. A precise study of political affiliations and rebellions, from the Soviet Revolution and the Basmachi uprising to collectivisation, and on to the post-Soviet era, would probably reveal the role played by regional struggles in political alignments, which, as in Afghanistan, are influenced by ethnic and regional differences.

The North-East of Afghanistan

The north-east of Afghanistan comprises the provinces of Kunduz, Baghlan and Takhar, formerly collectively known as Qataghan, and the province of Badakhshan.[5] The region to the north and east of Faizabad is ethnically homogeneous, peopled by Tajiks, but this term covers a number of groups and self-designations; the Pamiri peoples are often classed separately, as we have seen, for linguistic and religious reasons. To the extreme north-east live the Pamir Kyrgyz. In

7

summer, the relative homogeneity of the region gives way to great ethnic plurality with the arrival of Arab, Uzbek, and Pashtun herders practising transhumance in the region of Ragh, Esh and Shewa. Qataghan and the banks of the Kokcha, on the other hand, have a very diverse population, which comprises communities of Dari-speakers (Tajiks, Hazaras and Baluchis), Turkic-speakers (Uzbeks, Moghols and Qarluqs), as well as strong Pashtun colonies, to mention only the principal groups.

While the north-east of Badakhshan and the high valleys of the Hindu Kush have retained an ethnic make-up similar to that which existed before the twentieth century, the foothills and loess hills harbour a chiefly Turcophone population pushed back by migrations onto the plains, and in this century by colonists who moved into the lands around Kunduz, Taliqan and Baghlan, and, further to the north-east, into the area next to the Amu Darya (Darkat, Dasht-i Qala, Yangi Qala). This new wave of migration was linked to the internal colonisation policy pursued by the Kabul government between 1920 and 1960, and the large-scale irrigation works that accompanied it; as a result unruly populations had to be settled, and a large area inhabited mainly by Uzbek herders had to be Pashtunised. These newly-colonised regions exhibit remarkable ethnic diversity, with Pashtuns predominating.

Let us take two examples: Rustaq District, situated among the loessial hills near the Kokcha, and Yangi Qala, further north, near the Panj. Both are in Takhar Province (Centlivres 1976a, Centlivres-Demont 1976).

Rustaq

Up to 1980, the Tajiks represented about a third of the 70 to 80,000 inhabitants of Rustaq District. Apart from an indigenous minority, their origins are varied: Badakhshan, Lower Qataghan, north of Kabul, the Kulyab region. They are merchants in the bazaar and farmers.

Under Babur (at the beginning of the sixteenth century), the Hazaras took up residence in the south of Rustaq, on the ravine-scarred slopes where they practise agriculture and pastoralism; there are not much more than 1,500 of them. Unlike the majority of Afghan Hazaras, those of Rustaq are Sunnis, and as such are traditionally and prudently allied to the Tajiks. The Baluchis (numbering about 10,000), who probably came from Badakhshan with the troops of the Afghan Shah Ahmad in 1768, spread out from Kishm in Afghanistan to Kulyab in Tajikistan, and speak the languages of their Tajik and Uzbek neighbours. The Baluchis of Rustaq live in the lowest part of the district, along the river. The Turcophones are divided into two population groups, the Uzbeks and the Qarluqs, which are almost equal in number with 13,000 people in each. They occupy the loessial hills on the right bank of the Kokcha; formerly herders, they now practise dry cereal farming with a little sheep- and horse-breeding. They are the neighbours and allies of the Uzbeks who came as conquerors in the sixteenth century; the latter cultivate the irrigated lands in the valley. Rustaq is too far from the irrigated lands of Lower Qataghan and the large axes of communication to have been much disturbed by Pashtun colonisation.

The Tajiks and their Hazara allies somewhat outnumber the Turcophones, which makes the Baluchis the arbitrators in the equation. Settled in an Uzbek area, they side most often with the Uzbeks and Qarluqs, no doubt to resist assimilation or subordination by the Tajiks.

Yangi Qala

In contrast to the relatively stable situation in Rustaq, where each group occupies and controls a defined space, the district of Yangi Qala (which comprises the border localities of Darkat and Dasht-i Qala) on the bank of the Panj, is a mosaic of little groups of varied origin. In this fragmented and unstable ethnic configuration, alliances tend to be formed according to economic rather than ethnic interests: there is a perennial struggle for possession of irrigated lands.

From the 1920s, King Amanullah's governors undertook irrigation works and encouraged colonisation by non-native groups. The Qandaharis, sheep- and camel-breeding Pashto-speakers, arrived from the north-west of Afghanistan. They belonged to tribes that Abdur Rahman had hoped to settle in the north-west at the end of the nineteenth century. At the same time, cultivators began to arrive from the south, either voluntarily or as a result of deportation. These were Pashto-speaking tribesmen who had periodically rebelled against the power of Kabul, which now displaced them and turned them into government-sponsored colonists.

These newcomers clashed with the Uzbek herders and the Tajik, Qarluq and Moghol agriculturists, who were pushed out of the irrigated lands up towards the loess hills where only pluvial agriculture is possible. The Qandahari herders, meanwhile, were driven away from the banks of the Amu, which were taken over for agricultural purposes. Colonisation and irrigation benefited the Pashtuns at the expense of the indigenous groups, and agriculture at the expense of animal-breeding. This was in fact the political aim of the Afghan authorities.

Politics

Although some ethnic groups in the region, such as the Baluchis for example, have been totally assimilated linguistically, and although ways of life tend to become homogeneous, the sense of identity, of belonging to a community distinct from other communities, is still acute, and is perpetuated by marriage choices and the use of ethnonyms. In politics opposition between neighbouring communities is the logic underlying the alliances and conflicts between the leaders.

In 1969, during the Parliamentary elections in Rustaq, the Uzbeks, Qarluqs and Baluchis had only one candidate, a Baluchi, competing against the Tajiks and their Hazara allies; he very nearly won, but the Tajiks employed a more up-to-date strategy. The Uzbeks and Qarluqs relied on their traditional ethnic and tribal patronage system, whereby arbābs, the petty chiefs of villages and tribes, make their clans vote according to kinship criteria. The Tajiks, on the other hand, managed to offer economic benefits, in the form of presents to prominent people, and thus attract minorities. Chief among these were the Moghols, who, despite sharing their language with the Uzbeks and occupying the same terrain, were anxious to mark their difference from the latter, and hence an easy prey for the Tajiks.

Under the Communist government (1978–92), political affiliations largely followed ethnic lines:

- The Qarluqs of Rustaq chose either the Kabul camp or Hekmatyar's Islamists, following the logic of opposition to the Tajik majority, who joined the Jamiat movement of the commander Massoud.
- The situation of the Pashtuns of Yangi Qala was played out on two levels, political and ethnic. The majority sided with the Mujahidin (Hekmatyar's Hezb-e Islami and Sayyaf's Ettehad-e Islami);[6] others were chased off their land by Tajiks and Uzbeks who took advantage of weak central power to try to regain the lands taken from them by the Pashtun powers in Kabul.

10

Within the Resistance, alliances and divisions worked in the same way. Since the Tajiks of Badakhshan, with the exception of the Ismailis (Emadi 1993), and of Qataghan rallied to Massoud and the Jamiat, the other ethnic groups affiliated themselves with other parties. The Tajiks' closest neighbours, the Moghols of Argu (south of Faizabad) and the Uzbeks of Aliabad, joined the Hezb-e Islami. Sayyaf and his Ettehad-e Islami had, and still have, supporters among the Pashtuns. Since the capture of Khwoja-e Ghar by Massoud in 1991, the region of Yangi Qala has been controlled by the Jamiat (1993).

For both Uzbeks and Tajiks, 'national' identity and the feeling of belonging to an ethnic group in the broad sense have probably emerged reinforced from the conflict. Over and above partisan-ethnic fragmentation, the aspiration to belong to a larger community is making itself felt. The rejection of Pashtun domination and the nationality policies of the Communist government have played their part in this process. In the north and north-west of Afghanistan, General Dostom symbolises for many Turcophones the aspirations of the Uzbek nation; the Uzbek and Moghol officers of the Hezb-e Islami, though ostensibly supporters of Hekmatyar, still take General Dostom as their authority.

Let us conclude by returning to the question of identity. Though it may be correct that the term Tajik is often a self-designation and a word used to claim membership of a nationality, it should be pointed out that Tajik ethnicity, in the sense of a clear, stable, indisputable sense of belonging, is less prominent than Uzbek or Turkmen ethnicity. In practice, those whom we describe as Tajiks often call themselves by regional names – Panshiri, Darwazi, Rāghi (Centlivres and Centlivres-Demont 1988c).

The Uzbeks have an ethnic history; they can be identified and recognise themselves in identities which are fairly substantial, evoking a precise origin and an etymology which, while perhaps mythical, still has some foundation and is drawn from an eponymous ancestor. The case of the Tajiks, on the other hand, is much more ambiguous. Tajik national identity lacks clarity. The obscurity of the term's origin is one indicator, among others (see Dupree 1978 and Orywal 1986, p. 22). *Tāz* or *Tāt*, indeed, seems to have been a term for 'Arab' in the Sassanid period, used by Iranians to designate the Arabs living in Iran, right up to Islamic times. Others take it to be a term used by the Arabs just after their conquest of Central Asia to designate the Persian-speakers there, as opposed to the Turkic-speakers. It may then have been used by the Turcophones to mean the Muslims of Central Asia, and after their own conversion to Islam, the name *Tāzik* may have referred to the Iranian-speaking sedentary population, in other words the section of the population which had not been Turkicised.

This process of designating others by the absence of a characteristic is similar to that which one sees today in many areas of Afghanistan, where *Tāzik* is used by the Pashtuns to mean non-Pashtuns, whether they are Persian-speakers or not. The case of Afghanistan is useful in showing that the term can have a great variety of referents, often groups which lack a positive identity, and is devoid of almost any ethnic significance (Centlivres 1976b). The ethnonym *Tāzik* has therefore, for better or worse, been constructed around a label attached to a variety of peoples. It would appear that in Afghanistan the term has historically been used, and in some cases still is being used, to designate diverse populations which do not belong to the (usually dominant) group of the speaker. The awakening of nationalities in Afghanistan and the situation in Tajikistan show that this state of affairs has not yet changed completely.

Notes

1 The Panj takes the name of Amu after its confluence with the River Vakhsh.
2 'Desert of the Qipchaqs', the region north of the Caspian Sea, around the lower Volga, where the Golden Horde, the western most khanate of the Mongol empire, established itself after the death of Genghis Khan.
3 The Basmachis were Muslim guerillas who resisted the Soviet Revolution in Central Asia in the 1920s and 1930s.
4 A Muhajir is one who voluntarily goes into exile, especially for religious reasons, when the regime in power does not allow the free practice of Islam.
5 Between 1966 and 1974, we undertook several research trips to the north-east, north and north-west of Afghanistan (Centlivres and Centlivres-Demont 1977 and 1988a). Our research was primarily concerned with ethnic identity and inter-ethnic relations; it was made possible thanks to financial aid from the Swiss National Foundation for Scientific Research.
6 The seven Afghan resistance parties recognised by the government of Pakistan largely follow two tendencies: 'moderate' and 'Islamic'. The parties of G. Hekmatyar and Sayyaf belong to the second tendency.

Bibliography

ATLAS NARODOV MIRA. Akademia Nauk SSSR, Moscow, 1964.
ATLAS TADZHIKSKOJ SSR. Dushanbe and Moscow, 1968.
BECKER, Seymour. *Russia's Protectorates in Central Asia: Bukhara and Khiva, 1865–1924*, Harvard University Press, Cambridge, Mass., 1968.

Tajikistan and Afghanistan

CENTLIVRES, Pierre. 'Les Uzbeks du Qattaghan', *Afghanistan Journal*, 2 (1), 1975, pp. 28–36.

—— 'L'histoire récente de l'Afghanistan et la configuration ethnique des provinces du Nord-Est', *Studia Iranica*, 5 (2), 1976a, pp. 255–67.

—— 'Problèmes d'identité ethnique dans le nord de l'Afghanistan', *Actes du XXIXe Congrès international des Orientalistes. Iran moderne*, Vol. 1, Paris, 1976b, pp. 8–13.

—— 'Groupes ethniques: de l'hétérogénéité d'un concept aux ambiguïtés de la représentation. L'exemple afghan', in Ehlers, E. (ed.), *Beiträge zur Kulturgeographie des islamischen Orients*, Geographisches Institut der Universität Marburg, Marburg and Lahn, 1979, pp. 25–37. (Marburger Geographische Schriften 78.)

CENTLIVRES, Pierre and CENTLIVRES-DEMONT, Micheline. 'Chemins d'été, chemins d'hiver entre Darwaz et Qataghan', *Afghanistan Journal*, 4 (4), 1977, pp. 155–63.

—— *Et si on parlait de l'Afghanistan?*, Institut d'ethnologie, Neuchâtel and Maison des Sciences de l'Homme, Paris, 1988a.

—— 'Frontières et phénomènes migratoires en Asie centrale: le cas de l'Afghanistan de 1880 à nos jours', 1988b, in *Et si on parlait de l'Afghanistan?*, pp. 247–74.

—— 'Pratiques quotidiennes et usages politiques des termes ethniques dans l'Afghanistan du Nord-Est', in Digard, J.-P. (ed.), *Le fait ethnique en Iran et en Afghanistan*, Editions du CNRS, Paris, 1988c, pp. 233–46.

CENTLIVRES-DEMONT, Micheline. 'Types d'occupation et relations inter-ethniques dans le Nord-Est de l'Afghanistan', *Studia Iranica*, 5 (2), 1976, pp. 269–77.

DUPREE, Louis. 'Tajik', in Weekes, Richard V. (ed.), *Muslim Peoples. A World Ethnographic Survey*, Greenwood Press, Westport, Col. and London, 1978, pp. 389–95.

EMADI, Hafizullah. 'Minority group politics: the role of Ismailis in Afghanistan's politics', *Central Asian Survey*, 12 (3), 1993, pp. 379–92.

KARMYSHEVA, B. Kh. 'Etnograficheskaja gruppa tjurk v sostave uzbekov', *Sovetskaja etnografija*, 1, 1960, pp. 3–22.

—— *On the history of population formation in the Southern areas of Uzbekistān and Tādjikistan (Ethnographic data)*, Nauka Publishing House, Moscow, 1964. (VII International Congress of Anthropological and Ethnological Sciences, Moscow, August 1964.)

ORYWAL, Erwin. *Afghanistan: Ethnische Gruppen* (map), Dr Ludwig Reichert, Wiesbaden, 1983. (*Tübinger Atlas des Vorderen Orients* (*TAVO*), A VIII 16.)

—— (ed.). *Die ethnischen Gruppen Afghanistans. Fallstudien zu Gruppenidentität und Intergruppenbeziehungen*, Dr Ludwig Reichert, Wiesbaden, 1986. (*Beihefte zum Tübinger Atlas des Vorderen Orients*, Reihe B 70.)

Chapter 2

The Premises for the Construction of a Tajik National Identity, 1920–1930

Guissou Jahangiri

How can one be Tajik? We are not dealing here with Montesquieu's question, prompted by astonishment at the exoticism of a people with strange customs; nor yet with that of the sociologist interested in the 'formation of national identity': rather, it was the substance of a project launched by the *Nezārat-e Mo'āref* ('Commissariat of Education') of Tajikistan[1] and its organs, a number of journals published in the Tajik language from 1924 onwards.

The main task of the Nezārat-e Mo'āref, under the direction of 'comrade' Abbas Aliev,[2] was to set up a huge education and literacy programme in the Autonomous Province of Tajikistan.[3] To do this, it was necessary to create a network in the *velāyet* (Russian: *oblast'*, 'province'), build and equip schools, mobilise and train teachers, produce teaching materials which conformed to Leninist precepts, and, finally, convince the population of the merits of a new Soviet education. The obstacles to such an ambitious project were monumental. How could an agricultural and mountain-dwelling population, over 99% of whom were illiterate, be mobilised *en masse*, in a region controlled by the local clergy and *bāy* ('rich landowners'), which was heavily involved in the *Basmachi* movement, and where road and rail communications were practically non-existent?[4]

The publication and dissemination of journals was intended to unify those involved in this educational initiative. But their role far surpassed that of a mere newsletter. The Leninist plan for the peoples of the East was founded on the emergence of autonomous nations, which presupposed the assertion of a native culture which could allow the emergence of a national identity. From this point of view, the journals were to act as an instrument for working out and asserting a Tajik national culture. Since the plan for the Persian-speaking population was relatively vague, and particularly because it involved

14

a change in status for Tajikistan from that of an Autonomous Republic within the Soviet Socialist Republic of Uzbekistan to that of a full Union Republic, the journals did not limit themselves to running through a predetermined programme, but became a forum for conflicting points of view. They were at once pedagogical magazines, academic reviews and a ready platform for the expression of a nascent Tajik nationalism.

Taken together, these journals represent, therefore, a quite extraordinary source for understanding the process of 'national construction' in the crucial period of the 1920s. They contain evidence of three kinds. The first relates to intellectual history: through their active participation in the formation of a Tajik national identity, these journals came to occupy a founding position in the intellectual debate of the period, marking a sharp break with the Tajik intellectuals trained in the *Jadid* and Pan-Turkic movements.[5] The second kind of information in these documents concerns the educational operation set up to rally the Tajiks round the Socialist project and the nationalist identity. However, these journals have a third, and transcendent, interest, in that they are in fact the only Tajik-language publications of the period, and one can read in them, between the lines which affirm the official doctrine, the problems that were encountered. We will here try to define the scope that was permitted at the time to such a position of national self-assertion, the groups which became its standard-bearers, and the effects it produced.

The study will be based on three publications:

Avāz-e tājik-e kambaghal ('Voice of the Poor Tajik'),[6] the mouthpiece of the Committee of the provincial Party and of the Provincial Executive Committee of Samarkand, a weekly that described itself as 'political, social and literary'. The journal was printed on four to six large-format pages, in a print run of 2,000 copies. The first issue was published on 25 August 1924.[7] The editor-in-chief was Abdolqayūm Ghorbi;[8] its office was at the premises of the Uzbek review *Zarafshān* in Samarkand.

Dānesh va āmuzegār ('Knowledge and the Teacher'), the first fortnightly Tajik review,[9] was the organ of the Nezārat-e Mo'āref, and claimed to be 'political, social, pedagogical, literary, technical, scientific and critical'. It had 36 pages, the first issue being dated 5 March 1926. Abbas Aliev, the Commissar of Education himself, was the editor-in-chief. The review was published in Dushanbe, which became the capital in 1924, at the offices of the Nezārat. It was chiefly aimed at teachers.

15

Dānesh-binesh ('Knowledge and Insight') was a monthly 'scientific and pedagogical' review published by the Nezārat, which comprised 42 pages and was first issued on 1 August 1927. It was published in Samarkand under the direction of an editorial board, and printed in 1,500 copies by the press of *Avāz-e tājik-e kambaghal*.[10] The journal later changed its name to *Rahbar-e dānesh* ('Leader of Knowledge'),[11] a monthly 'social, pedagogical, technical and literary' review, also emanating from the Commissariat for Education. Thirty-six pages long, it was published for the first time on 1 September 1927 in Tashkent. An editorial committee was in charge of the review, whose print run was 1,500 copies. The journal concentrated primarily on the science of education and pedagogy.

I We are Tajiks!

Any political project which refers in any way to tradition comes up against the same problem: it is trying to bring about something that, to justify itself, must be supposed to exist already. Whence the paradoxical nature of the arguments: one must assert that the thing one seeks to establish has been there all along. This tension was particularly prevalent in the case of Tajikistan, so that the editors of these reviews had to devote a good deal of energy to refuting charges, sometimes even levelled by Tajiks who subscribed to Pan-Turkic ideas, that there was no such thing as a specific Tajik identity.

1 The Tajik People and its Territory

The definition of 'Tajikness', and of the territory on which the Tajik population lived, were questions open to lively debate. Definitions based on identity papers were discussed, as several Tajiks had been forced to declare themselves Uzbeks,[12] as well as those based on the use of the language, since the Uzbeks claimed that a large part of the population was Uzbek-speaking. The question was particularly relevant to the inhabitants of the centres of Tajik civilisation, Samarkand, Khojent and Bukhara.

On this issue, Esmā'ilzāde[13] had to reply to the arguments of Biktāsh, a Tajik sympathetic to the views of the Pan-Turkists.[14] Biktāsh apparently disagreed with one inhabitant of Samarkand who thought that, since the majority of the inhabitants of his city were Tajiks, there should be Tajik-language schools, newspapers and publications. Esmā'ilzāde stressed that despite some elements of

Uzbekification (such as declarations on personal documents), the people were still Tajiks:

> The Tajiks are third in number after the Uzbeks and Kyrgyz. Who, after all, are the inhabitants of the Pamirs, of Samarkand, of Khojent, of Bukhara and of Karategin? What does it matter if they have taken Uzbek names instead of their Tajik names? As if the inhabitants of the Pamirs were not Tajiks. These words are only used by strong nations in order to trample on the rights of others.

Some months later Biktāsh was on the offensive again in an article published in the Turcophone review *Zarafshān*,[15] asserting that only 25% of the inhabitants of Khojent spoke Tajik: 'Why is there so much fuss made trying to denounce the fact that the Tajiks do not study in their own language? Young and old alike speak Uzbek there.' Referring to his own experience as a teacher, Mohammad Hassani contradicted these claims, insisting that the majority of children did not speak Uzbek, and that the use of this language was limited to the children of wealthy merchants. According to him, poor people and peasants did not know Uzbek. Furthermore, he cited this as the reason why the Uzbek newspapers in Khojent were so little read. In support of his argument, he drew a chart of the Tajik, Uzbek and Kyrgyz populations of Khojent and Ura-Tyube, based on a census conducted in 1924.[16] The Tajik population of Khojent comprised 34,846 inhabitants (96%), compared with 501 Uzbeks (1.05%); the figures for Ura-Tyube were 15,197 (80.09%) and 3,473 (18.03%) respectively.

The language question also came up with reference to the city of Bukhara:

> After the creation of the Central Asian republics, this question [of finding out if the inhabitants of Bukhara were Tajiks or not] took on great importance and one can say without a doubt that in the future, the Party and the Soviet government will consider the resolution of this problem as an important factor in the nationality question, and will try very seriously to remedy it, since the present situation in Bukhara as well as the present state of the question are wrong.[17]

The author of this article, E. Mohiyedinov, noted that in fact, in the results of the Uzbek population questionnaires of 1926, all the inhabitants of Bukhara and its environs were counted as Uzbeks, apart from a depleted population, called '*fārs-tājik*', which was only a small group of Shiite Muslims and did not include all the Tajiks in the city. These statistics astonished Mohiyedinov, who wondered how nationality could possibly be founded on religion.[18] He suggested that the reader address this question to the Statistics Office of Uzbekistan. People were already saying that Bukhara had fallen into the hands of Uzbekistan through political betrayals, blunders and omissions committed by officials who had been influenced by Pan-Turkism and Pan-Islamism during the final years of the Republic of Bukhara.[19] Another section of the population had also been counted as Tajik, namely the Jews of Bukhara; according to Mohammadjān Shokuri,[20] it was thanks only to their existence that the term 'Tajik' figured in Uzbek censuses. Demonstrations against the results of the census were organised by the Tajik population. In response, a special commission was set up in Moscow under the direction of Kuybyshev to settle the dispute. However, although a second commission was set up by Stalin after the war, the question remained unresolved, some say because of Uzbek pressure.

A second argument against the Tajik nation was that the criterion of language did not help to define a unified and contiguous territory. Indeed, out of an estimated population of 1,240,000 (the Tajiks of the Republics of Turkestan and of Bukhara),[21] 800,000 were left outside the newly delimited Autonomous Republic. Moreover, the mountainous regions of Karategin and Machah remained isolated because of the lack of communications; this explains why roads and a railway line had to be built straight away. The territorial problem was highlighted by the difficult question of where to locate the journals, particularly because the Tajiks' intellectual centres, the cities of Samarkand and Bukhara, were not to be included in the essentially rural Autonomous Province of Tajikistan. 'Since Samarkand is the centre of the Tajiks of Turkestan,'[22] the Central Committee of the Party encouraged the launching of *Avāz-e tājik-e kambaghal* there. Moreover, in the contribution which the Uzbek Republic and its officials were to make to the construction of Tajikistan, it was decided at the meeting of the Sub-Commission of the Central Commission on National and Regional Divisions on 24 July 1924 that the large Tajik towns – Bukhara, Samarkand and others – should become temporary cultural centres used for training the cadres who would then go on to work in eastern Bukhara.[23]

The response to this challenge to the specificity of Tajikistan also included the promotion of research about the region. For 'he who does not know what he possesses is not its owner'. Subjects such as the history of Tajikistan, its geography, resources, peoples, folklore and traditions, were promoted by these journals as a new science, '*molk shenāsi*' ('knowing one's country').[24] It was largely a case of inventing a discipline since there were no books specifically about the new Tajikistan, apart from a Russian work produced by a 'Tajikology' association of European scientists which met in Tashkent in 1925.[25] The only reliable and valuable source was translated fragments of the works of V. Barthold.[26] The first appeals for the production of a history of the Tajiks were thus regularly made in *Avāz-e tājik-e kambaghal*. Often the articles would have to start with an explanation such as 'this is who we are, this is where we are geographically situated, we have such and such regions and this is what we cultivate in each region' etc.[27] It was also necessary to increase the standing of the territory and create a sense of local pride. 'The mountain-dwellers are still of the Aryan type and have a purer language than others.'[28]

2 The Tajik Language

Critics would go even further and call the Tajik language into question. The first type of argument consisted in labelling it not a local language but the contemptible leftovers of an external influence. The inhabitants of Bukhara, Samarkand and Khojent had, so the argument went, lost their original Turkic language as a result of Iranian oppression, which had forced them to speak Persian.

> These people were originally Uzbeks who became Tajik speakers under the influence of Persian civilisation and literature. We are bringing them back to their original language and nationality ... Uniformity is a condition of progress; if we 'Uzbekify' the Tajiks of Bukhara we are doing civilisation a service ... Although Pan-Turkic and Pan-Islamic ideas have lost their currency today, they have been replaced by a form of neo-nationalism [*now mellat-chigi*] of Uzbekism.[29]

Sadriddin Aini's work, *Nemune-ye adabiyāt-e tājik* ('A Sample of Tajik Literature'), which exhumed the works of Persian-speaking poets and writers who had lived in Central Asia, was a response to this argument.

This supposed return to an original language was presented as the true path to progress. A writer in the journal *Turkestan* considered that 'wanting to use the Tajik language is only moving further away

19

from the modern world, using a language which has become rare and is superfluous. It is vital that the Tajiks revert immediately to the Uzbek language and stop pursuing the specific Tajik language, for the Socialist movement of history has settled its fate.'[30] Biktāsh put this change in the context of a general process of integration: 'We are certain that the strong attraction of Uzbek civilisation will soon put an end to these disorders. We have seen similar examples in a number of cases. The Tatars of Lithuania, in particular, mingled with Russian society and lost their language.'[31] In response, Esmā'ilzāde stressed that the Tatars lost their language not through peaceful contact with the Russians but because of the latter's 'despotic reign, the watchword of which was imperialism'. The author then went on to criticise this attitude in the name of Communism and of the Soviet government, and added: 'The Uzbek civilisation which is progressing thanks to the Soviet government and our Party should turn to the smaller peoples which today want to open their eyes and influence them in a good way, not a bad'.

Another criticism, springing from *proletkult* ideas, challenged a language that had not produced a literature which suited its revolutionary principles. Thus, for example, it was written in 1928 that the Tajiks had left only a few works of poetry and anthologies of classical literature. Gholām Rezā Alizade[32] maintained in an article written in 1930 that there was only ever a feudal and bourgeois literature which served these classes and which was inaccessible to the proletariat, polluting, in fact, the proletarian way of thinking.[33]

A third argument concerned the unity of the language. It was noted that this included different dialects or pronunciations: Khojenti, Pamiri (Tajik spoken by peoples who had other mother tongues), Samarkandi, standard Persian (too Arabicised, according to these writers, to count as an ancestral language, and deemed incomprehensible to the working masses) or Karategini. The journals tended to respond to these questions with a plan of action. The language would have to be invented collectively:

> Today the primary duty of Tajiks is to prove the existence of the Tajik nation, and to construct under the Soviet banner an Autonomous Tajik Province. The question of language will follow: it will be the work not of individuals but of the Tajik nation itself, of the Tajiks who of their own free will shall assemble under the Tajik banner. They will choose the language which they will then define and adopt through their own consultations.[34]

II How Can One Become Tajik?

The arguments of these reviews thus made way for an organised project which would put some flesh on the bones of a nation simultaneously shattered and dominated by its Uzbek neighbour. Within this framework, a certain number of tools were to be employed: first of all, the journals, which were to serve as links between the grass-roots promoters of the project, as well as contributing to civic education. Secondly, there was to be a language initiative on three levels: simplification, to make the language accessible to the working classes; promotion of a literature which would lend dignity to the standing of the language and enhance national consciousness; and romanisation (the language was written in Roman script from 1928 to 1940), which would allow the language to achieve modernity. Finally, a transition was to be made from Quranic to Socialist schooling.

1 The Role of the Journals

A newspaper is the tongue of a people, it is the crystal ball that reflects the world, the companion in solitude, the bringer of justice for the oppressed. A newspaper is the source of vigilance, the awakener of the people. Long live education, long live the press.[35]

The launch of Persian-language reviews, albeit in very limited numbers, in Turkestan, where the official language was Chagatay Turkic, or in the heart of the Republic of Uzbekistan, was received by the educated Persian-speakers of the region as a breath of fresh air.[36] A newspaper was considered not simply a means of communication, but an antidote to the oblivion the Tajik people were experiencing.

Indeed, since the Revolution of 1917, apart from the publication in Persian of the weekly *Sho'lē-ye Enqelāb* ('The Flame of Revolution') between 1919 and 1921,[37] the Tajiks of the mountains and rural areas who, unlike those living in the larger towns, did not speak 'Uzbek', were deprived of information about the many upheavals affecting their regions, left untouched by the message of the Revolution, and reduced to a silent minority within the new structure of Turkestan society.

The nations of Russia have progressed and acquired liberty thanks to the Soviet government. But after the annihilation of

21

the old regime, the Tajiks have still not made the progress they should have made: they have been unable to do so. These last few years they should have been mobilising themselves in science and education ... The Tajiks have suffered many blows and borne them all. The peasants have not as yet understood the principles of Soviet government and continue to suffer at the hands of the governors and landowners. What are the goals that the Soviet government is heading towards? What is it that it seeks? It is highly unlikely that you would find one person among the Tajiks of the mountains who could answer these questions.[38]

This neglect could be explained by the fact that the authorities did not believe the Tajiks had a future in the formation of Turcophone republics; they were supposed to 'Turkify' or 'Uzbekify' themselves. This stand was not only taken by the Turcophones in charge, but by a large proportion of the Tajik intellectual élite. The few Tajik leaders involved in the Communist movement were heavily influenced by Pan-Turkic and regionalist ideas and considered themselves Turkestani.[39] It was not until October 1924,[40] with the formation of the Autonomous Soviet Socialist Republic of Tajikistan as a subordinate unit within Uzbekistan, that the question arose once again.

In a letter published in the first issue of *Avāz-e tājik*, Sadriddin Aini expressed his astonishment at the inferior position occupied by the town-dwelling Tajiks, who languished in the most humble low-paid manual jobs while 'others in Turkestan are blessed with newspapers, *maktab*, science and literature.[41] But the Tajik *qowm* ['people'] is neither aware of the state of world, nor in possession of the means to make itself heard. In the era of liberty this is obviously an evil.'[42] Knowledge of the rights of peoples would permit the Tajik élite to start making demands for their nation. 'Seven years on [from the 1917 Revolution], we have neither journals nor schools. How can we make the Tajiks understand ... their rights? How can we inform them about the doctrine and laws of the Soviet government?'[43]

The publication of newspapers and reviews constituted the only real cultural activity undertaken by the Party at that period with regard to the Tajiks. In accordance with Leninist cultural policy, *Avāz-e tājik-e kambaghal* had established its objective as fighting ignorance, illiteracy and superstition, and eliminating the savage and obscurantist customs practised in the name of religion and the Shari'a, so that thought could be developed, education broadened and the people led to the light of civilisation. *Avāz-e tājik* wrote in the name of the dispossessed, the workers and the proletariat (*bichāregān*, *zahmatkeshān* and *ranjbarān*), against the cruel bāys and the *mollā-namā* ('those who disguised themselves as mullahs').[44] The publication aimed on the one hand to allow the voice of the Tajiks, hitherto mixed in with those of the Turcophones and the Uzbeks, to reach the ears of the 'just' government of the Soviets; and on the other to inform the Tajik *qowm* for the first time of the overarching principles and ideas of the government and the Communist Party. Those in charge hoped to rally the Tajiks, and especially the poor, around the magazine.

Given that less than 1% of the Tajik population was literate, these reviews (including *Dānesh-binesh* in Samarkand) targeted teachers as intermediaries. After the creation of the Nezārat in December 1924, its mouthpiece *Dānesh va āmuzegār*, which was succeeded by the publication in Tashkent of *Rahbar-e dānesh*, had not only to fulfil the tasks that *Avāz-e tājik* had set itself, but also to maintain close links with the teachers, as agents of social change, in order to ensure the establishment of Soviet structures. Since one of the most pressing problems was the dearth of school textbooks, it was through these journals that teachers, often trained very quickly, could learn the 'science of pedagogy' beloved of Communists, as well as Marxist-Leninist principles, and receive guidance as to the content of the instruction that they were supposed to give young people and adult illiterates.

> Our review must be a useful guide for teachers at all times. Since teaching is still new in Tajikistan and the Tajiks do not understand very literary Persian, our journal should, as far as possible, be simple and written in a language close to that of the indigenous population. May we not be considered men of letters, but may every teacher understand us.[45]

This goal called for change to the language itself, to make it more accessible.

2 The Promotion of Modern Tajik

The criticism regarding the multiplicity of accents and dialects in Tajik touched a raw nerve with the promoters of this movement. If it was language which constituted the specific identity of a country, it ought to tend to unify itself into a modern Tajik tongue.[46] Moreover, inasmuch as standardisation had to affect the whole population, it

23

would have to begin with a process of simplification. The 1920s are generally considered the first stage in the *nowsāzi va bonyādkāri* ('renovation and foundation') of the language.[47] However, this trend tied in with a movement to simplify the literary language and bring it closer to the vernacular (*zabān-e umumi-ye khalqi va avām*) which had been inititated by men of letters at the beginning of the twentieth century.

A completely separate language was needed. Tajik had, therefore, to be freed from over-use of Uzbek loans. 'In Samarkand, the Tajik currently spoken is mixed with Uzbek. Quite obviously no Tajik would accept this language. Although the languages of Ura-Tyube and Khojent are slightly purer, they are not completely separate from Uzbek.'[48] It was also necessary to try and counter the Arabic influence which originated in the *medrassa* under the watchful eyes of the ulama, as well as to distinguish Tajik from literary Persian (although there was a trend which supported the promotion of the Persian language of Iran, which, it was claimed, would facilitate the export of the Revolution to the East). It was then necessary to simplify it so that it could become the language of the labouring masses, and so call in question for all time the distinction between the scholarly language of the privileged intellectual classes who produced culture, and the language of day-to-day life destined for the masses.

The first attempts at a language accessible to the masses were demonstrated in the language of *Sho'lē-ye Enqelāb* (the first Tajik newspaper), as well as in the first works of *ustād* Aini, *Nemune-ye adabiyāt-e tājik* (1925), *Adine* (1924) and *Dokhunde* (1930).[49] These attempts were later renewed in the language of *Avāz-e tājik-e kambaghal* and in journals, manuals and stories produced during the years that followed.[50] Moreover, Aini suggested that prose was superior to poetry from this point of view, and discouraged young authors of the period such as Ekrāmi and Oluqzade from working in this form.[51]

The leading lights of this movement did not take the risk of trying to choose between the different regional dialects and idioms. This was a particularly sensitive issue. It was not enough to draw on the language of Samarkand or of Khojent, which was used by the majority of those writing for the reviews, since between 1924 and 1929, the period which particularly interests us here, Tajikistan was made up of former eastern Bukhara: the provinces of Ura-Tyube, Penjikent and the mountains of Badakhshan, and did not include those towns. In fact, in its experiments with writing in modern Tajik, the Association of

Linguists chose as the basis of the language the *miānkālat* dialect of Persian (from the region of Miānkāl, halfway between Samarkand and Bukhara), which was used by Aini in his works. Gradually through the 1930s, and with the arrival of a new generation of teachers, journalists and writers after the war, the written language also adapted to include the dialects and accents of the mountains.

3 Literature: Between a Return to Sources and Socialist Realism

The contents of literary works also had to adapt to this desire for a Socialist renewal of language. Writers and poets had to seek their inspiration, as much for content as for form, not from the bāys and the clergy, as before, but from the *khalq* ('people'). Two areas were thus opened up: reference to an ancient culture, and Socialist Realism.

The first was represented by Aini in his seminal anthology *Nemune-ye adabiyāt-e tājik*. This was the first re-evaluation of 'Tajik' culture. The tenth-century poet Rudaki, who is considered the father of Persian poetry and lived on the territory of present-day Tajikistan, featured prominently, but so too did Persian writers whose links with Central Asia and Tajikistan were less obvious, such as Ferdowsi (who came from Tus), as well as lesser-known contemporary writers. Denounced by the Uzbeks as a celebration of the Emir (because of a poem by Rudaki) and banned by the Uzbek Party Plenum, this work had to be published in Moscow in 1926, after intercession from the Iranians.[52]

Socialist Realism also makes its appearance in the reviews. Tajik writers now abandoned Romanticism in favour of this new literary trend. Aini's story *Tājik-e kambaghal* ('A Poor Tajik'), which was published in *Avāz-e tājik-e kambaghal*, is an example, as is *Faqir-e zan va kolub-e zanān* ('The Beggar Woman and the Women's Club'), by M. S. Ekrāmi.[53] This is a story about a Tajik woman whose husband, a worker, has just died. She sells all her possessions in order to bury her husband and braves the snow with her two barely-clothed children to go and reclaim money owed by the bāy for work done by her husband, whence she is unceremoniously turned away. Weeping in the street, she passes a (Soviet) women's club. The woman running the club instantly offers her work, and sends her children to a state-run boarding school. By taking reading classes in the evening after work, she gets promoted and ends up working for a women's cooperative. A fine example of didactic literature.

25

4 Romanisation

Let us respectfully return this worn out *yarāq* ['weapon', i.e. the Arabic alphabet] to the Arabs themselves, and take up a new weapon.[54]

The project to simplify the language naturally involved challenging the Arabic alphabet, which is in fact not very well adapted to Persian pronunciation. Some sounds cannot be transcribed, while others are represented by several different letters, causing difficulties in spelling. Contrary to the experiences of the relevant Uzbek authorities, who had been trying to tackle the same problem since 1918,[55] the Tajik *emlā' tāze chi* ('renovators of writing') seem rapidly to have gained the upper hand over the *emlā' miāne chi* ('reformers of writing'), who foresaw an intermediary period during which a modified and abbreviated Arabic alphabet would be used. The position that was upheld was that of going straight to a Roman alphabet without trying to reform the Arabic alphabet.[56]

In Tajikistan this debate surfaced in 1925 among the senior officials of the Commissariat for Education, and reached the Tajik journals one year later, although there had been several conferences on the subject in Tashkent, Bukhara and Azerbaijan at the beginning of the 1920s.[57] The decree on the romanisation of the language was published in April 1928, and was applied in the 1930s, until 1940, when Cyrillic was substituted for the Roman alphabet.[58] In this context it should be mentioned that the originators of the movement in the region were Azerbaijani, Tatar and Anatolian Turcophones, who had been agitating about this question since Mirzā Fatali Khān Akhūndov in 1858.[59] This was not a question of managing tensions with those who denied the existence of Tajik, but, on the contrary, of signing up to a 'progressive' movement across the Soviet Union and of serving as a model for the 'obscurantist' Persian-speaking neighbours to the south. Romanisation was supposed to facilitate the process of teaching illiterate adults and children to read.[60] 'Red Tajikistan will have more experience on this path than other Tajik-speaking countries [*sic*], and will be able to act as a symbol to them, since achieving the literacy of the impoverished peasants (in a short time span) constitutes the main aim of the Soviet government. It will only be possible when the Roman alphabet is adopted.'[61]

Romanisation was also part of a drive for national self-assertion. It allowed links to be rediscovered with the Persian tradition, as opposed to the 'obscurantist' Arab world, while at the same time marking a visible difference between Tajik and Persian, which, as we have seen, was tenuous as far as the canon of writers was concerned. Emphasis was laid on Persian nationalism, since romanisation was only a reflection of the modernisation of Persian and its ability to expand with the times. In order to maintain the idea of a Tajik nation that was the heir apparent to the glorious history of Persia in the region, an inventory was hastily drawn up of the pillage and destruction of historic monuments, as well as burning of Persian books and manuscripts, committed by the Arab conquerors. 'The Arabs seduced the Persian-speakers by forcing Arabic words into their mouths.' For all that the authors accepted the inevitability of foreign words creeping into a language, the introduction of a foreign alphabet was quite intolerable to them: 'It is becoming obvious that the reason for the backwardness of the Persian-speaking nation [*mellat*] is not only the fact that Arabic words have been adopted, but, more importantly, that Arabic letters are used.'[62]

Romanisation posed technical problems and in a way forced a reassessment of the sensitive question of the language of reference. The main points in contention were: the choice of which Roman letter would best represent the different local pronunciations[63] and not reproduce the shortcomings of the alphabet that had been cast off; the use of capitals and small letters; and the creation of new letters.[64] Another matter for consideration was whether to preserve in part or wholly abandon certain features of the various dialects and pronunciations which distinguished the town-dwellers from the mountain Tajiks.[65]

The review *Rahbar-e dānesh* played a central role in the romanisation project. It became the place where experiences on the subject were exchanged, and published in 1928 the first text, six pages long, in the new alphabet. The problems, however, were manifold. Communist activists met with local resistance to Soviet schools (the clergy took a dim view of the loss of their monopoly on the education system and writing), and therefore tried to emphasis the role of 'progressive' mullahs who supported the change of alphabet. But the first and most important task was the training of those who were to propagate the new alphabet. Teachers took some time to adapt to it; in the early years even the journals did not really get to grips with it. Although the Arabic script was banished from the Union c.1929, the first attempts to introduce the new script were limited to titles in the Roman alphabet or the publication of a few articles in the new transcription, while the majority of articles continued to be written in

27

Arabic script, even those that asserted the necessity of changing the alphabet.

5 From Medrassas to the New Maktabs

Faqat bi maktabi dar asr-e hāzer
kami māne' shod az parvāz-e tājik
'Only the lack of schools at that period
somewhat hampered the flight of Tajik'[66]

The Nezārat, as well as the *sorkh* ('Red') Association of Teachers, saw their primary task as being the establishment of a new system of schooling in Tajik, which would be secular, public (free) and unshackled by the monopoly of the clergy, but which also had to be able to provide precise local information to the authorities.[67] In order that teachers themselves should be the repositories of the 'Socialist spirit', 'Our teachers must be mainly attached to the villages [in the absence of local proletarians, peasants would have to be trained instead], the teachers must be linked to the projects of the Soviets and close to the Party. They must be agitators.'[68] This plan, however, came up against two main obstacles. On the one hand, the Uzbek authorities tried to hinder the development of teaching in Tajik. On the other, it was difficult to establish contact with the rural population.

There were no Tajik-language teacher-training colleges until 1924, when the central government of Turkestan established its teacher-training college in Tashkent. The *talab-e* ('adult students') studied Russian and Tajik, pedagogy, mathematics, history and geography. The chief concern of Tajik militants regarding the territories remaining under Uzbek jurisdiction was the scarcity of schools in which the teaching was conducted in Tajik, and the fact that Tajik pupils had to attend Uzbek schools in a language they did not understand.[69] The few Tajik teachers, even if they were bilingual themselves, used the reviews to denounce the action of the Uzbek authorities, which, while not perhaps amounting to an actively negative policy, still neglected or lacked initiative in promoting teaching in Tajik (planning of curricula, allocation of funds, recruitment of Persian-speaking teachers, and so on). Even on the level of teacher-training a number of problems were evident. One of the students at the college in Tashkent, where 180 future teachers were being trained, complained of the lack of space and equipment, making comparisons with other Uzbek training colleges to highlight the backwardness of the Tajik teacher-training college.[70] The development of these colleges therefore remained limited. In July 1929, the fourth Association of Tajik Teachers met to consider urgent matters of education and teacher-training, as well as to assess the experience gained since 1924. The progress made in education and civilisation was acknowledged to be unimpressive. There were very few teachers, and they were the product of old schools, often trained in Uzbek and in a religious framework. In 1921 there were only 31 schools and twice that number of teachers for a population of approximately 800,000, which was an obviously ridiculous disparity. In the next ten years, the number of schools increased tenfold, but with 12,000 elementary school pupils to cater for, these figures were still modest; 11.8% of school-age children attended elementary school. Three teacher-training colleges were established, the first in Tashkent in 1925.[71]

Schools[72]

	Number of schools	Teachers	Pupils
1921–22	31	61	904
1925–26	67	85	2,287
1926–27	154	184	5,024
1927–28	258	–	9,070
1928–29	307	393	12,000

Schools for teaching literacy

	Number of schools	Pupils
1925–26	63	1,400
1926–27	140	2,100
1927–28	271	7,400
1928–29	318	12,400

Once established in the villages, the teachers also found it difficult to be accepted by the communities. For example, they were not welcomed in the local tea-houses, and their own Communist *chāikhāne* were not popular. The authorities expected the teachers to involve themselves fully in local activities in order to instruct the peasants on a variety of subjects, from the validity of the cooperative system and the introduction of machinery to boost production, to the importance of silk-worms and the illnesses that could be spread by locusts.[73] To judge from the reports from teachers, which often took the form of letters to the journals, working conditions and practices were very different from the image that had been promoted. For example, a teacher named Jalālzāde confessed in a letter that the principal and other teachers at his school in Doāb, in a remote region, were not interested in the 'pupils' fathers' or the general life of the inhabitants. The pupils could easily miss school to go to *bozkashi* ('marriage feast') or *tuy* ('circumcision feast'), and this suited the teachers. Religious people avoided Soviet teachers and kept their children from going to these schools. Moreover, at the end of the year, having failed to attract enough pupils, the teachers were forced to lie about the numbers (claiming they had sixty pupils instead of thirty).[74]

Conclusion

How can one be Tajik? If one now asks this question from a sociological point of view, the activity of the Nezārat-e Mo'āref represents a key moment. For the first time an assertion of a specific Tajik identity was made and validated by the journals it launched, with their attention to the questions of Tajik culture, territory and especially language. This movement found its social expression in the teachers mobilised by these journals, who, living as they did in direct contact with the rural communities, were particularly inclined to make a break with the urban Tajik intellectuals.[75] To assert that one was Tajik was in effect to part company with the Pan-Turkic movements which had inspired a large number of the country's intellectual élite.

The position of the pro-Tajiks of that period seems to have been relatively weak within the intellectual spectrum of the region. The divide which becomes apparent in the theoretical debates in the journals was played out in a more significant way in the discussions on the definition of the nation. The stands taken by these journals, which tended to justify the creation of an Autonomous Republic, ran counter to those maintained by some of the country's élite. It is interesting here to juxtapose some of the militants' arguments with those which were put forward in debates about the formation of an Autonomous Republic, recently exhumed by Masov from hitherto inaccessible sources. Even at the decisive moment of the partition and allocation of the regions which would form the area under Tajik jurisdiction, there were ongoing disagreements among the Tajik representatives themselves. Some 'inter-regionalists' proposed a plan for the future of the Tajik nation which was more 'regionalising' and sprang from a logic of economic and cultural dependence on 'Greater

Uzbekistan'.[76] Masov notes that these representatives even used Socialist arguments to support the idea of a hierarchy of peoples. The civilisation of progress had initially been brought to Central Asia by the Russian avant-garde, which had liberated its backward brothers and comrades in the region from the yoke of the Emir, the mollā-namās and the bāys. But within Turkestani society, the Uzbek brothers were considered a more advanced people, a model to follow, and later to challenge. Abdollah Rahimbāyev, the Secretary of the Central Committee of the Communist Party of Turkestan, thought that: 'Central Asia is constructed on a national basis in which certain nations such as the Uzbeks and the Kazakhs and the Turkmen are superior, and the various small peoples [*khalqā-ye khord*] follow.'[77]

It is therefore difficult to analyse this awareness as a gradual process of mobilisation of the country's élite, in which a nation was formed in opposition to the forces of Russian colonial domination. The facts described above offer more support for the 'Machiavellian' theory that the Russians played on national feelings to assert their power. It is interesting that the liveliest polemic between these journals and those that defended the assimilation of the Tajiks into the surrounding Turkic world was played out between two papers which shared the same premises: one can almost imagine the insults ringing out from one end of the corridor to the other. On the strength of the evidence, the Russians played a key role. Their support was expressed early on through the orientalists who published, against the advice of the Uzbeks, Aini's anthology of Tajik literature, and the first ethnological history of the Tajiks, and also participated in the debates on the use of the Roman alphabet. They may have had to moderate their position somewhat because of the Basmachis, who were fighting a war of resistance, based particularly in the Pamirs. 'Since the Basmachi movement was strong in our country and the government newly formed, we could not talk about a new Roman alphabet.'[78]

Was this movement then the expression of a Socialist project or a nationalist project? The models seem ambiguous. It was a time of tests and trials, and references to Pan-Turkic movements, Jadids, nationalists and internationalists were not yet circumscribed by an authoritarian ideological power. There was the Leninist model, which advocated a focus on the mother tongue, but it was also perfectly possible to put forward, in the name of Socialist principles, a hierarchy of peoples in the order of their acceptance of Socialism. Uzbek officials, who cherished Pan-Turkic and Pan-Islamist ideas, thought that the strength of the region lay in its unity, insisting on

31

Uzbek as a common language, and on the fact that the Tajik language had become obsolete, thus making redundant the whole idea of a separate Tajik state (a 'scientific and materialist' discourse on the progression of history). The project for a nation-state, inspired also by Atatürk, mostly strengthened the Pan-Turkists who opposed a separate Tajik identity. The struggle against religion was half-hearted, and the elements which could have given people a sense of belonging had not yet been assailed. Moreover, in one debate, a senior Turkestani official had emphasised the necessity of using Pan-Turkism and Pan-Islamism as progressive elements in the context of Central Asia.[79] This same group defended the idea of creating republics for the Turkic peoples.

But having noted all this, the question still remains. How was it possible that the Tajiks took this definition of their identity on board, and how did a point of view that was obviously marginal at the start of the 1920s gradually gain the upper hand?

In fact, the intellectuals later came into line with each other on this position. Aini's development affords a good example. A product of the Jadid movement, sympathetic to Pan-Turkism, he gradually came to take part in the journals and join in their projects, particularly through the promotion of the Persian heritage and the simplification of the language. In 1926, he became a member of the Central Executive Committee of the Tajik SSR.[80] Like Lāhuti, he was elected as one of the fifty members of the Organisation Committee of the Union of Writers, which contained all those who had opposed that movement's Tajik nationalism. The same was true of Biktāsh,[81] who in September 1927 became a member of the editorial board of *Dānesh-binesh* (along with Hassani and Uyqur), as well as of the Scientific Council of the Republic of Tajikistan. Hassani, who had often been in conflict with Biktāsh, found himself on the team for the new alphabet, under orders from the Communist Party of the Republic, as did Nosratollāh N. Makhsum[82] (who became the head of the Central Executive Committee of the Republic of Uzbekistan), Mohiyedinov (who was also the Deputy Director of the Revolutionary Committee of Tajikistan), Momen Khojayev, Deylami and Fitrat;[83] Emāmov (thought to be the one who 'sold off' large parts of Tajik territory cheaply) became the Secretary in charge of the Communist Party office in Tajikistan.[84] Finally, Mohiyedinov as good as made an admission of guilt by confessing that at the outset of the creation of the Republic of Bukhara, Jadids like him had been strongly opposed to the Tajik language, as it threatened the unity of a greater Turkic government. Even though at the end of its life the Republic made some attempts to open Tajik-language schools (it being their mother tongue), by all accounts this had raised very little interest. He admitted to having been wrong in the past, and hoped that the Party would redress the balance. 'For the Tajik workers of Bukhara have not reached such a degree of activity that they can raise their own voices in protest. Again, we are to blame for this, since we did not advance as much as we ought the work of the Party.'[85]

This alignment cannot of course be explained solely by the force of the militants' conviction, nor by the practical success of the nation-building project among the people. The distribution of schools remained very limited, and their impact patchy. The dispersion of the Tajik populations in remote mountainous regions, the absence of communications infrastructure, the publication in Uzbek of journals, decrees and propaganda on the message of the Revolution and the Bolshevik movement, as well as the lack of militants and agitators in these regions, the continuation of Basmachi activity and the presence of hostile religious leaders, all constituted serious obstacles to the dissemination of revolutionary ideas and of information about the changes which had happened. The move to a Roman alphabet was similarly slow to materialise. On the whole, the Uzbeks were always opposed to the idea of the emergence of a Tajik identity. In particular, they tried to hamper the progress of education in Tajik. 'Who says that in the mixed regions the people are Persian-speaking, whereas the majority of them speak Uzbek? And moreover the Tajiks have neither schools nor proper representatives, apart from which their Tajik is highly Uzbekified, they were originally Turcophone peoples who were forced by Persian influence to become Tajiks, etc. ...' The Uzbeks made concerted attempts to withhold the means of development from the Tajiks, and then deduced from the weakness of these means of development that Tajikistan could not constitute an autonomous entity. The decision to create an Autonomous Republic of Tajikistan unquestionably had an important influence.[86] It certainly encouraged a number of supporters of the Pan-Turkic argument to change their positions enough to take up jobs within the government of the new Republic. It also helped many institutions, such as universities, museums and libraries, to spring up, which could underpin local identity.[87]

Nevertheless, against a background of indeterminate models, these journals managed to stamp a frame of reference onto the face of 'Tajikness'. Perhaps it is particularly those things which were not

33

thought about, which were never aired in these debates, that we are encountering today. These reviews are indeed silent about the discrepancy between the territorial delimitation of the Republic of Tajikistan and the definition of Tajik identity. Thus, *Avāz-e tājik-e kambaghal*, in Samarkand, had to defend the idea of a nation which could never have its centre in that city. The 'Tajikistan of their dreams' had to leave out the great cities of the plains: Samarkand, Bukhara and Khojent; but neither could it really incorporate the mountains of the Pamirs, where the Basmachis were hiding, and whose inhabitants spoke languages which, though of Iranian origin, could not be understood by other Tajiks. The actual Tajikistan of the Autonomous Republic was ultimately to integrate Khojent and the Pamirs, and the tensions between the different regions were to constitute one of the main elements of the dynamic of crisis in the 1990s.

Notes

1 Created by the Revolutionary Committee of Tajikistan, it was made official on 14 December 1924 and set up its headquarters two months later in Dushanbe.
2 As a child, Aliev had worked in the Bukhara Komsomol. He was the second Tajik after Fitrat to gain the title of Professor, and studied in Moscow after being appointed Commissar of Culture of Tajikistan. He was imprisoned in 1935, and later taught history in Dushanbe, but gave it up under local pressure and left in 1946, to live first in Kirgizia, then in the Ukraine and Alma-Ata.
3 Its territory was the eastern part of the old Bukharan Emirate: the velāyats of Hissar, Kulyab, Garm, Kurgan-Tyube, the Pamirs, part of the velāyat of Samarkand, the *raion* ('districts') of Penjikent and of Ura-Tyube. See Rahmatzāde, 'Jomhuriat-e Tājikestān' ('The Republic of Tajikistan'), *Dānesh va āmuzegār*, no. 3–4, 15–20 July 1926, p. 10.
4 The Basmachis were resistance fighters linked to the exiled Emir of Bukhara, who led a war against the Soviet powers.
5 See Stéphane Dudoignon, 'Changements politiques et historiographie en Asie centrale. Tadjikistan et Ouzbékistan, 1987–1993', *CEMOTI*, no. 16, July-December 1993, pp. 86–132. The Bukharan Jadid ('new', 'modern') movement grew up in the early twentieth century. It campaigned for educational modernisation, established 'new-method' schools, and later demanded political reforms.
6 The same journal continues to be published in Uzbekistan. Its name was changed to 'Haqiqat-e uzbakestān' ('Truth of Uzbekistan'), but changed back to the original title in January 1993, with the omission of the word *kambaghal* ('poor').
7 Two months after the Tajiks were given autonomy.
8 One of the youth of Samarkand, Ghorbi also made forays into poetry, without much success.

9 It became a monthly after the second issue because of lack of funds.
10 The board consisted of Musavi, Hassani (an Iranian), Uyqur, Jabbāri (a teacher from Samarkand), and Biktāsh.
11 The new generation of Tajik Soviet and nationalist writers was born from this review.
12 To the census agents' question, 'Who are you?', people often replied '*Alhamdollāh* ['Thank God'], I am a Muslim.' In response they were told to go to Arabia. At a second attempt, the answer might be, 'I am a Persian speaker.' 'Then go to Iran,' they were told. 'I am a Tajik': 'Then get out of Uzbekistan.' 'But Bukhara (or Samarkand) is my native town.' 'Then declare yourself an Uzbek.' This account was given to me by Mohammadjān Shokuri at one of our meetings in Dushanbe in the summer of 1992. On the question of the connection between nationality and identity papers, see Gerard Noiriel, 'L'identification des citoyens', *Genèses*, 13, 1993, pp. 3–28.
13 Esmā'ilzāde, 'Mas'ale-ye tājiki' ('The Question of the Tajik Language'), *Avāz-e tājik-e kambaghal*, no. 5, 28 September 1924, p. 4.
14 Published in *Zarafshān*, no. 182, cited by Esmā'ilzāde, *loc. cit.* A Samarkandi, Biktāsh (a pseudonym) was a translator, critic and writer. He often exchanged polemics with Sadriddin Aini and accused him of being a Jadid.
15 Cited by Mohammad Hassani, 'Ahāly-e Khojand va Ura tappe aksaran tājikand' ('The Inhabitants of Khojent and Ura-Tyube are Predominantly Tajik'), *Avāz-e tājik-e kambaghal*, no. 8, 21 October 1924, p. 4.
16 *Ibid.*
17 E. Mohiyedinov, 'Mardom-e shahr va atraf-e Bokhārā tājikand ya uzbek' ('Are the People of the Town and Environs of Bukhara Tajiks or Uzbeks?'), *Rahbar-e dānesh*, nos. 8–9 (11–12), second year, August and September 1928, pp. 16–18.
18 Mohiyedinov published an open letter on the subject addressed to Stalin in *Za Partiyu* ('By [or For] the Party'), the organ of the Communist Party Bureau in Central Asia. The letter remained unanswered. Interview with Mohammadjān Shokuri in Paris, December 1993.
19 Rahim Masov, writing much more recently, presents a similar analysis, looking for the answers in betrayals by several Tajik figures of the period who were too hungry for power. *Istoriya Topornogo Razdeleniya* ('History of a Carving-Up with an Axe'), Nashriāt-e Erfān, Dushanbe, 1991, p. 48.
20 Interview with Mohammadjān Shokuri, December 1993.
21 Masov, *op. cit.*, p. 42.
22 *Ibid.*, p. 1.
23 *Ibid.*, pp. 41–43.
24 Klemchitsky, 'Molk shenāsi va mo'alemin' ('Knowing One's Country and the Teachers'), *Dānesh va āmuzegār*, no. 3–4, 15–20 July 1926, p. 20. Klemchitsky, a Russian historian, subsequently worked in the Tajik branch of the Academy of Sciences. He 'disappeared' in the 1930s.
25 This association compiled the first book on the Tajiks. However, Sadriddin Aini was active in gathering and disseminating knowledge of the Tajiks' past and present. Moreover, his works contribute to a great

extent to the modern history of the Tajiks. Aini, 'Keshvar shenāsi' ('Knowing One's Country'), *Dānesh-binesh*, no. 1, 1 August 1927, pp. 29–31.

26 See the translations which the Iranian Communist Deylami published in *Dānesh va āmuzegār*, no. 2, 29 March 1926, p. 15. Deylami was arrested in 1937, and ended his career working in the press and radio in Tajikistan.

27 See amongst others Rahmatzāde, *op.cit.* [note 3 above], pp. 10–12.

28 *Ibid.*, p. 10.

29 Mohiyedinov, *op. cit.* [note 17 above], p. 17. This was a common belief at this period, promoted by those Mohiyedinov describes as neo-nationalist Uzbeks. Mohiyedinov does not adhere to this belief himself but is exposing it in his article; however, later in his life he admitted that he had been somewhat influenced by such ideas in his early activities.

30 *Turkestan*, 2 January 1924. Quoted by Masov, *op. cit.* [note 19 above], p. 34.

31 Quoted by Esmā'ilzāde, 'Bāz dar atraf-e mas'ale-ye Tājiki' ('Once Again On the Question of Tajik'), *Avāz-e tājik-e kambaghal*, no. 6, 5 October 1924, p. 4.

32 A Communist militant, Alizade was liquidated in the purges of the 1930s.

33 A. Seyfollāyev, 'Enqelābi now' ('A New Revolution'), *Sedā-ye Sharq*, no. 4, 1968, pp. 107–8, quoted by Jiři Becka, *Sadriddin Ayni Father of Modern Tajik Culture*, Istituto Universitario Orientale Seminario Di Studi Asiatici Series Minor V, Naples, 1980, p. 27.

34 Esmā'ilzāde, *loc. cit.*

35 Assadolāh Kāshāni, 'Mojde va tabrik' ('Tidings and Congratulations'), *Avāz-e tājik-e kambaghal*, no. 3, 12 September 1924, p. 4. Kāshāni was a Central Asian Iranian, descended from a group who had been emigrating there since the eighteenth century.

36 Until 1925, and even in 1930, the Persian and Tajik-Persian languages were spoken of interchangeably. This can be confirmed by reviewing the literature of the period.

37 This was halted officially for technical reasons (lack of paper and printing machines), but Masov says that it was a token of the Pan-Turkists' lack of interest in Tajik language and culture. Masov, *op. cit.*, p. 34.

38 'Vazifehā-ye mā' ('Our Duties'), in *Avāz-e tājik-e kambaghal*, no. 2,4 September 1924.

39 One could mention here the role of the revolutionary Iranian poet Abolqāsem Lāhuti, who was heavily influenced by the ideas of the Young Turks. During his long stay in Turkey, from 1913 to the end of the war, he was deeply impressed by the modernity and progress that these movements had brought about. The role of Sadriddin Aini was also significant: the product of a multilingual society, he wrote many of his works in Uzbek, due to the lack of Tajik journals. He, too, lacked a ready-made Tajik identity which distinguished itself from Turkic culture.

40 Declaration issued after an extraordinary meeting of the Central Executive Committee of Turkestan, *Avāz-e tājik-e kambaghal*, no. 5, 28 September 1924, p. 1.

41 There had been a series of Turkic-language reviews in Samarkand since 1913: *Samarkand* in 1913 (banned after 6 months), followed by *Ayine*,

which started before the 1917 Revolution and was banned in 1919, and *Horiyat* (which lasted only a year due to lack of financial means). In 1918 the Workers' Party of Samarkand brought out *Mehnatkeshān-e Oqi*, which became *Zahmatkeshān-e Tavosi* and then, until 1922, *Kambaghalar Tavochi*; this became *Zarafshān*, which continued to be published. See 'Eyd-e dosāle-ye jaride-ye Zarafshān' ('The Second Anniversary of the Journal *Zarafshān*'), *Avāz-e tājik-e kambaghal*, no. 8, 21 October 1924, p. 1.

42 *Avāz-e tājik-e kambaghal*, no. 1, 25 August 1924.

43 *Ibid.*

44 'Dibāche va marām' ('Preface and Programme'), *ibid.*, p. 1.

45 'Maqsad-e mā' ('Our Aim'), in *Dānesh va āmuzegār*, no. 1, 5 March 1926, p. 2.

46 Tajik has four dialects (*guyesh*): 1) central: the region of Zarafshan, Rashta and Sokh; 2) southern: Badakhshan, north and south Kulyab, Karategin; 3) northern: Samarkand, Bukhara, east and west Ferghana, Ura-Tyube and Penjikent; 4) south-eastern: Darvaz. See Afshār Sistāni Iraj, 'Moqadame-yi bar shenakht-e qom-e tājik' ('An Introduction to the Tajik People'), *Simorq*, no. 7–9, first year, Mordād-Abān 1369, p. 69.

47 Mohammadjān Shokuri, *Har sokhan jā-yi har nokte maqām-i dārad* ('Every Statement Has its Place and Every Point its Status'), Nashriāt-e Erfān, Dushanbe, 1985, pp. 8–9.

48 'Dar bāre-ye ketābhā-ye maktab-e tājikān' ('On Tajik Schoolbooks'), *Avāz-e tājik-e kambaghal*, no. 3, 12 September 1924, p. 1.

49 For an analysis and historical overview of the collected works of Aini, see Becka, *op. cit.*

50 The Persian-speaking reader from Iran would be bemused at first sight of the works written during this period, such as, for example, Aini's novel *Marg-e sudkhor*, or those works of poetry and prose produced in later years when a new attempt was being made to re-establish a deliberately simplified language. This language could be considered infinitely limited and impoverished, especially if one takes into account the massive gradual injection of Russian, into both grammatical forms and vocabulary.

51 Interview with Satem Oluqzade, summer 1992, Dushanbe. He and Ekrāmi are probably the most famous and popular writers at present. Ekrāmi has recently disappeared (1993). Oluqzade, who is very ill and aged, has been in Moscow since the intensification of the civil war in Tajikistan.

52 Banned from being circulated in the region, this work was hastily prepared for publication by two Iranians, Lāhuti and Dorāj (a printer). Interview with Mr Dorāj (a 93-year-old Communist who left Iran at the age of fifteen), Dushanbe, summer 1992.

53 Ekrāmi later became a teacher in Tajikistan.

54 Sābt Monāfzāde, 'Tājikān va alefbā-ye now' ('The Tajiks and the New Alphabet'), *Rahbar-e dānesh*, no. 2, first year, 1 October 1927, p. 4. Monāfzāde, an Iranian from Ashghabat, also worked in Baku. He was a teacher who wrote textbooks. He was called to Tashkent to work on *Rahbar-e dānesh*. In 1937 he was liquidated, accused like other Iranian Communists in the main cities of Turkmenistan of being an Iranian spy.

55 The Central Executive Committee of the Uzbek Republic decided that a national Roman alphabet should be in use by the end of 1932 in all organisations, schools and publications. The equivalent date for Azerbaijan was 1929. *Rahbar-e dānesh* Roman script edition), no. 8–9 (11–12), second year, August-September 1928, p. 4.

56 'Nakhostin anjoman-e moa'lemin-e tājikestān' ('First Meeting of the Teachers of Tajikistan'), *Dānesh va āmuzegār*, no. 3–4, 15–20 July 1926, pp. 1–5.

57 A second conference on the new Tajik alphabet took place on 27 October 1928 at Tashkent, after the one in Samarkand, to resolve differences on technical details. Envoys from the Tajik Autonomous Province and the Tajik regions of Uzbekistan were invited, as well as Professors of Iranology. The meeting was meant to debate the new romanisation law, draw up an account of the measures taken and propose a five-year plan for the new alphabet. 'Elān' ('Announcement'), *Rahbar-e dānesh*, no. 8–9 (11–12), second year, August September 1928, p. 67. The first six pages of this issue of the journal were produced for the first time in Roman characters.

58 It was at this time, between 1920 and 1930, that the Roman alphabet was introduced in Turkey. The rapid development of publications there reinforced a strong linguistic nationalism, which was distinct from the Islamic religious tradition. In Iran the movement to romanise the language did not see the light of day, even though Rezā Shah did attempt to purify the language of Turkish and Arabic roots. J. P. Derriennic, *Le Moyen-Orient au 20ème siècle*, translated into Persian by F. Ardalān, Sāzmān-e Enteshārāt-e Jāvidān, Tehran, 1368, pp. 103–4 and 117.

59 Malkolm Khan and the Adamiat Committee should also be mentioned for comparison with Iranian intellectuals and the Persian-speakers of India; Aliev, 'Mas'ale-ye alefbā-ye tāze' ('The Question of the New Alphabet'), *Dānesh va āmuzegār*, no. 3–4, 15–20 July 1926, pp. 6–7.

60 Aini said the new alphabet should be so simple that every Tajik child would be able to master it in one month. 'Donyā-ye now va alefbā-ye now' ('A New World and a New Alphabet'), *Avāz-e tājik-e kambaghal*, no. 171, 1927, p. 1).

61 Monāfzāde, *loc. cit.* [note 54 above].

62 Aliev, *op. cit.*, p. 10.

63 For instance 'u/ū' or 'i/e' and the long and short 'a'.

64 For the 'sā'et' sounds such as eyn (') and the h (*hotti*) used for example in the word '*hayāt*' in Persian, which is different from the h (*havvaz*) in '*hodhod*'.

65 See 'Alefbā-ye now Avāzhā-ye lahjey-i tājiki' ('The New Alphabet, Tajik Accents'), *Rahbar-e dānesh*, no. 1, third year, 1 January 1929, pp. 18–19, or Fitrat, 'Lāyehe-ye alefbā-ye now-e tājiki' ('The New Law on the New Tajik Alphabet'), *Rahbar-e dānesh*, no. 3, first year, November 1927, pp. 12–14.

66 From Aini's poem 'Avāz-e tājik' ('Voice of the Tajik'), published in *Avāz-e tājik-e kambaghal*, no. 2, 4 September 1924, p. 3.

67 By official order from the Commissar for Education, teachers had to take a census of their pupils by means of questionnaires to establish their

names, educational levels, ages and family status. 'Farmon-e 42 az Nāzer-e mo'āref Abbās Aliev', *Dānesh va āmuzegār*, no. 2, 29 March 1926, p. 36.

68 The words 'of the honourable Comrade Talpigo', who was the spokesman for the Tajik Communist Party at the annual Festival of Education, 'Jashn-e sāliāne-ye mo'āref va maqāsed-e mā' ('The Annual Festival of Education and Our Goals'), *Dānesh va āmuzegār*, no. 2, 29 March 1926, p. 3.

69 On 14 July 1918, the Central Committee of Turkestan ratified the ascendancy of the official languages (Uzbek and Kyrgyz) over Russian. On 14 July 1924, in view of the numerous peoples constituting the population of Turkestan, the three principal languages – Uzbek, Kyrgyz and Turkmen – were designated the languages of administration. J. Hasanov, *V. I. Lenin i turkbiuro*, CC BKP (b), Tashkent, 1969, pp. 32–3, quoted by Masov, *op. cit.* [note 19 above], p. 15.

70 'Darolmo'ālemin'-e tājikān dar Tāshkand', ('The Pedagogical Institute in Tashkent'), *Dānesh va āmuzegār*, no. 3–4, 15–20 July 1926, p. 22.

71 Some students, often selected from the villages, later became very famous, notably the writer S. Uluqzāde and the poet M. Tursonzāde.

72 Mohammad Seyedov, 'Anjoman-e chahārom moālemin-e tājikestān', ('Fourth Meeting of the Teachers of Tajikistan'), *Rahbar-e dānesh*, no. 8 (23), third year, August 1929, pp. 1–3.

73 See for example 'Qeshlāq, kermak dāri va abrishamchegi' ('The Provinces, Silkworm Cultivation and Silk Production'), *Rahbar-e dānesh*, no. 1, third year, 1 January 1929, pp. 14–17.

74 'Jalālzāde, az rāyon-e Boyson', *Rahbar-e dānesh*, no. 2 (29), fourth year, 1 February 1930.

75 Picking out the militants who ran these journals merits further investigation, but one can state that their public was primarily composed of teachers, since journals such as *Dānesh va āmuzegār* and *Rahbar-e dānesh* were set up specifically to help teachers. This class of teachers was very small, its power to act limited, and its establishment in the countryside laborious but real. One must also recognise the links established with the first promoters of the *kolkhoz* ('collective farms').

76 See the intervention of Ch. Emāmov, a member of the Tajik Sub-Commission created along with the temporary bureaux of the republics and provinces, to the Bureau of the Central Committee of Central Asia on 15 July 1924. (The Tajik Sub-Commission had consultative voting status on the Central Commission on National and Regional Divisions: there was thus no Tajik representation, despite what had been decided beforehand.) Masov, *op. cit.* [note 19 above], p. 46.

77 *Ibid*, p. 32.

78 Aliev, *op. cit.* [note 59 above], p. 7.

79 This was the response of T. Ryskulov (a Kazakh), who, at the second Russian General Meeting of the Communist Turkic Peoples in Moscow in 1921 showed his disagreement with Lenin, who spoke about the need to fight Pan-Islamism and similar movements. Ryskulov declared that Pan-Islamism and Pan-Turkism were very important for the Muslim peoples, and that this was the reason why they were looking towards Atatürk. Quoted by Masov, *op. cit*, p. 30.

80 Aini would often recite his favourite poem by Bidel, which could be summarised thus: 'Life has become weighty, what should Bidel do? Happy or unhappy, one must live.' He received the Red Banner in 1931.

81 Biktāsh was forced to resign his position at the Pedagogical Institute in Tajikistan in 1934 and returned to Samarkand.

82 Makhsum was a native of the mountainous region of Garm; he was executed in1937.

83 Born in Bukhara, Fitrat was at that time teaching Turcophone literature. In an open letter of 1929, he criticised himself for his 'Pan-Turkic' stance. He was executed in 1937.

84 Before the Revolution, the city of Bukhara had four famous millionaires. The Emir escaped, as did the fathers of Fayzollāh Khojayev, Mohiyedinov and Arabov. They could all be considered as belonging to the Jadid movement and as supporters of a social and economic upheaval in their society. Having become Communists and architects of Tajik society, they gave all their money to the Party, only to be executed finally during the purges, in 1937, 1934 and 1932 respectively.

85 Mohiyedinov, *op. cit.* [note 17 above], p. 18.

86 In 1924, Checherin, Russia's Minister of Foreign Affairs, even suggested the creation of a Greater Tajikistan, within which Uzbekistan would have had the status of Autonomous Republic. His proposal was rejected by Stalin.

87 One should note for example that 1929 saw the establishment of the first National Drama Theatre by Lāhuti, and 1931 that of the Public Pedagogical University, the first institute of higher education in Tajikistan, initially with only one faculty. There were twelve teachers. In 1931 the University of 'Mive sabzivatshenasi' was built on the model of the Central Asian University of Agriculture in Khojent; in 1934 it became a University of Agriculture. The Republic's first scientific centre was built in 1932, called the Tajik Section of the Academy of Sciences of the Soviet Union; the Dushanbe City Library was opened in January 1933 and renamed Ferdowsi in 1934 on the occasion of the celebrations for his millenium. In 1934, the Public Museum of History, *keshvar shenāsi* and *behzād* art was opened (to exhibit the Republic's economic and national achievements, in nature, history until the Revolution, in the Soviet period, etc.) In 1937, the Russian language National Mayakovsky Theatre was opened, and in 1948 the National University of Tajikistan, etc.

Select Bibliography

JOURNALS:

AVĀZ-E TĀJIK-E KAMBAGHAL, a weekly political, social and literary journal. Samarkand, 1924–25.

DĀNESH-BINESH. Nezārat-e Mo'āref-e Tājikestān, Samarkand, 1927.

DĀNESH VA ĀMUZEGĀR, a political, social, educational, pedagogical, literary, scientific, technical and critical fortnightly journal, which became a monthly after the third issue. Nezārat-e Mo'āref-e Tājikestān, Dushanbe, 1926.

The Premises for the Construction of a Tajik National Identity

MARDOM GIĀH, an academic and popular cultural review. Dushanbe, 1993.

RAHBAR-E DĀNESH, monthly. Nezārat-e Mo'āref-e Tājikestān, Tashkent, Stalinabad, 1927–32.

SIMORQ, monthly. No. 7–9, first year, Mordād-Abān 1369, Tehran.

BOOKS AND ARTICLES:

AINI, Kamal S. *Kārnāme-ye Ostād Sadriddin Aini*, Nashriāt-e Erfān, Dushanbe, 1978.

AINI, Sadriddin. *Marg-e Sudkhor*, Nashriāt-e Dowlaty-e Tājikestān, Stalinabad, 1956.

BECKA, Jiři. *Sadriddin Ayni Father of Modern Tajik Culture*, Istituto Universitario Orientale Seminario Di Studi Asiatici Series Minor V, Naples, 1980, 111 pp.

BENNIGSEN, Alexandre and BROXUP, Mary. *Mosalmānān-e Shoravi*, translated by Kaveh Bayat, Daftar-e Nasr Farhang-e Eslāmi, Tehran, 1370, 287 pp.

DERRIENIC, J. P. *Le Moyen-Orient au 20ème siècle*, translated into Persian by F. Ardalān, Sāzmān-e Enteshārāt-e Jāvidān, Tehran, 1368, 497 pp.

GAFFUROV, Bābājān. *Tojikon, okhirhoy-i asr-i miyona va dawray-i naw*, Vol. 2, Nashriāt-e Erfān, Dushanbe, 1985, 414 pp.

HAERI, Abdolhādi. 'Mafhum-e Novin-e Azādy hāy-e Siāsi va Ejtema'i dar neveshtehay-e Pārsi-e Asiay-e Miāne', *Simorq*, no. 7–9, first year, Abān-e 1369, pp. 3–25.

'Naqsh-e zabān-e fārsi bishtar khāhad shod', interview with Albert Karamov. *Adine*, no. 67, Bahman-e 1370, Tehran, pp. 13–15.

LANGERUDI, Shams. *Tārik-e Tahlili-e She'r-e no: Az mashrutiat tā Kudetā (1284–1332 hg)*, Nashr-e Markaz, 1370, 659 pp.

MASOV, Rahim. *Istoriya Topornogo Razdeleniya*, Nashriāt-e Erfān, Dushanbe, 1991, 190 pp.

RAKOWSKA-HARMSTONE, Teresa. *Russia and Nationalism in Central Asia. The Case of Tadjikistan*, The Johns Hopkins Press, Baltimore and London, 1970, 293 pp.

SHOKUROV, Mohammadjān. *Har sokhan jā-yi har nokte maqām-i dārad*, Nashriāt-e Erfān, Dushanbe, 1985, 368 pp.

SHOKUROV, Rostam. 'Septāmbr-i sāl-i 1920 dar Bokhārā she hādisay-i ruy dād?' *Sedāy-e Sharq*, no. 9, 1990, Dushanbe, p. 113.

TOYROV, T. 'Bombēbārān-e Bokhārā', *Sedāy-e Sharq*, no. 9.

41

DIVISION AND
CONFLICT

Chapter 3

Perestroika as seen by some Tajik Historians

Michel Hammer

The following remarks are a synthesis of the conversations, and especially of the correspondence, which the present author has had with some Tajik historians.[1] The aim of the article is to recreate the tone of the discussions, which in fact confirm and concur with my own analyses of the situation. Two of these historians, the Academicians R. Masov and F. Jumayev, have taken a public stand in the debate on Tajikistan in the monthly review *Sukhan* ('Word'), founded in February 1990. Their stance is aligned to that of the nationalist opposition.[2] A. Safarov, F. Kadyrov and A. Baimuradov do not have strong political affiliations; they see themselves as close observers of the evolution of the Soviet scene, in the broad sense. Baimuradov in particular often shared his feelings with me until his hospitalisation in Moscow in March 1990. Unfortunately the data end at this moment, coinciding with the riots which bathed Dushanbe in blood. Such questions as *Birlik* (Uzbek movement) cannot be dealt with here.

The essay is constructed around two main themes: firstly, general ideas about perestroika; secondly, the particular case of Tajikistan from the perspective of the changes taking place in the USSR.

On 11 March 1985, even before Chernenko had been buried, Gorbachev was elected General Secretary of the Communist Party of the Soviet Union. Schematically speaking, his actions up to 1990 aroused four types of reaction in my interlocutors: 1) disappointment; 2) amazement mixed with exasperation; 3) anxiety; 4) hope.

Disappointment

This reaction was prompted by the following seven factors:[3]

1. *The same stock phrases were still being used.* In his first speeches, for example, Gorbachev used the concept of

45

perestroika (whose future fortunes we are all familiar with) just as Andropov had.[4]

2. *Conceptual vagueness.* As the months passed, the term perestroika took on the quality of an emblematic formula, the exact meaning of which was impossible to pinpoint. The terms Bolshevism, Socialism, Leninism and Communism were used loosely. This semantic imprecision was a reflection of the hesitant thinking and confusion clouding the entire project. In November 1989, in a long theoretical article, Gorbachev conjured up a new image of Socialism as not only humane but democratic.[5] Once certain imperfections had been set right, the authorities would have to embark on the phase of rebuilding (*peredelka*) the whole edifice, from its economic foundations right through to the superstructure. This new concept did nothing to clarify the venture.

3. *Schematisation and reductionism.* Perestroika was opposed to *zastoi* ('stagnation'). At the XXVII Party Congress in April 1986 Gorbachev attacked the bureaucracy, delaying mechanisms and the administrative command system to explain the stagnation. It was made to look as though, thanks to him, the country was embarking upon a new era, a golden age, while the Brezhnev era had produced nothing but negative results.

4. *Silence on the question of dissidents.* On 8 December 1986, A. Marchenko died in prison. However, on the twelfth of that month, Sakharov was permitted to return to Moscow.

5. *The absence of any fundamental change regarding the war in Afghanistan.* It was only during a speech given in Vladivostok in July 1986 that the decision to withdraw six regiments was made known.

6. *Silence about the turmoil occurring outside the centre.* Despite the riots in Alma-Ata in December 1986 and the troubles in Tajikistan at the beginning of 1987, there seemed to be no awareness whatsoever of the national and religious issues. Even when he met the Uzbek authorities in Tashkent, Gorbachev did not produce any analysis of the situation worthy of the name, even though some weeks previously, in talks with the Orthodox Patriarch, he had outlined the absolute necessity of aligning believers with perestroika.[6] His heavy didactic insistence and fondness for circumlocutions led him to make a rambling speech peppered with tautologies and contradictions. 'We must not decrease our efforts in the field of restructuring; on the contrary, we must multiply them, taking into account the experience acquired during restructuring...'[7]

7. *'Westernisation' in the reform movement.* The expression 'common European home' seemed to ignore the cultural and economic aspirations of Central Asia and the tact required for the solution of such problems.

Amazement mixed with exasperation

In September 1985, Gorbachev declared: 'The Party's policy on matters of nationality has been a resounding success. The fifteen Republics are booming.' On 25 February 1986, he elaborated his thought: 'We have done away, once and for all, with national oppressions and inequalities. Unshakeable friendship among our peoples and respect for national culture and national dignity have been asserted and are firmly anchored in the minds of millions of men.'[8] He did concede, however, that the achievements should not make one think there were no problems. Nevertheless, all things considered, multinationalism was a source of strength more than of weakness or disintegration. In terms of nationalities, the USSR stood out as a unique example in the history of human civilisation.[9]

The glorification of Russia was another source of surprise: 'Throughout its history, the Russian people has shown vivid proof of its internationalism and respect for other peoples.'[10]

Finally, on another level, in June 1989[11] a Russian nationalist, Valentin Rasputin, advocated Russia's secession from the Soviet community, blaming the ingratitude and indifference of the peoples of the USSR towards the sacrifices made by Russia.

Anxiety

The passage of the months brought more and more vividly to light the chasm between rhetoric and positive achievements: all the economic indicators were unfavourable and poverty was increasing. Where was Gorbachev headed exactly, with his daydreams and his vacillations? He had managed to convince even the most sceptical Westerners, yet failed to win over those who needed conviction most – the inhabitants of the country he was leading.[12]

In February 1988 nationalist demonstrations broke out in Yerevan and Tallinn. Yet on 14 September, A. Yakovlev claimed that the national factor was an added driving force of perestroika. On 16 November 1988, the Estonian Parliament proclaimed the ascendancy of its laws over those of the USSR. Gorbachev deemed this measure unconstitutional and annulled it on 26 November. On 8 and 9 April 1989, the security forces dispersed peaceful demonstrators in Tbilisi. 'Is Gorbachev really a true liberal, dedicated to pluralist democracy?'[13]

In an article in *Izvestia* on 30 November 1987, Yakovlev asserted: 'To be opposed to perestroika is as good as saying you are a supporter of corruption, opposed to social equality and justice.'

On 12 December 1989, the Congress of Deputies refused, at Gorbachev's instigation, to hold a debate on the abolition of the leading role of the Communist Party (Article 6 of the Constitution). A painful scene of confrontation between Sakharov and the Soviet President ensued: 'On one side was a man exhausted by years of struggle and humiliation; on the other, a man of power, authoritarian, outraged, intransigent and contemptuous.'[14]

Nonetheless the main preoccupation remained the question of nationalities. On 27 July 1989, the Supreme Soviet conferred economic autonomy on Estonia and Lithuania. 'It is not enough,' stressed F. Kadyrov.[15] The separatists' requests should have been acceded to, and those of Vilnius particularly should have been supported in their confrontation with the Kremlin. Gorbachev should have removed all traces of the German-Soviet treaties of 23 August and 28 September 1939. The legal identity of the Baltic states had survived annexation.

As for Tajikistan, it belonged in a renewed federation, with autonomous status. Its position was not comparable with that of the Baltic countries.

Hope

In the autumn of 1989, after months of procrastination, one of Gorbachev's chief advisers, Grigorii Revenko, was made responsible for devising a new Union treaty in the spirit of the reforms. It was to institute a remodelled decentralisation, underpinned, as the European Commission would say, by the condition of subsidiarity. Legal clarification, the redistribution of jurisdictions and a revision of the levels of jurisdiction were to guarantee the survival of the USSR.

Revenko's initial plans envisaged three levels of jurisdiction:

1. The centre would be in charge of defence, foreign policy, monetary policy, energy supply, transport and protection of the environment.

2. Certain issues would be under the jurisdiction of mixed commissions of decision-makers. Moscow and Dushanbe, for example, would jointly examine the question of water:[16] a large part of Central Asia's water system is on Tajik territory. Military service, in territorial formations, could also be organised on this level.[17]

3. Finally, there were to be matters of purely Republican jurisdiction: Tajikistan would have had its own religious policy and an education system designed to halt Russification, promote the Arabic-Persian alphabet and encourage the establishment of an Islamic university.[18] On the commercial front, Dushanbe would have been allowed full scope to develop its exchanges with Iran, Turkey and China, along the lines of the Protocol of Agreement it had signed with the Chinese minister Zheng Tuobin in 1988.[19]

Tajikistan subjected to the hazards of perestroika: the factors which explain the Tajik historians' pessimism and fears[20]

1. The Tajik entity is a product *par excellence* of the Soviet era, and does not have a historical tradition of its own.[21] On 14 October 1924, Tajikistan was joined to Uzbekistan as an Autonomous Republic. It became a Soviet Socialist Republic on 5 October 1929. Seventy years later, this decision arouses bitterness in Tashkent as well as in Dushanbe, as memories are reviewed and the scars of history are assessed. It also illustrates the potentially dangerous phenomenon of frontiers which do not coincide with ethnic distribution.

2. It is more helpful to speak of a sum of Persian-speaking Sunni communities than of a Tajik *ethnos* as such. The territorial patchwork that makes up Tajikistan is reflected in the vividness of its regional differences. Local cultures have developed. Kurgan-Tyube Province is strewn with pockets of 'Wahhabism' (hence the troubles of March 1987).

3. More revealing of the precariousness of Tajikistan's position is the situation in the Autonomous Province of Gorny Badakhshan, where Ismailis greatly predominate. The danger represented by this region as a hotbed of instability is not so much religious as political, with the growth of a movement in Khorog calling for greater autonomy.

4. The demographic structure of Tajikistan is also unstable, with 1.2 million Uzbeks and about 380,000 Russians for 3.2 million Tajiks,

according to the 1989 census. Cohabitation between Tajiks and Uzbeks is more or less troubled, depending on the region. In Leninabad it is slightly more harmonious, but on the whole, the level of intermarriage is dropping, with a tendency to endogamy.[22]

5. Tajikistan has no external pole of attraction or point of support: no country fully shares its culture, religion and language. Neither Iran nor Turkey can take on that role. For the Tajik entity to survive, caution demands that the question of the Afghan Tajiks is left untouched, and that noisy irredentism about the Persian-speakers of Bukhara and Samarkand is avoided.

Only a coherent project for a confederative union guaranteed by the Kremlin could save Dushanbe from the threat of a territorial reorganisation of the region. In the latter scenario, the major risk would be the assertion of Uzbek hegemony under the banner of a new Pan-Turkism.[23] Masov and Jumayev were sympathetic to some of the hypotheses outlined above, though more vehement in their denunciation of the Turcophone Uzbeks; but they seemed much more worried about the fate of Tajiks living outside the present-day borders of the Republic. In their view, the stability of Central Asia could only be ensured if frontiers were declared sacrosanct, but this can only happen with the mandate of the electorate, in referenda by secret ballot.[24]

Fifteen years ago, H. Carreère d'Encausse wrote, and I quote the gist of what she said: 'The Muslims clearly have the feeling that they belong primarily to the Muslim nation, and only then, in the heart of this nation, to a specific nation.'[25] However, an assessment of the issues involved in the Tajik problem testifies to the contrary: the ethnic component has played a dominant role in the years 1985–90. One of the characteristics of Tajikistan seems to be that it is a 'quasi-state': it can only survive and be maintained through the benevolence and indulgence of its neighbours.

Notes

1 In the context of symposia on Tsarist policy in Turkestan, held in Moscow (September 1979 and September 1987), Samarkand (October 1979) and Dushanbe (September 1987).

2 See *Revue du monde musulman et de la Méditerranée*, 1/2, 1991.

3 My personal notes: see the analyses of Baimuradov (October 1988, September 1989, January 1990), Safarov (December 1989) and Kadyrov (January 1990).

4 *Pravda*, 11 December 1984 and 12 April 1985.

5 *Pravda*, 26 November 1989.
6 M. Gorbachev, *The Success of Restructuring is in the Hands of the People*, Novosti, Moscow, 1988.
7 *Ibid.*, p.5.
8 *Pravda*, 26 February 1986.
9 Gorbachev, *Péréstroïka. Vues neuves sur notre pays et le monde*, Paris, Flammarion, 1987, p. 167.
10 *Ibid.*, p. 169.
11 At the first meeting of the Congress of People's Deputies.
12 Remark by Baimuradov. Personal notes.
13 *Ibid.*
14 Remark by Kadyrov. Personal notes.
15 *Ibid.*
16 Suggestions by Safarov. Personal notes.
17 *Ibid.*
18 Suggestions by Baimuradov. Personal notes.
19 The Minister of Foreign Affairs of the People's Republic of China, Qian Qichen, confirmed to me that this would be possible 'when the time came', since there was 'no Tajik question in the province of Xinjiang'. Beijing, September 1992. Personal notes.
20 Baimuradov's analysis. Personal notes.
21 See Guissou Jahangiri, 'Le Tadjikistan, éléments pour la construction d'une nation', *Le Trimestre du Monde*, no. 20, fourth quarter 1992, pp. 154–66.
22 Remark by Kadyrov. Personal notes.
23 *Ibid.*
24 See the analysis of S. A. Dudoignon in 'Vers une fédération de l'Asie Centrale', *Le Trimestre du Monde*, no. 20, fourth quarter 1992.
25 H. Carrère d'Encausse, *L'Empire éclaté*, Flammarion, Paris, 1978, p. 306.

Chapter 4

Political Parties and Forces in Tajikistan, 1989–1993[1]

Stéphane A. Dudoignon

The study of the alternative political organisations which appeared and disappeared in Tajikistan over the course of these five years is a subject that begs the historian's attention today. The Communist offensive launched in autumn 1992 and the subsequent joint armed intervention by Russia and Uzbekistan ended in the re-establishment of an old-style Communist government in Dushanbe and the brutal elimination of any form of opposition, after four brief years of relative pluralism and six months of government by the former opposition parties, whose authority extended over the central regions of the country and the Pamirs. The formation of these movements and their repression constitute an episode of contemporary Central Asian history that has unfolded before our very eyes: the issue is by no means over, but we are already able to draw the first lessons from it, for it has brought to light hitherto undreamt-of determinisms, whose respective importance in the cause and resolution of Central Asia's political conflicts can now be assessed.

On the one hand, the movements which sprang up in Dushanbe in the perestroika years were strongly conditioned by the history of Tajikistan itself, a former Soviet Republic which surfaced on the map *ex nihilo*, after the ethno-territorial division of Central Asia under the aegis of the Russian Bolshevik party.[2] The primary characteristic of the Tajik situation was that the Republic's national intelligentsia, which was to play the leading role in the changes that took place in the 1980s, did not have available to it any political references of its own in modern history other than the Communist heritage. Firstly, because the difference between Communists and non-Communists in the political élite of Tajikistan in the last five years has been reduced to the distinction between those who are and those who have been.

Secondly, because the intellectual reformers in Dushanbe saw themselves hamstrung in their quest for a political genealogy by the fact that Tajikistan was entirely the creation of Bolshevism: before the October Revolution, the Tajik territory had been a rural region fought over by the Khanates of Bukhara and Kokand. The Tajik intelligentsia therefore found itself deprived of the memory of independence, whereas in other 'Muslim republics' of the USSR, such as Azerbaijan, Kazakhstan or neighbouring Uzbekistan, the non-Communist political organisations at the end of the 1980s could claim that they were going back to the spirit of modernist (*Jadid*) national movements of the beginning of the century, and indeed of brief periods of independence before Sovietisation.[3] Even the descendants of the few dozen literate Tajiks who had taken part in the Jadid renaissance in Central Asia before disappearing in the Stalinist purges had difficulty getting in touch with this pre-Communist heritage, since Jadidism belonged to the period before the ethnic and linguistic division of the region, on which the legitimacy of present-day Tajikistan is based.[4]

On the other hand, the political organisations which have flourished in Dushanbe in the past few years have certainly tried to compensate for their lack of historic roots by staying open to relatively varied external influences originating in different regions of the former Soviet periphery, from the Baltic states to Yerevan (which the Russians now call 'the new near abroad'). However, these influences produced contradictory effects in the different Central Asian republics (Tajik nationalists, for example, were sensitive to the Armenian cause, whereas their Uzbek counterparts embraced the Azeri cause). These divisions finally put an end to the coordination of the national opposition movements in Central Asia, and prevented the emergence of a united front such as existed in the Baltics, despite appeals for union uttered by Uzbek and Kazakh reformers.

The history of Tajikistan's alternative political movements, isolated from their neighbours by the ideological barriers created by Sovietisation, has been caught up in the ancient determinisms of a rural society dominated by traditional grandees whom the Russians, and later the Communists, had wooed and won over as allies. The strength of the rifts within Tajik society has proved the greatest barrier to political revival in Tajikistan, and is the second feature that distinguishes it from the other new Central Asian states.

A Paradoxical Avatar of Perestroika

The Crucial Impact of External Influences

The political renewal of Tajikistan had its origin in a number of external factors, the most decisive of which was certainly the constant and increasingly obvious weakening of Russia (*imperiya-yi fartūt*),[5] and its gradual economic detachment from its southern periphery. One of the first indications of this was the reversal of migratory fluxes, beginning in the mid-1970s, when Russian-speaking minorities began to outmigrate.[6] The concomitant demographic explosion in the Central Asian republics led to the appearance and exponential growth of unemployment, and at the same time definitively shattered the myth of the ultimate fusion (*slijanie*) of the nations through Russification. The national intelligentsias, hard pushed to mobilise themselves, were faced with the essential work of reconstructing the national identity, a task which, in the early days, devolved upon official writers and poets. The resurrected historical novel could now exalt, within the limits of Soviet decency, the greatness and past of the dominant people in each republic.[7] In the historical literary portraits by Sātim Ulughzāda (born in 1911 and a great devotee of the Russian orientalists of the 1930s), the Tajik reader is asked to identify with his distant 'ancestors' the Sogdians,[8] an Iranian-speaking people with an outstanding culture, whose capital had been situated at a crossroads on the Silk Route during the sixth to eighth centuries AD; the author, who for a long time was in semi-disgrace, was the direct originator of the recent fashion for the 'Sogdian novel', and one of the spiritual fathers of Dushanbe's young intellectuals. The poet Bāzār Sābir (born in 1938), who was latterly the most eloquent bard of the Tajik national revival until his imprisonment in early 1993, started toppling Communist idols during the same period and calling for a renewal of civic awareness based on national points of reference.[9]

The official organisations of the intelligentsia (*tvorcheskie sojuzy*, 'creative unions': Writers, Cinema, Theatre, etc.) were a driving force behind the first renewal of identity, which could not yet be political. In September 1988, they banded together to form a united front of the 'Friends of Perestroika', each institution of which soon had an independent press organ. At the head of this revival were to be found, apart from the Union of Writers and the poet Lāyiq Sheralī's Persian-Tajik Language Foundation, the authors of the law which made Tajik the state language (June 1989), an Association of Young Historians,[10] and the Cinema Union, which rallied round Dawlat Khudonazarov, the future champion of the joint opposition. These pioneering institutions were later joined by academic circles, which would make up for their tardiness with an excess of nationalist zeal which soon strayed into drawing up territorial claims.

At the same time a schism occurred at the very heart of the Tajik Communist Party, once considered among the most placid in the USSR. On the orders of his superiors, and over a number of years, the official video-maker Evgenij V. Kuzin had been making confidential films, for the exclusive attention of the apparatchiks, documenting the appalling dimensions of collapse and decay in the Republic's economic infrastructure and social fabric.[11] The division between the reformers, alerted by this vision of disaster and the Party's loss of legitimacy, and the conservatives, who closed ranks behind the First Secretary of the Party, Qahhār Mahkamov (who supported the political *status quo* after a brief effort at perestroika), came to a head during the violently repressed demonstrations of 11–13 February 1990, in an attempt at a palace revolution. This was inspired by Otakhon Latifi, the regime's ideologue, and Nūr Tabar, the young Minister of Culture, and aimed to bring to power Būrī Karimov, the forty-year-old Director of Services of the Republic's Plan.[12]

Anti-Russian feeling had been the motive for the big demonstrations in Alma-Ata, Kazakhstan, in December 1986,[13] which confirmed the failure of the Russian nationalities policy in Central Asia; it was also the common denominator in the demonstrations which followed in the huge squares of the Tajik capital from February 1989. The Tajiks had been on the outposts in the war with Afghanistan: the incessant round of cargo-planes landing at Dushanbe airport were a reminder, even to the least observant, of the proximity and scope of the conflict; in addition, many young Tajik intellectuals had served as translators in the main trouble-spots of the Afghan battlefield, and not all of them had returned with their devotion to the Soviet regime intact. The impact of the war on people's minds was so great, and the trauma of it such, even for an intelligentsia not slow to admit its debt to Russia, that the Afghan war was the only really taboo subject of conversation in Dushanbe after the abolition of the USSR. Russia, hitherto a generous benefactor, now appeared to young Tajiks as the cause of their country's innumerable problems: pollution, malnutrition, expansion of the unofficial economy, a rise in crime and an infant mortality rate suggestive of a Third World country. The rumour of a wave of immigration by Armenian refugees from Nagorno-

Karabagh, 'deliberately set off by Russia's intervention in Transcaucasia',[14] unleashed the demonstrations of February 1990 in Dushanbe, which were the crucible for the national opposition.

The Contradictory Pressure of Soviet Institutions

In Tajikistan, the watchwords of perestroika rapidly turned into a huge public debate about relations with Russia and the construction of national, economic and political sovereignty. Gorbachev's words continued to be quoted for quite some time in order to maintain a Socialist legitimacy that was still indispensable, but it was the Indian Muslim poet, Muhammad Iqbāl (1877–1938), the herald of the reawakening and modernisation of Islam, who became the ultimate point of reference for all alike.[15] The issue of the national language, a symbol of de-Russification, was the first one adopted by the forces who were to become the opposition to the left-overs of Communism.

The CPSU's double-dealing and systematic obstruction of reforms were soon exposed.[16] The demonstrations in Moscow by Crimean Tatars claiming their rights (July 1987), the first 'anti-nomenklatura' offensives mounted against the Communist Party by economic and academic circles in the 'centre' (the election campaign to the People's Congress, from December 1988 to March 1989), and the marches by Sajudis for Lithuanian self-determination (February 1989), gradually led to the realisation that there was room for political movements outside the Communist Party. At the same time, Russian reformist circles, who had for long been in the minority in Moscow itself (see the events of 1992–1993), looked for support to the intelligentsia in the apparatus and the KGB in the republics;[17] this 'second level' of the Soviet political system was, from autumn 1989 to autumn 1992, able to act with relative freedom and with the blessing of the Ministry of Order.

An aside should be added here about the leading role played by the KGB in the organisation and launching of the popular fronts on the periphery of the empire. Boris Pugo, the head of the KGB and later First Secretary of the Party in Latvia,[18] and a future protagonist in the putsch of August 1991, set up the popular front in his own republic[19] before going to Dushanbe in February 1990; he strongly advised his Tajik counterpart to satisfy the symbolic demands of the demonstrations organised by the academic intelligentsia. The alternative political organisations and parties in Tajikistan were initially tolerated because they were thought to provide so many necessary and convenient outlets for the frustrations of the country's urban population, and ensure that these did not escalate into inter-communal violence.[20]

But collaborative links between the 'organs' (the KGB) and academic circles were not a new phenomenon: they had been established in the 1970s, when the KGB of the USSR had begun to take over the Party's job of recruiting intellectual élites. These links were rapidly strengthened by a shared hostility towards the institutionalised corruption of the upper echelons of the USSR's leaders in the second decade of the Brezhnev era. This is how, for a time, the KGB came to be close to the most fervent supporters of reform, the intelligentsia and some of the economic nomenklatura. And this is why in Tajikistan the Pamiris allied themselves collectively with the 'Islamic-democratic' opposition against the apparatchiks, even though they were hostile to Islamist parties in general (and Afghan ones in particular) extending their influence into Central Asia. Since the mid-1970s, the Ismaili communities of the Pamirs have made up the bulk of medium-level officers in the security forces in Tajikistan (not surprisingly, given their religious particularism and phobia of fundamentalism); moreover, they harboured an instinctive animosity towards the black market networks which had been developed, under cover of the Party, by provincial officials in Kulyab, in the south of the Republic – a region entirely overlooked by Soviet industrial investment.[21]

The Pamiris' support for the 'anti-nomenklatura' is one explana-tion for the regional (not tribal, as it is too often described) character assumed by political conflicts in Tajikistan, and later by the civil war. Their alliance did not, however, make these mountain-dwelling KGB agents a decisive support for the anti-Communist cause, since the Pamiris' chief preoccupation was with preventing the confiscation of the Republic's resources by the networks of officials on the plains, and with defending, eventually with Russia's help, their strategic region's own interests against the mafia-like centralism of the Communists in power in Dushanbe. The bitterness of the conflict made the Pamiri communities the main target of the bloody score-settling that followed normalisation.[22]

The backing of the KGB and the tacit support of the Soviet authorities had a very different effect on the development of Tajik opposition organisations in Dushanbe, by bringing about a rapid radicalisation of the political demands formulated by the academic circles – especially after the Congresses in Moscow (the first of which was elected in March 1990) had aired the evils of the system to their hearts' content, and suggested the urgency of radical reforms. The Tajik opposition parties rapidly won huge popular support – as their Russian 'counterparts' never did – and became true parties of independence and 'decolonisation' in a way wholly unpredicted by the daring strategies of the 'organs'.

Indeed the initial support of the KGB for the 'academocrats' and the reform fringe of the economic nomenklatura had originally been aimed at providing a channel for popular demands, while maintaining Tajikistan's position under Russia's wing. After all, were not the academic intellectuals, who were to be at once the originators and the gravediggers of the Tajik political revival in the 1980s, the only social group in all the Soviet republics who had an interest in maintaining the institutions and political space handed down by the USSR?

At first, the relatively homogeneous milieu of the academies allowed for the establishment, in almost all the Union's republics, of Democratic Parties which, the 'organs' hoped, would rally nascent public opinion under the authority of 'approachable' leaders, none other than the technocrats and official writers of the Soviet regime. Tajikistan was no exception: here the Democratic Party of Tajikistan, which had sprung up in the halls of the Academy of Sciences,[23] was placed under the authority of the official philosopher Shādmān Yūsuf [Yusupov] (the author of a thesis on Karl Marx's spiritual quest).[24]

The fondness felt by many Tajik intellectuals of the apparatus for the institutions and political sphere handed down by the USSR can be explained in part by their awareness that radical political reform would fell the branch on which they were comfortably perched: the intellectual mediocrity prevalent in Dushanbe, as in all the Soviet provincial capitals, precluded any hope of the intelligentsia's survival outside the national Socialism of which it had made itself the official custodian (it was soon to be joined on this battlement by the new economic nomenklatura, which was also quick to start spouting about national values). In the particular case of the Tajiks, this worry was compounded by the awareness that any discussion about the legitimacy or viability of Tajikistan as a political entity, or about the ideological heritage of the Soviet era, was no more nor less than a death sentence for the 'national' intelligentsia of the former Soviet Republic. This is why the reformers within the Tajik apparatus always thought of de-Communisation in terms of personal purges (which did, moreover, become convulsively violent in Dushanbe), rather than of an attempt to bring about long-lasting institutional reform. Personal attacks of remarkable inanity – which the KGB soon began to stir up with the aim of discrediting all and sundry – and rhetoric about the 'national whole' pervaded every nook and cranny of the public debate; especially virulent were those who felt weighed down with remorse about their erstwhile Soviet orthodoxy. This rhetorical violence remained inversely proportionate to the energy expended in denouncing former privileges, and thus Tajik nationalism became in its final phase a factor for the conservation of the 'values' and structures of the old regime.

Turkestanism and Tajikism

The direct influence of the Sajudis press, which the originators of the first Tajik opposition movements could read regularly at the National Library of Dushanbe (it officially subscribed to Vilnius newspapers, thanks to the Soviet registration of copyright), can be readily discerned in the programmes of these organisations. In particular, the insistence of the radical Lithuanian intelligentsia on the desperate necessity of escaping from the Russian sphere of influence was loudly echoed in the Tajik nationalist press. The popular fronts in the Baltics also had a less direct influence on the Tajik revival. In fact, the 'Birlik Popular Movement' in Uzbekistan was born in the wake of the Baltic fronts; it was set up in November 1988, and the large demonstrations it staged in Tashkent the following spring caused a mighty reverberation throughout Central Asia, leading in turn to the upsurge of a multitude of alternative organisations.

Birlik hoped to unite the popular movements throughout Central Asia, since the Uzbek reformers saw here great cultural and political scope for setting up a democracy.[25] In the short term, the Birlik leaders set themselves the goal of resisting both the temptation of an ultra-nationalist swing, which would be sure to grip all the young intelligentsias in each republic, and the threats of inter-ethnic violence that had been brewing since the end of the 1970s, and which erupted sporadically between 1987 and 1991. Birlik tirelessly emphasised the common goals of the Central Asian intelligentsias, urging them to muffle their conflicts and animosities.[26] With the aim of presenting a united front of alternative forces, the Uzbek popular front practised a policy of permanent contacts with the new political organisations in neighbouring republics, which principally took the form of inter-party meetings at regional level, particularly in the sensitive Ferghana region, divided as it was between Uzbekistan, Kyrgyzstan and

Tajikistan. It is difficult to appreciate the role that these permanent consultations played in the apparent decrease in inter-communal violence from autumn 1991; it certainly contributed extensively to the circulation of ideas between the republics.

However, Birlik, a vast, inorganic constellation of intellectuals who had been bred in the apparatus, never got anywhere near positions of political power in Uzbekistan, however minimal. The country stayed in the hands of a hereditary group of the old regime, overtly hostile to the alternative movements led by intellectual reformers which had begun to spring up all over Central Asia. The Tajik reformers saw from the outset that the continuing power of the Uzbek 'conservatives' posed one of the gravest threats to their political survival.[27] Their fear of intervention in Tajik affairs by Islam Karimov's regime[28] unfortunately expressed itself as increasingly violent anti-Uzbekism,[29] with recriminations and disputes dating back to the start of the Soviet era and the ethnic and territorial division of Central Asia. One Tajik opposition party, made up of former orthodox apparatchiks short on legitimacy and inspiration, even tried to use it to stir up the masses.

These feelings had a decisive influence on the whole alternative movement in Tajikistan, from its points of reference to its political practice. Thus, Birlik, completely engrossed in its struggle against the Russian empire and the dubious game it was playing on its fringes, declared its solidarity in early 1992 with the government of the Azerbaijani Popular Front (the APF was prey to an invasion of fighters from Stepanakert which called into question the whole democratic process in Transcaucasia), and set up a Karabagh Committee in Tashkent to provide aid to Azeri civilian refugees;[30] Tajik reformers expressed their sympathy for the Armenian cause to anyone who cared to listen. This turning-point was broadcast by the steadily more frequent publication of articles glorifying Armenian culture in the academic reviews in Dushanbe, which maintained an impenetrable silence on the subject of the Turkic world. Everything was used as a pretext to denounce the 'hegemony' of the Turks who had dominated Central Asia and the Islamic world since the eleventh century. The Indo-Europeanism of the nationalist tribunes in Dushanbe bred a geopolitics of the enclave, based on the threat of political, as well as cultural, assimilation into a Turkic universe. This explains the insistence of Tajik reformers on gaining the support of the 'democrats' in Moscow for their struggle against the old order, as a guarantee against the potential machinations of the 'conservative' Uzbek powers; it also explains their affection for the political space of

Sovietisation, which offered them a buffer against cultural disappearance, pure and simple: they always denounced its imperfections, beginning with the layout of the inter-republican borders, without ever challenging the principle of it.

From Perestroika to Bāz-sāzī

Before it strayed into rhetoric about the national whole, perestroika ('reconstruction') was still interpreted in Tajikistan as a reconstruction (*bāz-sāzī*) of politics: decolonisation coupled with de-Sovietisation. The rise of parties which gathered together members of the intelligentsia of the apparatus in opposition to the Communist Party was a completely new phenomenon, for Soviet Central Asia had never experienced the dissidence typical of the European regions of the USSR. The only organised opposition movements there had been those defending the rights of the deported Meskh and Crimean Tatar minorities.[31]

The economist Tāher 'Abdujabbār formed the first nucleus of political opposition worthy of the name in the Supreme Soviet, gathering together a tiny group of five deputies in 1989. He then founded the Rastākhez movement, a group of 'intellectual patriots' (*ziyāyān-i watanparast*),[32] launched on 14 September 1989.[33] Confined to illegality until 21 June 1991,[34] Rastākhez brought itself to the attention of nascent public opinion from summer 1990 by demanding the banning of all Communist Party activity in the state apparatus of the Republic.[35] It played the dual roles of spur to public life and rallier of opposition parties, gathering under its wing representatives of the main alternative movements. The Democratic Party of Tajikistan came into existence on 10 August 1990;[36] it was destined to be the standard-bearer for the opposition in future electoral failures, and was enriched by the arrival of numerous defectors from the Tajik Communist Party. At the same time, the political clubs (*mahāfil-yi siyāsī*) which had sprung up during perestroika: the reformist *Rū ba Rū* ('Face to face') in Dushanbe and the 'conservative' *Āshkārā* ('Glasnost') in Kulyab, revealed the rifts at the heart of the apparatus and hinted at the regionalist foundations of the ideological disagreements that would soon drag the country into civil war.

Each organisation immediately equipped itself with a bilingual press: the monthly *Rastākhez/Vozrozhdenie* alternated articles in Tajik and Russian, while the DPT initially printed two separate newspapers, *'Adālat* and *Svoboda*, before withdrawing the latter. The first independent periodicals, banned in the Republic, were published abroad (*Rastākhez* was issued from Lithuania, as was the monthly '*Adālat,* which was printed on the press of the daily *Respublika*), or behind the screen of figureheads like the newspaper *Duniyā,* published in Dushanbe from May 1991, which was the unofficial forum for Rastākhez.

In this new press, perestroika was reviewed and modified into a construction of national sovereignty. The Tajik ex-apparatus reformers proposed turning the USSR into a commonwealth of independent states, long before the term existed, and then making the CIS an 'internal common market' (*bāzār-i yagāna-yi dākhilī*).[37] They hoped to enjoy all the benefits of political independence while receiving from Moscow all the grants necessary for the maintenance of the Tajik economy which the Soviet system had so long guaranteed them.

The publicists of Rastākhez and the DPT knew perfectly well that economic independence was the first condition for any political sovereignty,[38] and to this end advocated the nationalisation of the raw materials and industrial infrastructures, transport etc.[39] The favourite economic theme of the new parties was decreasing dependence on cotton by drastically reducing monocultured lands,[40] and implementing a national textile industry which, it was believed, would be achieved more quickly if financial autonomy of production units and diversification of forms of ownership of the means of production were established. This liberalisation of the economy, verging rather on nationalisation, was supposed to achieve the detachment of the Republic and bring about the conditions for real political democratisation.[41] The essence of this programme, aside from the national packaging, was in fact nothing more than a carbon copy of Gorbachev's 'new thinking' on economic matters, which was itself the legacy of a series of abortive reforms of the Soviet integrated economic system;[42] moreover, it was first put into practice by the Tajik Communist Party after its comeback in autumn 1992.

The Tajik reformers were more articulate about the construction of political independence, quickly advocating, for example, that military service should take place in Tajikistan (mostly, in fact, to put an end to the murder of Central Asian conscripts in the Russian garrisons of the Soviet Army),[43] followed by the nationalisation of the armed forces,[44] with the formation of national guards (*gurdān-i jumhurī*) and a Defence Ministry at the sole disposal of the Tajik head of state – an idea steadfastly rejected by the Tajik Communist Party, which saw, quite rightly, that the presence in Tajikistan of the 201st Russian

Division was the only real guarantee of political stability.[45] The first stage of change in Tajikistan was to be the organisation of free general elections, merely in order for the reformers to get rid of the Brezhnev-era government.[46] Next, a new constitution would safeguard human rights, freedom of the press and political pluralism (*nizām-i chandhizbī*),[47] and make provisions for all central and regional positions of power to be electable.[48]

The central role set aside for 'persons of higher education' in the future institutions gives one some idea of the place the university-educated urban intelligentsia intended to give itself in the new regime, at the expense of those rural officials who had been favoured before by the Communists – bemedalled heads of kolkhozes and Stakhanovite cotton-pickers who had once lent their inimitable rustic style to the Tajik Supreme Soviets. The plan for a society dominated exclusively by the academic intelligentsia conformed perfectly with the idea of post-Soviet society dreamt up by the Muscovite theoreticians of perestroika: a republic of scholars and philosophers (of the apparatus), inspired by the ongoing dream of building universal Socialism.

Between a Persian-Islamic Synthesis and National-Communism

The Appearance of an Islamic Party

The apparatus intelligentsia which had been converted to the cause of reform was soon, however, to come up against a partner/adversary of an unusual type, in the shape of the Islamic Rebirth Party. The IRP, a body which initially covered the whole territory of the Soviet Union, was created at a Congress which met in Astrakhan on 9 July 1990 by North Caucasians, led by 'Abbās Kebedov, the chief of the Organisation Committee, based in Qizil-Yurt in Dagestan, and Muhammad Bahāuddīn, who presided over the 183-strong assembly of delegates from the entire USSR.[49] The new Party was effectively directed by a fifteen-strong Council of the 'ulamas', elected at the suggestion of the all-powerful Organisation Committee (*orgkomitet*), and comprising intellectual Islamists rather than the traditional ulama.[50] Its functioning was more reminiscent of the first Bolshevik organisations than of Islamist parties in other Muslim countries, and its official (and minimalist) credo was to unite Muslims throughout the USSR to defend their freedom of conscience.[51] However, using a terminology which was itself fairly well-worn (Islam was 'humanist', 'pacifist' and 'progressive')[52] the IRP's discourse was classically neofundamentalist, particularly emphasising its vocation of proselytism, leading an offensive against the official clergy of the Soviet era and advocating social justice based on the redistribution of riches through the Islamic taxes of *zakāt* and *sadaqa*.[53]

In Tajikistan, where it was called *Hizb-i Nahzat-i Islāmī*, the historic roots of the IRP lay in the Islamic counter-society of the Soviet era. Indeed, in this disinherited rural Republic, the 1980s had seen the resurgence of alternative social phenomena, as witnessed by the blossoming of numerous underground cultural and sports clubs, where Far-Eastern martial arts were taught alongside didactic texts by the classical Persian poets Hāfiz and Firdawsī.[54] This phenomenon also found expression in fundamentalist propaganda by the very high-profile mullahs in the southern regions of the Republic, which were the poorest and closest to the Afghan border; among them was 'Abdullāh Sayyidov, who argued for the creation of an Islamic state inside the borders of Tajikistan.[55] The strength of the network created by these young mullahs, trained by reading the Quran and the Sunna in small alternative *madrasa*, was demonstrated on 6 October 1990, when they emerged from hiding to found the Tajik branch of the IRP in the Lenin suburb of Dushanbe, where the Naqshbandi sanctuary of Mawlānā Ya'qūb Charkhī is situated. Although it was initially illegal, the Party was to take part in the presidential elections held one year later.

In Tajikistan, the IRP set itself up primarily as the determined opponent of the apparatus intelligentsia, as well as of the Republic's *qaziyat*, a classical religious institution which had recently been revitalised by the youthfulness of its leaders and the appointment as its head of the dashing Hājji Akbar Tūrajānzāda. The *qāzī kalān* ('High Cadi') of Tajikistan received a Saudi subsidy and had at his disposal a publication which disseminated Islamic sacred texts and thus offered a useful complement to the work of the mullahs. Presiding over the organisation of the annual pilgrimage and attracting increasingly large crowds of the faithful to its 'Imām Termezī' mosque-*madrasa*, and adjoining 'Islamic market', which became hotbeds of social and political life, the *qaziyat* represented the main socialising force of Islam. The caution of the High Cadi in political matters, and the cleverness with which he kept his options open, made Tūrajānzāda a person whom it was very difficult to get around.

The 'Persian-Islamic Synthesis' and its Interpretations

The Tajik fundamentalist movement was gradually prompted to break with its headquarters in Moscow, which practised a *realpolitik* of alliance with the Communists, aiming to reduce as far as possible, in all the 'Muslim republics' of the USSR, the popular audience for the radical intelligentsia that had sprung up out of the apparatus. The separatist nationalism of the latter ran counter to the interests of the autochthonous nomenklaturas, but their growing success in public opinion was also harmful to the establishment of the fundamentalist party. Throughout the Muslim fringes of the empire, systematic campaigns to discredit the radical opposition were creating a political vacuum which favoured the Islamists.

Nevertheless, when the federal Islamist leader Haydar Jamāl called the Tajik electorate to a 'revolutionary vote' in favour of the Communist leader Nabiev in the presidential elections of October 1991,[56] the Tajik branch of the IRP seceded from its Moscow headquarters and moved closer to the organisations of the Tajik intelligentsia, partially espousing the nationalist and 'democratic' discourse of Rastākhez and the DPT – despite the philippics with which the President (*amir*) of the IRP of the USSR and his lieutenants had constantly bombarded the 'democrats' and other 'nationalists'.[57] This rapprochement was all the more easily achieved because the Dushanbe intelligentsia had itself been affirming the vitality of autonomous re-Islamisation since the early 1980s,[58] and even the most pro-Communist writers had begun appealing for a rehabilitation of the 'Islamic' tradition which they saw as an indispensable factor in social regulation[59] and presented as an integral part of the 'national' (or community: *millī*) cultural heritage.

The Tajik branch of the IRP borrowed its new, and thereafter more 'national', campaign themes from its opposition partners, beginning with the racist crimes committed in the Soviet army and the call for a national military service.[60] For the IRP and Rastākhez alike, religion became the ideological cornerstone of the anti-Russian, anti-colonial struggle.[61] They both used the same references to Islam's fight against the West, from Sayyid Jamāl id-Dīn al-Afghānī (1838–1897), an advocate of union against the colonial powers, to Muhammad 'Iqbāl, mentioned earlier, prized by well-read Tajiks for his theory of the reconstruction of identity (*khudshināsī*) and his exhortation to put up resistance to the European powers. Rastākhez's pleas for a re-evaluation of the status of women, 'tarnished' by the Russian and

Western media, and a return to 'ancestral customs',[62] echoed the sermons of the IRP on the 'foreign' (*'ajamī*) origin of the *faranjī*, the Central Asian version of the *chādor*, and their recommendation that women and adolescents should wear the *hijāb*, a simple veil covering the head, which was touted as conforming better to Tajik 'national' customs.[63]

Dushanbe academics and Islamist intellectuals adopted similar positions in wholeheartedly rejecting Turkish-style secularisation and elaborating on what the present author still hesitates to call a 'Persian-Islamic synthesis'.[64] They also denounced the role, real or imagined, of the USA in giving humanitarian aid to 'feather the nest of the Turkish model' (*model-i turkī*)[65] and 'lead the Muslim world astray'.[66] This hostility was bred of the Tajiks' fear of being absorbed into a greater 'Turkestan' under the joint aegis of Ankara and Tashkent, and greatly complicated the mission of discreet Turkish diplomacy in Tajikistan.[67] Brought up on Stalinist and Pan-Slavist reading, the reformist or Islamist intellectuals in Dushanbe could not conceive of the USSR's giving way to anything other than great confederations of 'pan' states, either Pan-Slav or Pan-Turkic, on a national basis constructed on the narrowest of ethnolinguistic parameters. This is why they chose to build bridges with 'all Persian-speaking states', that is principally Iran,[68] in which they saw primarily a future economic partner, with the common language ultimately facilitating the transfer of technology.

The two protagonists in the public debate, reformers and Islamists, nonetheless maintained very different interpretations of this 'Persian-Islamic synthesis'. The former saw it as a source of cultural renaissance (with the emphasis on Iranian Islamic culture: *farhang-i irānī wa islāmī*),[69] born of their residual fear of Turkicisation. The IRP, on the other hand, despite its Wahhabite origins, was looking for national political moorings in Tajikistan, presenting itself as the trusty defender of the newly-independent country's interests. Paradoxically, it was by adopting Khomeynist points of reference (Persian nationalism and anti-Western rhetoric)[70] that the IRP attempted to correct its internationalist 'image' and dissociate itself from the Soviet chaos, seeking an alliance with the Islamic Republic in order to limit the influence of the *qāzī kalān* Tūrajānzāda, the favoured client of the Saudis.

The typically urban – or suburban – reformist parties and IRP found themselves in competition with each other in the countryside, where their respective propaganda accompanied, rather than created, the renewal of ritual. They both fought for the allegiance of traditional community elders, whose support turned out to be decisive at election time.[71] In fact, Tajikistan is the most barren terrain imaginable for a fundamentalist organisation, because, with the notable exception of Dushanbe, it is practically bereft of the large modern towns and industrial suburbs where classic Islamist movements have traditionally flourished. In neighbouring Uzbekistan during the same period, 'Islamist organisations' (*islomiy uyumalari*) thrived in the large industrial cities of the Ferghana Valley, and the proto-Islamisation of some municipalities took place. In the Tajik countryside, however, the establishment of the IRP remained weak; the Party, led first by Muhammad-Sharīf Himmatov and then by Dawlat 'Usmān, encountered great difficulties in its relationships with the traditional élites there, the families of local and regional chiefs who had overall responsibility for networks of ancient Sufi brotherhoods.[72] It was thanks to its establishment in the central regions of Tajikistan, and its presence in Dushanbe itself and its large, sinister suburbs (550,000 inhabitants in 1990, almost double that today after the influx of refugees), that the Tajik IRP managed to be so influential in political events – which were principally played out in the capital – and to become such a major player in the opposition's rise to power in May 1992. Government by the Tajik Islamists chiefly meant a tremendous reinforcement of Iranian influence in Dushanbe; however, the IRP had to tone down its fundamentalist slogans demanding the creation of an Islamic state, since the latter was not part of the programmes of Rastākhez and the DPT, its partners in the anti-Communist coalition.

Towards a Set of Themes Based on the 'National Whole'

The reformist parties, which hinged their programmes on religious freedom for all creeds, saw in 'national' culture a condition for the resurgence of community spirit and civic conscience. However, in ascribing all the ills of Central Asia to cultural confiscation, the publicists of *Rastākhez* and *'Adālat* let the politicians off scot-free. They also remained dependent on *mirāsism* (from the Arabic word meaning 'heritage'), a sort of identity reconstruction, well known in Soviet Islam, which had already been tried out during de-Stalinisation (1956–1964) in some Muslim regions of the USSR, especially the Tatar world.[73] *Mirāsism* advocates the protection and illustration of the cultural heritage (in Tajik *ehiyā-yi zabān u farhang*)[74] as a weapon of de-Russification. Favouring the strictly identity-based elements of

67

the public discourse to the detriment of purely political claims, *mirāsism* was fundamentally a cultural revivalism which was encouraged in times of crisis by the central power of the Soviet state itself. It was essentially based on exalting the dominant ethnic group in each republic, and was favoured by the 'centre' because, as well as being apolitical, it sustained and deepened the fragmentation of the different peoples on the outskirts of the empire. The temptation for Soviet élites to veer into a discourse of the national whole was greater during the years of the collapse of the USSR because central power seemed to have weakened, and perestroika tended more and more to restrict itself to arousing nationalist passions. These were intended to hinder the creation of 'political oppositions formulated in political terms',[75] and thus create as many trouble-spots as possible, so that it would then be legitimate to call for the normalising intervention of Russian tanks.

Mirāsism, which, as already mentioned, was devoid of any historical and intellectual genealogy apart from Sovietism, was the only reference point that the Tajik national intelligentsia had available to it. The political heritage of the Jadids remained taboo in Tajikistan longer than it did in Tashkent, and its appropriateness continues to be problematic for the post-Soviet Tajik intelligentsia, whose debates on the role of the Jadids, fuelled with Stalinist histories, keep stumbling over the supposed Jadid inclination towards 'Pan-Turkism'.[76] This Pan-Turkism, contracted by the young Bukharan scholars who went to study in Istanbul between 1907 and 1914, apparently made them 'forget' the specific cause of the 'Tajiks' in favour of a Turkestanism which was beneficial to the more numerous Turcophone people of the region, the Uzbeks. This is why Tajik intellectuals preferred to exhume the memory, obliterated by Stalinist criticism, of the nationalist Bolsheviks of the 1920s and 1930s.

Dushanbe thus rehabilitated the last leaders of the Tajik SSR before the Russification of the apparatus, Nusratullāh Maqsūm and 'Abdurrahīm Hājībāyev, who had been executed in 1938, and every reference to whom had been expunged from the Republic's few modern history textbooks. They then dragged out of obscurity the Tajik Communist theoreticians who had specialised in the national question, 'Abd ul-Qādir Muhiddīnov and 'Abbās 'Aliyev. At the end of the 1920s they had tried to mount a belated resistance to the allocation of the historic centres of Persian culture in Central Asia, Bukhara and Samarkand, to Turcophone Uzbekistan. These first leaders of the Republic, promoted to the status of great ancestors of the present national intelligentsia, were henceforth presented as heroic defenders of Tajik national interests against 'Uzbek hegemony' and Russia's reprehensible 'favouritism' towards Tashkent.

The themes of the Tajik-Uzbek border, the alienated Tajik minority in Uzbekistan and the irredentism of the 'Tajik cities' of Bukhara and Samarkand were one of the main ideological threads of Dushanbe's reform movements from their conception until their elimination from the political scene.[77] This theme of rescuing Bukhara and correcting the borders, which could have been very threatening if it had found an echo outside the literate circles of the capital, seems to have remained, in Central Asia, peculiar to the Tajik nationalist parties. Indeed, even if the 'Uzbek zones' of Kazakhstan had a special place in the hearts of the Birlik tribunes, both as a hideout to which they could escape from Islam Karimov's police, and as a territorial claim, this was not a theme that was systematically developed by the Uzbek opposition, unlike what happened in Tajikistan. This Tajik claim seems to have expressed primarily the lack of political references available to the Tajik intelligentsia of the apparatus, apart from 'national Communism'. It caused long-term damage to relations between Tajik and Uzbek reformers, and contributed to the isolation of supporters of change in Dushanbe, despite the willingness of their Uzbek counterparts to establish close coordination among opposition movements throughout Central Asia.

The Triumph of Classic Determinisms

The Permanence of Localism

In Tajikistan, unlike the large Islamic nations where the political forces at play are backed by antagonistic social categories, the Democratic Party and Rastākhez, products of the intelligentsia of the Soviet period, on the one hand, and the Islamic Rebirth Party, created by a clandestine network of Islamist intellectuals, on the other, essentially fought over the same constituency, in the Dushanbe suburbs and the most impoverished parts of the Tajik countryside, which were divided into networks of regional and local solidarity dominated by the hierarchies of traditional chiefs. This search for an identical social foundation, in the absence of any alternatives, explains to a great extent why their respective discourses were so similar, and an alliance possible, despite the fact that their initial ideological postulates seemed irreconcilable. Neither the Tajik

Islamist movement nor the reformist organisations gained the support of any particular social class with its own history and collective imagination, which could have informed the discourse of their respective tribunes.

Thus when the civil war broke out in autumn 1991, the armed conflict between the opposition and the Tajik Communist Party was rapidly resolved through a confrontation between those local community leaders who had allied themselves with the forces of change, and the others, the majority, who ever since the 1920s had been the representatives of the Communist Party's authority in the countryside. The military leaders in both camps were impervious to the ideological arguments going on in the capital. The conflict rapidly developed into a confrontation between loyalist and rebellious leaders, along regional fault-lines which sometimes seemed to reproduce exactly those of the first civil war which had engulfed the Tajik valleys between 1917 and the beginning of the 1930s, pitting the regions which supported the Emir of Bukhara against those taken over by the Reds.

However, the Tajik opposition had tried hard to dispel the danger of segmentation, which was liable to perpetuate a weak state and the Communist Party's position as the only instrument of national unity. Rastākhez and the DPT vied with each other to flay the relics of 'localism' (*mahall-garāyī* or *mahallchīgī*), a political practice which allowed the local Communist Party to keep control over the countryside by preserving the old hierarchies of rural grandees. Their former power as big landowners was usually compounded by the residual prestige attached to literate people affiliated to hereditary lines of Sufi sheikhs; their authority as chiefs, which had structured local communities since the time of the khanates, had already been carefully preserved by the Tsarist regime during colonisation. The links of family and regional solidarity (*'asabiya*) in Tajikistan were even faithfully reproduced, during the Soviet period, by the sophisticated system of regional allocation of senior administrative positions (culture, that is propaganda, fell to the scholarly families of Ferghana, Bukhara and Samarkand; the political police, from the 1970s onwards, to the Ismailis of the Pamirs; while formal government had remained since the 1930s the monopoly of apparatchiks from the prosperous merchant centre of Khojent, the only real city that Tajikistan possessed until after the Second World War).

The persistence of these traditional local segmentations and of the regional chiefs' authority is the reason for the hostility of the reformist intelligentsia in Dushanbe towards the Islam of the Sufi brotherhoods.

Indeed, intellectuals trained in the Communist Party, even when they had rehabilitated the intellectual heritage of an enlightened Sufism[78] as a possible defence against the ritualism of the mullahs and the fundamentalism of the IRP, indefatigably denounced the lingering influence in Tajikistan's political power-play of the traditional chiefs, led by the *īshān* (heads of the brotherhoods), and the territorial fragmentation of politics which they encouraged.

The Rastākhez movement's calls for the formation of a united Tajik nation, and its appeals for unity against external danger, represented by the threat of Uzbek Communist intervention, were not enough to thwart fate. The Tajik opposition parties never had much of an audience except in those regions where they had a real social base, that is essentially in the capital Dushanbe (because it was the seat of the academic institutions, as well as being the melting-pot of the Republic, and as such served as an arena for the confrontations of the last few years), and in the provinces where Rastākhez and the IRP could count on the allegiance of community chiefs who had been converted to political Islam: Hissār and the high valley of Garm in central Tajikistan, and Gorny Badakhshān, where the great Ismaili families, for reasons described earlier, went over to the opposition of Dawlat Khudonazarov, formerly an official (and fairly orthodox) film-maker at the Tajikfilm studios.

The recent civil war has shown that the rifts between the Tajiks of Kulyab and those of Garm are more decisive than any opposition between Tajiks and Uzbeks living in the same region. This is why the localist base of the opposition was both its surest asset and a serious drawback, insofar as three quarters of the useful territory of the Republic remained in the hands of magnates allied to the Communists. The Pamiris, who participated in the political struggles in Dushanbe through the separatist party *La'l-i Badakhshān* ('The Ruby of Badakhshān'), could have turned out to be a weighty ally, despite being a very small minority on a national scale, thanks to their links with the 'organs'. However, they were pursuing very different goals from those of the radical Dushanbe intelligentsia, with whom relations deteriorated during the period when they shared power (May to November 1992), to the point where the fact that the majority of Pamiris are Ismailis seemed once again to the Sunnis of the plains an important differentiating factor, and contributed to limiting the Badakhshān representatives' audience in the heart of the country. In private conversations, and less frequently in the columns of the

Rastākhez newspaper, the peculiarities of Ismaili dogma were dwelt on more and more.[79]

The Battle of the Sheikhs

One year before the triumph of reaction, one of the foremost players in the political revival of Tajikistan[80] warned: 'A terrifying, infamous tragedy awaits us.' He had begun to see that his country was the promised land for neo-Bolshevism. The Tajik Communist Party was soon to extricate itself, at the close of a war which would pit the citadels of the oppostion (Dushanbe, Hissār and Garm) against the provinces of Khojent and Kulyab, respectively the richest and the most impoverished provinces in the country; and would make a battlefield of the cotton-growing plains of Kurgan-Tyube, which had been since the 1930s the site of immigration by the mountain-dwelling populations of the foothills of the Pamirs, who recreated in this region the conflicts which had riven the leaders of their communities for generations.

The actions of Sangak Safar (1928–1993), the leader of the Communist militias until his tragic death on 4 April 1993, are in this respect exemplary. Bābā Sangak was the grandson of an *īshān* from Upper Wakhiyā, a mountainous valley on the northern periphery of Darwāz, who had successively embraced the cause of the Basmachis (supporters of the Emir) and the Communists, before being killed by his rival from the neighbouring valley of Garm. Sangak's main adversary in the present conflict was the grandson of the Basmachi chief who had killed his grandfather. It was in his capacity as Sheikh and traditional chief of a local community, who also had access to an important network in the unofficial economy, that Bābā Sangak was called to serve the Communist President Rakhmon Nabiev in his election campaign in autumn 1991, before becoming the leader of the conservative camp in the civil war.[81]

The desire of the Communist victors to build a strong central power on the rubble of the Soviet institutions came up against the fragmented, regional reality of Tajikistan, and the absence of a strong national identity and culture. Since it was impossible, as had been the tradition in the Soviet era, to appoint a Khojenti head of state, a 'parliamentary' regime, dominated by a Supreme Soviet, was created on the ruins of the old Soviet Republic, in which the main allied region, Kulyab, obtained the over-representation demanded by its apparatchiks to make up for three quarters of a century of neglect and contempt by the northern city.

After a year during which everything remotely resembling a radical or Islamist intellectual was mercilessly and painstakingly chased out, subsequent months again witnessed the appearance of new political parties, this time remote-controlled by the regime and without any links of affiliation with the alternative movements of 1989–92, since they were intended by the authorities solely to fill the vacuum created by the civil war, to give the illusion of pluralism, and to 'reconcile the divided sections of society'. Thus the mysterious 'People's Party of Tajikistan' (Hizb-i Khalq-i Tājīkistān) came into being, a so-called supporter of 'parliamentary democracy',[82] which, however, seems more than a little inspired by a technique of internal lobbying within the apparatus, initiated in the neighbouring state by the inventive Uzbek President Islam Karimov.[83]

Garmis against Kulyabis and Khojentis: Three Scenarios for Life After the Soviet System

The armed confrontation between the people of Garm and Kulyab, and the tensions today between the latter and their allies from the north (Khojent), have certainly brought to the fore, as has already been emphasised, regional divisions, but also social differences, which only partially match up with the former.

A fundamental difference of orientation is apparent in the embryonic economic programmes drawn up by both sides since 1989. On one side were the agricultural communities of central Tajikistan, threatened by a precipitate fall in revenue from individual plots of land as a result of the policy at the 'centre' of freeing industrial prices,[84] and a budding class of liberal traders and small entrepreneurs, none other than the presidents of kolkhozes. Often members of the emigrant (*muhājir*) communities from the foothills of the Pamirs who had migrated to Garm or Machā on the plain between the 1930s and the 1960s, these peasants and traders, destabilised by the crisis, converted to political Islam in order to set up networks of economic solidarity parallel to those of the Party-state, which were dependent on the Soviet space, in the hope of ridding themselves of the burdensome national nomenklatura.[85] On the other side were the economic nomenklatura of Khojent, who had been in power since 1924, led at first by the agricultural engineer Qahhār Mahkamov (First Secretary of the Tajik Communist Party from December 1985 to September 1991). They were intent on establishing a market economy in the proper way, that is, ensuring that the economic apparatchiks retained their mastery over the Republic's large agro-industrial complexes; this path was conditional on maintenance of preferential economic links with Russia and the former-Soviet republics.

Tajikistan's economic nomenklatura was the only beneficiary from the conversion of the apparatus to business and the 'privatisation' of the Communist Party's possessions. Its membership chiefly came from the northern province of Khojent, the most industrialised in the country (hence renamed Leninabad). After several perestroikist whimsies, it ultimately reassociated itself with the cause of the continuity of the institutions inherited from the USSR. The Tajik *Komsomol* ('Communist League of Youth') and KGB also played the conservative card, after trying that of alternation within the Party.[86] The national Communist Party seemed to them the only guarantee of survival for the Tajik entity and its élites, since there was a gaping lack of a truly 'Tajikistani' tradition of statehood and no hope of economic autonomy outside the CIS.

Three members of the Tajik Communist Party, all in their forties or thereabouts, who represented different tendencies in the economic nomenklatura, each played an emblematic role in turn; their successive trajectories illustrate the gradual shift of a whole class, from its temptation towards ideological secession to its return to the Communist fold.

Burī Karimov (born in 1957), from the Dushanbe suburb where the Tajik IRP was founded in 1990, was the Director of the Republic's Gosplan[87] at the time of the anti-government demonstrations of February 1990 in Dushanbe. His name was put forward as a successor to Mahkamov, and seized on by the crowd of demonstrators, at the suggestion of a group of young apparatchiks from the central regions, who were trying to get rid of the ruling team, three quarters of whom were Khojentis. The reaction of the police and the tough line taken by the Tajik Communist Party after a few symbolic concessions threw the audacious 'forty-year-olds' of this premature Tajik Spring back into obscurity, and put a temporary stop to the national destiny of Burī Karimov, who was relegated to work on his economic doctoral thesis.[88]

More fortunate than Karimov was the industry boss Sayf-id Dīn Turaev (born in 1945 in Ura-Tyube, to the south of Khojent), a candidate for office in the alternation process, who enjoyed an unusual monopoly of the limelight in politics and the media in Tajikistan from the presidential campaign of October 1991 to the Communist reaction of the following autumn, and this without support from any party at all. This media success, begun under the Soviet regime, made some people think that Turaev might be one of the 'Trojan horses' that the CP and then the KGB used to introduce into the electoral arena in order to neutralise opposition parties which were judged excessively separatist.[89] During the perestroika years, Sayf id-Dīn Turaev had been the head of the Tajik Ministry of Consumer Industries,[90] which he started 'privatising'[91] in 1991, and turned into a vast industrial complex called *Khizmat* ('Services'), with numerous specialities and ramifications, and outlets outside the CIS, notably in the Near East. As the head of a network of enterprises which were fitter than others to seize the opportunity of leaving the Russian orbit, Turaev gradually aligned himself with the nationalist and Islamist parties and seems to have played an independent political role which was intended to further the designs of an oligarchy of former economic apparatchiks, redeployed in fruitful import-export operations with Muslim countries. Lacking any support from the political nomenklatura of the south, which was firmly anchored in the ex-Soviet space, he disappeared from the political scene when the Communists regained power.

Less appealing to the media than the enterprising Turaev, but a perfect example of the high-ranking apparatchik converted to business, Abdumalik Abdullojonov (born in 1949 in Khojent) became the Prime Minister of Tajikistan after the Communist reaction of December 1992, thanks to a *modus vivendi* arrived at by the Kulyabis and Khojentis, which reserved the post of head of government for the latter. Born into a family of party functionaries in Khojent, and the brother of a powerful provincial Party Secretary known for his recent and very large fortune, for one year he pursued a policy of transforming the big units of the industrial apparatus into state-owned capital enterprises. However, his manners, too loud for the 'rustics' of the south, and his rather sulphurous reputation as a big financier in the Republic, precipitated his removal from the government in December 1993.[92] It is also likely that disagreements that arose with the invading Kulyabis about the tricky business of dividing up the goods of the Party-state (a problem which was pinpointed by Russian strategists as the primary source of armed conflict on the periphery)[93] had a decisive influence on this government reshuffle.

Thus it is the Kulyab nomenklatura, consisting mainly of party and administration officials, who seem to have had the last word. These apparatchiks, from a province which, having no industrial infra-

75

structure, is economically dependent, are at once still closely tied to the practices of the parallel economy and viscerally attached to preserving the workings and symbols of the old regime – all the things which the economic nomenklaturas of the north and the centre were ready to get rid of.[94] These divergences allow the possibility of future discord between these erstwhile allies, despite the consensus on the necessity of moving to a market economy under the sole control of the legatees of the single Party, following the model of neighbouring Uzbekistan.

The likelihood of a conflict between Kulyabis and Khojentis was not entirely removed by the reallocation of government posts which was carried out after the military victory of December 1992. This was especially so since the 'neo-Communists' of north and south Tajikistan saw the institutions they were respectively gaining control of as competing sites of power, governed by one and the same rule, worthy of the Bolshevik heritage: 'Who will end up eating who?' The complete absence of separation between the executive and legislative powers, as shown by the activities of a Parliament led by a very 'Khazbulatovian' President, the Kulyabi Imomali Rakhmonov, prevents any clear division of competences at the summit of the state. In Tajikistan, much more than elsewhere in the former Soviet Union, state functions, which formerly devolved on those satraps who seemed best able to apply the CPSU's latest policy, seem no longer to exist, except in their allocation *a priori* to the head of one faction or another.

Have we, then, witnessed in Tajikistan the final victory of local party potentates and the industrial apparatus, to the detriment of the state's already minimal cohesion? And are we now at the threshold of the (perfectly logical) territorial explosion of a former Soviet Republic utterly lacking in historicity? Paradoxically, even the segmentations of traditional society in Tajikistan further the maintenance of a centralised Party-state, as well as the territorial unity of the old Soviet Republic. There is no one political power that is capable any longer of imposing its diktat on the whole country, yet the idea of partition entertained by everyone in Dushanbe only recently is now greeted with general dread. The irreversible weakening of the Tajik Communist Party means that its activists can no longer exclude a 'national reconciliation' with some leaders of the former opposition, starting with the prudent Cadi [Qazi] Tūrajānzāda. The viability of the Republic of Tajikistan depends to a great extent on the future of the current negotiations.

Whatever the eventual outcome of current developments in Tajikistan it is not the radical intelligentsia, who have today deserted the political field, who will benefit from the situation. The historic curse of the reformist intelligentsias of Central Asia seems to have been repeated in Dushanbe.

Turkestani Jadidism, which appeared on the political scene between 1905 and 1920, between two crises of the Russian colonial system, was oppressed by the Emirs of Bukhara, then censored by the Tsarist regime, and finally swallowed up by the Bolsheviks. The Jadids of Bukhara and Samarkand owed the failure of the first autonomous attempt at modernisation in Central Asia to their ultra-minority position in indigenous society, to the lack of a national industrial bourgeoisie which could have financed their programmes, and to the hostility of the traditional grandees. Today, while the Uzbek reformers are developing a trans-ethnic nationalism which claims to be the heir to Jadidism, the Tajik intelligentsia remains bogged down in the contradictions of a mono-ethnic nationalism, somewhat abstract and ill-adapted to the rural nature of the new state, which is segmented into 'countries' still dominated by the aristocracies of grandees, jealously guarding their regional powers.

Without real historical or sociological roots, the movements of ideas which have swept through Tajikistan in the last five years seem like interchangeable pieces of conceptual machinery, without any great influence on the course of events. The combinations of imported discourses rehearsed by the orators of Rastākhez and the Islamic Rebirth Party have proved incapable of taking hold of the body of society, and the Tajik population has shown immense indifference to the unproductive themes of a freed Bukhara and the fundamentalist slogans of the Nahzat. Unable to arouse any real social mobilisation, the reformist and Communist parties of Tajikistan have finally contented themselves with embodying different sections of the apparatus, and the conflict which has pitted them against each other with ever greater violence has tended to reproduce the social and ideological rifts between the sections of this élite. These are similar to those which existed throughout the empire between the state apparatus, the economic bureaucracy and the party nomenklatura. It appears in retrospect that Rastākhez and the Democratic Party of Tajikistan, and before them the informal groups which had influence in the Communist Party, have struggled less hard in trying to gain the allegiance of the population than in the internal lobbying of various competing sections of the political leadership.

The interplay of regional oligarchies and their alliances and the monopoly of the Communist and Stalinist legacy over the minds of an intelligentsia without a history have finally facilitated the exclusion of the reformists from the political arena, and the return to power of the national Communist Party, to the great advantage of Russia, which sees Tajikistan as its most precious outpost in its continued advance towards the south. Put off the centrifugal temptation which was moving it closer to the Persian-speaking world, Tajikistan is now more than ever integrated into a CIS which has been revised and modified into a military alliance. And it is preparing to join the other newly sovereign states of the region under the Uzbek banner, in a Turkestani economic whole in the making,[95] brought back to life by the 'neo-Communist' ideologues of Tashkent, who also know so well how to accommodate the favourite themes of their failed opposition.

Notes

1 In conformity with the new alphabet laws passed in Tajikistan in 1989 and Uzbekistan in September 1993, although these were not retrospective, I have transcribed Tajik according to the Arabic-Persian written form, using the 'e' of Eastern Persian, and used Uzbek directly in the Roman alphabet established last autumn. Russian transcription follows the simplest international standards. [The editors have changed transliterations of the most common geographic and personal names.]

2 The Tajik Sub-Commission, which was entrusted in summer 1924 with tracing an outline for the new Autonomous Republic of Tajikista's borders with Uzbekistan, put forward a plan very similar to the present-day map of the Republic, with the exception of Khojent Province in the north. It was this Sub-Commission which gave up the claim to the ancient capitals of Bukhara and Samarkand, inhabited by a marked Tajik majority, and chose instead the territory of former eastern Bukhara – mostly 'bare mountains', as reported by Uzbek, Kazakh and Kyrgyz observers, who were astonished at the lack of attention paid by the Tajik Communists to the economic viability of their future state (see the minutes of the session of the Territorial Commission, dated 21 August 1924, reproduced by Masov, Rahim, *Istorija topornogo razdelenija* ('History of a Carving-Up with an Axe'), Dushanbe, Irfon, 1991, pp. 47–8).

   Some authors today are tempted to see in the delimitation proposals of the Tajik Sub-Commission, whose inexperience and lack of preparation have been emphasised by the historian R. Masov (*ibid.*, p. 41), evidence of the Tajik representatives' 'collective will' and of a socio-political reality predating Sovietisation, which therefore confers a sort of historical depth on the present-day outline of the borders: in setting up the Republic of Tajikistan, the Soviet regime was only fulfilling the legitimate desire for autonomy of the populations of eastern Bukhara. This is to subscribe to a form of historicism and apologetics which seeks in the past factors to justify the present; it overlooks the fact that before 1920 aspects of ethnicity and regionalism existed in the collective mind of the inhabitants of eastern Bukhara and not given rise to any sort of political expression, even during popular movements heavily coloured by regionalism, such as the jacquerie of Mu'minābād led by 'Abu ul-Wāsī' at the end of 1880s, or the Baljuan uprising north of present-day Kulyab in 1916. See Iskandarov, B. L., 'Vosstanie krest'janskih mass Tadzhikistana pod rukovodstvom Vose' ('The Uprising of the Peasant Masses of Tajikistan under the Leadership of Wāsī'), and Mukhtarov, A., 'Vosstanie krest'jan Bal'dzhuanskogo bekstva v 1916 g.' ('The Peasant Uprising in the Baljuan Province in 1916'), in Mukhtarov, A. (ed.), *Iz istorii narodnyh dvizhenij v Srednej Azii* ('Pages from the History of Popular Movements in Central Asia'), Dushanbe, Izdatel'stvo Donish, 1988, pp. 7–25 and 35–42 respectively; and Pirumshāyev, Haydarshā, *Ta'rīkh-i āmūzish-i shūrishi-i Wāsī* ('History of the Interpretation of Wāsī's Uprising)', Dushanbe, Nashriyāt-i 'Irfān, 1992, pp 11–36.

For all that, the Soviet archives open today show that the ethnic and territorial partition of Central Asia was entirely conceived and carried out by high-ranking Party apparatchiks, and presented to the masses later. Among the peoples of the region, the Tajiks were outstanding by virtue of their 'passivity', according to some documents of the Central Committee of the Bolshevik party's Central Asia Bureau. See Eisener, Reinhardt, 'Some Problems of Research Concerning The National Delimitation of Soviet Central Asia in 1924', in Fragner, B. G. and Hoffmann, B. (eds), *Bamberger Mittelasienstudien, Konferenzakten, Bamberg 15–16 Juni 1990*, Berlin, 1994, pp. 109–16 (Islamkundliche Untersuchungen, Band 149). Moreover, the early Tajik Communists themselves seem to have had no clear notion of national and territorial identity, and quickly came to regret their initial 'error', embarking upon a futile rearguard battle to reincorporate Bukhara and Samarkand into the Tajik SSR (Muhiddinov, A., 'Tadzhiki ili Uzbeki naseljajut gorod Buharu i ego okrestnosti? V porjadke obsuzhdenija' ('Is it Tajiks or Uzbeks who Inhabit the City of Bukhara and its Environs?'), in *Za Partiju*, no. 9 (13), September 1928, reproduced by R. Masov, *op. cit.*, pp. 146–51).

3 The Azeris had the *Musavvat* government at Baku from 1918 to 1920; the Uzbeks had the autonomy of Kokand from October 1917 to February 1918, and indeed the People's Republic of Bukhara from September 1920 to September 1924; and the Kazakhs had the *Alash Orda* government in winter 1918–19.

4 The inter-ethnic national ideal of the Central Asian Jadids, their concern to create a modern civilisation that would be truly Turco-Persian, was perfectly expressed by their most high-profile spokesman, Mahmūd Khwāja Behbūdī (1875–1919), 'Ikki imās turt til lāzim' ('We Need not Two but Four Languages'), in *Āyīna* (Samarkand), no. 1, 1 Shawwal 1331/20 August 1913, p. 13.

5 'The Wormeaten Empire' in 'Abdujabbār, Tāher, 'Wāy bar mā!' ('Woe to Us!'), in *Duniyā* (Dushanbe), no. 1, May 1991, p. 4.

6 See the texts edited by Alain Blum, *Démographie et politique en Russie*, Paris, La Documentation Française, 1993, pp. 17–26 (Problèmes politiques et sociaux, no. 711).

7 See Dudoignon, Stéphane A., 'Changements politiques et historiographie en Asie Centrale (Tadjikistan et Uzbekistan, 1987–1993)' in the *Cahiers d'Etudes sur la Méditerranée Orientale et le Monde Turco-Iranien*, no. 16, July-December 1993, pp. 83–134.

8 Ulughzāda, Sātim, *Riwāyat-i sughdī* ('Sogdian Tale'), Dushanbe, Adib, 1977 (reprinted 1984).

9 See Musulmāniyān, Rahim, 'Adabiyāt wa tafakkur-i ghulāmāna' ('The Literature and Ideology of Servitude'), in *'Adālat* (Dushanbe), no. 2, November 1990, p. 7.

10 Brown, Bess, 'The Public Role in *Perestroika* in Central Asia', in *Central Asian Survey*, Vol. 9, no. 1, 1990, p. 93.

11 Kuzin, Evgenij V., *Kto pomozhet bol'nym?* ('Who will Help the Sick?'), Dushanbe, Videofilm, 1987; *Materialy dlja XII s'ezda Tadzhikskoj Kommunisticheskoj Partii* ('Documents for the XII Congress of the Communist Party of Tajikistan'), Dushanbe, Videofilm, 1987. These films were widely cited in the documentary *Asie Centrale, Etats d'urgence*, by S. A. Dudoignon, L. Segarra and J.-M. Meurice, SFP, 1991, broadcast on FR3, 4 March 1992.

12 *Rasshirennyj XVII Plenum CK Kompartii Tadzhikistana, 15–16 fevralja 1990 g.*, *stenograficheskij otchet* ('The Enlarged XVII Plenum of the Central Committee of the CP of Tajikistan, Stenographic Report'), Dushanbe, Irfon, 1990, 152 pp.; *Rasshirennyj XVIII Plenum CK Kompartii Tadzhikistana, 3 marta 1990 g.*, *stenograficheskij otchet*, ('The Enlarged XVIII Plenum of the Central Committee of the CP of Tajikistan'), Dushanbe, Irfon, 1990, 184 pp.

13 Kuzio, Taras, 'Nationalist Riots in Kazakhstan', in *Central Asian Survey*, Vol. 7, no. 4, 1988, pp. 79–100; Lemercier Quelquejay, Ch., 'Le monde musulman soviétique d'Asie Centrale après Alma-Ata (décembre 1986)', in *Cahiers du monde russe et soviétique*, Vol. XXXII (1), 1991, pp. 117–22.

14 'Barnāma-yi sāzmān-i Rastākhez' ('Programme of the Rastākhez Movement'), in *Rastākhez* (Dushanbe), no. 4, October 1990, p. 3.

15 The first anthology of his poems had already been published in Dushanbe, one year after S. Ulughzāda's Sogdian novel. Iqbāl, Muhammad, *Sadā-yi Mashriq*, Dushanbe, Nashriyāt-i Dānish, 1978 (in Persian, with Cyrillic script). During one of the first demonstrations for proclaiming Tajik the state language, the academician Tāher 'Abdujabbār read Iqbāl's famous poem on the rebirth of Islam to close his summing up (video document by E. V. Kuzin, Dushanbe, Videofilm, 1989).

16 Yūsuf, Shādmān, 'Zarurat-i ta'sis-i hizb' ('On the Necessity of Founding a Party'), in *'Adālat*, no. 1, September 1990, p. 2.

17 Thom, Françoise, *Les fins du communisme*, Paris, Critérion, 1994, pp. 50–6.

18 Marie-Schwartzenberg, Nadine, *Le KGB (des origines à nos jours)*, Paris, PUF, 1993, p. 44.

19 Retrospective testimony by Colonel Alksnis in *Den'*, no. 33, 1992, cited by Françoise Thom, *op. cit.*, pp. 54–5.

20 The same may be said for the Tajik inhabitants of neighbouring Uzbekistan, whose cultural claims were cautiously channelled by 'democratic' movements encouraged by Tashkent, which acted as safety-valves, such as the 'Samarkand Social and Cultural Movement', or the Tajik National Cultural Centre in the same city: Rahimov, R. R., 'K voprosu o sovremennykh tadzhiksko-uzbekskikh mezhdunarodnykh otnoshenijakh' ('On the Current Inter-Ethnic Relations between Uzbeks and Tajiks'), in *Sovetskaja Etnografija*, no. 1, 1991, p. 22.

21 The Tajik detective novel, emerging in the mid-1980s and generally written by agents of the security forces, was a gibe against the reigning anarchy and called for the country to be taken firmly back in hand; it regularly featured virtuous officers from Darwāz or Badakhshān, two regions of the Soviet Pamirs, battling against all forms of misappropriation of public funds in southern Tajik towns: see *Sūz-i dil* ('Burning in the Heart') by Safaralī Kenjayev (who later became the Communist leader in the north before the opposition seized power), Dushanbe, Nashriyāt-i 'Irfān, 1991; and the collection of novels by Lieutenant-Colonel N. Tillizādā, *Qissa-yi portfel-i surkh* ('The Story of the Red File'), Dushanbe, 'Irfān, 1992.

22 See the account by the British anthropologist Gillian Tett, *Financial Times*, 19 February 1994, p. xiii.

23 The Democratic Party of Tajikistan, founded in August 1990, was to be an ally of the Democratic Parties in neighbouring countries; it welcomed at its founding conference delegations from Uzbekistan (Tashkent and Samarkand), Kyrgyzstan and Lithuania. See 'Nawid-i zādrūz' ('A Happy Occasion'), in *'Adālat*, no. 1, September 1990, p. 1; 'Ayinnāma-yi Hizb-i Demokrātī-yi Tājīkistān' ('Statutes of the Democratic Party of Tajikistan'), in *'Adālat*, no. 1, September 1990, supplement, p. 1. On the first anniversary of its founding on 10 August 1991, the DPT invited the leader of the Russian Democratic Party, Nikolaj Travkin, as well as his Kyrgyz and Turkmen counterparts, to Dushanbe. It took an active part in the formation of a 'Union of Democratic Parties' in the former Soviet countries: *Duniyā*, no. 2, (September) 1991, p. 1.

24 Sh. Yūsuf later wondered about the real intentions of the 'centre' towards him, and about the nationalist 'drift' of N. Travkin's party (after the crisis in the Russian state, Travkin became the most heated supporter of the 'rights' of Russian-speaking communities on the periphery): 'Chego zhe hochet rossiskoje pravitel'stvo v Tadzhikistane' ('What does the Russian Government Want in Tajikistan?'), in *Charāq-i rūz* (the old autonomous daily of the young Tajik intelligentsia, published in Moscow from January 1993 to January 1994), no. 3 (72), 1993, p. 14.

25 The creation of a huge coalition of alternative political movements in Central Asia was the most lasting aspiration of the Uzbek popular front. See Dudoignon, Stéphane A., 'Les médias autonomes d'Asie Centrale pendant la dislocation du système soviétique. I – Le *Mustaqil Haftalik* (janvier-novembre 1992)', in *Bulletin de l'Association des Anciens Elèves et Amis des Langues Orientales* (Paris), November 1993, pp. 107–18.

26 This is what Yaacov Ro'i does himself in 'The Soviet and Russian Context of the Development of Nationalism in Central Asia', *Cahiers du Monde russe et soviétique*, Vol. XXXIII (1), January March 1991, p. 139.

27 Mīrrahim, Mirbābā, 'Muqarrabān-i 'prezident', yā khud pirāmun-i fāji'ae ki ba mā tahid mekunad' ('The 'President's' Favourites: a Few Words on the Tragedy that Threatens Us'), in *Adālat*, no. 12, 1991, p. 3.

28 'Ūrtāq Karimov chī mekhāhad?' ('What does Comrade Karimov Want?'), in *Adālat*, no. 30 (42), 1992, p. 6.

29 The Tajik historian of Jadidism in Central Asia, Rasul Hādizāda, later deplored this, in 'Istiqlāl-i mā. Imrūz wa fardā-yi ān' ('Our Independence, Today and Tomorrow'), in *Jumhuriyat*, 26–27 August 1993, p. 3.

30 Anonymous, 'Ōzbekistonda 'Qorabog' qomitasi', in *Mustaqil Haftalik* (Moscow), no. 5, March 1992, p. 1; Qarobogiy, Sulton, 'Xalqni xalqqa qarsi qoyisyapti', *ibid.*, no. 6, August 1992, pp. 1–2.

31 See Alekseeva, L., *Istoria inakomyslija v SSSR* ('History of Dissidence in the USSR'), Vilnius and Moscow, Vest', 1992, pp. 93 114.

32 'Abdujabbār, T., 'Peshguftār yā haqiqat-i hāl dar bāra-yi Rastākhez' ('Foreword, or the Truth about the Rastākhez Movement'), in *Rastākhez*, no. 4, October 1990, p. 2.

33 'Barnāma-yi sāzmān-i Rastākhez', *op. cit.* [note 14 above], p. 3.

34 'Sāzmān-i Rastākhez nāmnawis shud' ('The *Rastākhez* Movement has been Registered'), in *Duniyā*, no. 2, (September) 1991, p. 1.

35 *Rastākhez*, no. 2, July 1990, p. 2.

36 'Nawid-i zādruz', *op. cit.* [note 23 above], p. 1.

37 'Barnāma-yi Hizb-i Demokrātī-yi Tājīkistān (HDT)' ('Programme of the Democratic Party of Tajikistan (DPT)'), in *Adālat*, no. 1, September 1990, supplement, p. 5.

38 'Barnāma-yi sāzmān-i Rastākhez', *op. cit.*, p. 2.

39 'Barnāma-yi Hizb-i Demokrātī-yi Tājīkistān (HDT)', *op. cit.*, p. 6; 'Barnāma-yi sāzmān-i Rastākhez', *op. cit.*, p. 2.

40 Rabe', 'Abdurāfe', 'Pakhtaghulāmān-hlopkoraby' ('Slaves of Cotton'), in *Duniyā*, no. 2, (September) 1991, p. 3.

41 Hamīdov, Khalīfabābā, 'Suxan dānista gū ...' ('Speak in Knowledge ...'), in *Rastākhez*, no. 3, August 1990, p. 2.

42 See Sokoloff, Georges, *La puissance pauvre. Histoire de la Russie de 1815 à nos jours*, Paris, Fayard, 1993, pp. 549, 576–7, 618, 647–8 and 669–70.

43 'Barnāma-yi sāzmān-i Rastākhez', *op. cit.*, p. 2; Ismā'īlī, Roziya, 'Marg-i askarbacha chand sūm?' ('How Much is the Death of a Young Soldier Worth?'), in *Duniyā*, no. 2, (September) 1991, p. 5.

44 'Payām ba mardum-i Tājīkistān' ('Message to the People of Tajikistan'), in *Adālat*, no. 1, September 1990, p. 5; 'Barnāma-yi Hizb-i Demokrātī-yi Tājīkistān (HDT)', *op. cit.*, p. 5.

45 In fact Tajik national armed forces were only instituted by a law passed by the Communist Supreme Soviet on 25 June 1993, six months after the Red militia and the Russian army had regained control of the Republic: *Jumhuriyat*, 29–30 July 1993, p. 2, and 3–4 August 1993, p. 2.

46 'Barnāma-yi sāzmān-i Rastākhez', *op. cit.*, p. 2.

47 'Barnāma-yi Hizb-i Demokrāti-yi Tājīkistān (HDT)', *op. cit.*, p. 5.

48 'Barnāma-yi sāzmān-i Rastākhez', *op. cit.*, p. 2.

49 After it was dispersed by the army, this Congress had to continue in what was then still Checheno-Ingushetia: see the intervention by Muhammad

Qādir at the Constituent Congress in Astrakhan, in *Hidāyat* (Moscow), no. 5, July 1990, p. 6.

50 Roy Oliver. 'Le renouveau islamique en URSS', in *Revue du Monde musulman et de la Méditerranée*, nos 59–60, 1991/1–2, pp. 140–2.

51 Anonymous, 'Dar bāra-yi anjuman-i hizb-i "Nahzat-i islāmi"' ('On the Islamic Rebirth Party Congress'), in *Hidāyat* (Moscow), no. 5, July 1990, p. 2; Dāwudī, Dawlatkhwāja, 'Kommunistān wa "wahhābiyān"' ('Communists and "Wahhabites"'), in *Charāq-i rūz*, no. 25 (46), 1992, p. 6.

52 Intervention by Muhammad Bahāuddīn at the Constituent Congress in Astrakhan, in *Hidāyat* (Moscow), no. 5, July 1990, pp. 5–6.

53 Résumé by Olivier Roy, *op. cit.*, p. 141.

54 The best documentary on these underground clubs, which were subject to numerous court cases in the 1980s, is still the anti religious propaganda film by the film-maker Pulāt Ahmatov, *S pervyh ruk* ('At First Hand'), Tajikfilm, 1989. It was revealing enough never to have been broadcast.

55 The Sayyidov case is cited by the film-maker Pulāt Ahmatov, who particularly shows the demonstrations organised in Kurgan-Tyube for his liberation. See also Rabiev, V., 'Idushchie v nikuda', in *Kommunist Tadzhikistana*, 12 February 1987, p. 3 (cited by Atkin, Muriel, *The Subtlest Battle: Islam in Soviet Tajikistan*, Philadelphia, Foreign Policy Research Institute, 1989, pp. 35–6).

56 See the analysis by Mullodzhanov, P., 'Islam i politika v Tadzhikistane' ('Islam and Politics in Tajikistan'), in *Maverannahr* (Moscow), (no. 1), August 1992, pp. 15–21.

57 Kebedov, A., 'Demokratija – demokratam, islam – musul'manan' ('Democracy for Democrats, Islam for Muslims'), in *Al-Wahdat* (Moscow), no. 2, March 1991, pp. 1 and 3–4.

58 On Nūr Tabar, see Atkin, Muriel, *op. cit.*, pp. 8–9.

59 On polygamy, see some thoughts by one official writer: Akābirov, Yūsuf, *Payām-i Danghara* ('The Message of Danghara'), Dushanbe, Irfon, 1990, pp. 53 ff.

60 Ghulāmzāda, S., 'Nāma-yi purgudāz-i mādar' ('A Mother's Heartbreaking Letter'), in *Najāt* (Dushanbe), no. 5 (August 1991), pp. 2–3.

61 Ismat, 'Abdughaffār, 'Maftun-i tazwīr, yā khud dasīsahā-yi dushmanān-i 'alayhi junbishhā-yi islāmi' ('The Inveterate Hypocrites, or the Intrigues of the Enemies of Islamist Movements'), in *Najāt*, no. 4 (July 1991), p. 3.

62 Mas'udi, Yazdāmehr, 'Khwān, chi daryāhāst dar pahnā-yi 'aql' ('Learn what Oceans Lie Hidden in the Mind'), in *Rastākhez*, no. 5, November 1990, p. 1.

63 Qurbān, Najmiddin, 'Hijāb yā faranjī' ('The Veil or the *Faranjī*'), in *Najāt*, no. 5 (August 1991), p. 2.

64 A sort of paradoxical analogy with the 'Turco-Islamic synthesis' (the Tajiks being anti-Turk): see Copeaux, Etienne, 'Le réve du Loup Gris. Les aspirations turques en Asie Centrale', in *Hérodote*, no. 64, January-March 1992, pp. 183–93.

65 Qanāt'at, Muhabbat, 'Mā wa Erān' ('Iran and Us'), in *Rastākhez*, no. 11, March 1992, p. 4.

66 Mas'udshāh, Muhammadbarāt Bakhtiyārzāda, 'Charā ū ba Turkiya raft?' ('Why did He Go to Turkey?'), in *Duniyā*, no. 2, (September) 1991, p. 6

(on the visit by Qahhār Mahkamov, then First Secretary of the Tajik Communist Party, to Ankara, 5–9 June 1991).

67 Erdivan, Orhan (Turkish Ambassador in Dushanbe), 'Turkiya istiqlāliyat-i Tājīkistānrā e'tirāf wa ehtirām mekunad' ('Turkey Recognises and Respects Tajikistan's Independence'), in *Jumhuriyat*, 2–3 September 1993, p. 3.

68 Qanāt'at, Muhabbat, *op. cit.*, p. 4.

69 Anonymous, 'Barnāma-yi sāzmān-i Kurush-i kabir' ('Programme of the Cyrus the Great Association'), in *Sāman* (Dushanbe), no. 14, 18 October 1991, p. 2.

70 'Ayūbī, Zayn id-Dīn, 'Tawāfuq-i siyāsathā' ('The Convergence of Politics'), in *Najāt*, no. 3 (June 1991), p. 1.

71 See the internal document of the Central Committee on the propaganda activities of the DPT, published by *Rastākhez*, no. 4, October 1990, p. 6.

72 These difficulties were revealed in early summer 1991 by the scandal of the *īshān* of Garm: see Safarzāda, 'Alī, 'Bāz yak fitna' ('Another Attempt to Divide Us'), in *Najāt*, no. 3 (June 1991), p. 1.

73 Lazzerini, Edward, '*Tatarovedenie* and the New Historiography in the Soviet Union: Revising the Interpretation of the Tatar Russian Relationship', in *Slavic Review*, Vol. XL, no. 4, 1981, pp. 629–31.

74 'Barnāma-yi sāzmān-i Rastākhez', *op. cit.* [note 14 above], p. 3. Tajik *mirāsism* was synthesised in a new review, *Meros-i niyāgān*, published from January 1992 by the Society for the Protection of the Historical Monuments and Culture of Tajikistan, made up of academics who were also the ideologues of the Rastākhez national movement.

75 Thom, Françoise, *Le moment Gorbatchev*, Paris, Hachette, 1989, p. 160.

76 See especially Sheralī, Lāyiq (dir.), 'Jadidizm dar dūrnamā-yi ta'rīkh' (round table), in *Sadā-yi Sharq* (Dushanbe), no. 3, 1990, pp. 129–39.

77 See two articles by Muhammadjān Shukūrov: 'Bukhārā, shād bāsh u der zi!' ('Long Life and Happiness to You, Bukhara!'), in *Rastākhez*, no. 2 (June 1990), p. 3, and 'Anchi bā tabar-i nāinsāfi tarāsh shuda ast' ('That Which the Sword of Iniquity has Felled'), in *Sadā-yi Sharq*, no. 10, 1990, pp. 92–110; also Masov, R., *op. cit.* [note 2 above], p. 189.

78 See Muhammedhodzhaev, A. (a member of the Academy of Sciences of Tajikistan), *Gnoseologija sufizma*, Dushanbe, Dānish, 1990, and *Ideologija nakhshbandizma*, Dushanbe, Dānish, 1991.

79 'Suhbat-i Dawlat bā Aghā-Khān' ('A Conversation between Dawlat [Khudonazarov] and the Aga Khan'), in *Rastākhez*, no. 36 (48), September 1992, p. 3. The author of this anonymous article chooses to compare Ismailism to Christianity, and the Aga Khan to the Pope.

80 Mirrahim, Mirbābā, *op. cit.* [note 27 above], p. 3.

81 Medvedev, Vladimir, 'Saga o Bobo Sangake, voine' ('The Saga of Baba Sangak, Warrior'), in *Druzhba Narodov* (Moscow), no. 6, (June) 1993, pp. 186–205, and my detailed account in the *Cahiers d'Etudes sur la Méditerranée Orientale et le Monde Turco-Iranien*, no. 16, July–December 1993, pp. 393–400. For a study of recurrent aspects of the Tajik civil war, based on the work of V. Medvedev, see also Eisener, Reinhardt, 'Zum Bürgerkrieg in Tadschikistan. Einige aktuelle und historische Dimensionen der Konflikte', in *Osteuropa* (Berlin), still to be published.

82 This goes without saying, since all power is concentrated in a Supreme Soviet which is both executive and legislative: see 'Izhārāt-i barnāmawī-yi Kumita-yi Sāzmāndeh-i Hizb-i Khalq-i Tājīkistān' ('Declarations of Principle of the People's Party of Tajikistan'), in *Jumhuriyat*, 21–22 September 1993, pp. 1–2.

83 On the improbable 'National Progress Party' (*Vatan Taraqqiyoti Partiyasi*) of Uzbekistan, see *Pravda Vostoka*, 19 May 1992.

84 Mullodzhanov, P., *op. cit.* [note 56 above], p. 17.

85 This aspect of the Islamist party's strategy still largely remains to be studied: see Malashenko, Alexei V., 'Islam versus Communism', in Eickelman, Dale F. (ed.), *Russia's Muslim Frontiers, New Directions in Cross-Cultural Analysis*, Bloomington and Indianapolis, Indiana University Press, 1993, p. 70.

86 'Alternation' here denotes an arrangement whereby different people from different political tendencies accede successively to power.

87 *Enciklopedija-i sovetī-i tājīk*, Vol. 8, Dushanbe, 1988, p. 536.

88 On this person, and his resistible rise, see Atāullā, Dādājān, 'Dām' ('The Trap'), in *'Adālat*, no. 2, November 1990, pp. 4–5, and no. 3, January 1991, pp. 4–6; anonymous, 'Būrī Karimov', in *Duniyā*, no. 2, (September) 1991, p. 3; and Mu'azzam, 'Nāz u niyāz-i bachcha-yi khūb-i khalq' ('The Charm and Seduction of a Real Child of the People'), in *'Adālat*, no. 30 (42), 1992, p. 8.

89 Sayf id-Dīn Turaev managed to get 5% of the votes in the Tajik presidential elections of November 1991, a very respectable score in view of the fact that the opposition parties' candidate gained 30% and that of the Communist Party 57%.

90 *Enciklopedija-i sovetī-i tājīk*, Vol. 8, *op. cit.*, p. 555.

91 This is the cavalier expression used by S. Turaev himself in describing the transformation of his Ministry into a 'private' enterprise, during an interview with the present author in May 1992.

92 And his replacement by another Khojenti dignitary, the economist 'Abdujalīl Samadov: *Jumhuriyat*, 30 December 1993.

93 See Bel'kov, O. A., 'Ētnopoliticheskie faktory voennoj opasnosti v SNG' ('The Ethno-Political Factors of Military Insecurity in the CIS'), in *Voennaja mysl'* (Moscow), no. 7, p. 18.

94 Maqsūd Ikrāmov, the Mayor of Dushanbe, popular across the board for his abilities as an administrator, brought down the statue of Lenin opposite the building of the Supreme Soviet of Tajikistan; it was replaced by a huge effigy of Firdawsī, the poet who originated the mediaeval Persian epic (the late head of Tajik Communist militias, Bābā Sangak, swore to blow it up as soon as he returned to the capital).

95 Abdullojonov, Abdumalik, 'Maqsad-i mā istiqlāliyat-i iqtisādist' ('Our Aim is Economic Independence') (interview), in *Jumhuriyat*, 16–22 October 1993, p. 1.

Chapter 5

The Civil War in Tajikistan,
1992 –1993

Bess A. Brown

When the Soviet Union disintegrated in December 1991, many foreign observers predicted that the new countries of Central Asia would be among the more unstable successor states. In the event, during their first two years of independence the Central Asian states have proved politically stable despite varying degrees of economic decline, with the single exception of Tajikistan. During the last six months of 1992 what had been the poorest of the republics of the USSR was ravaged by a civil war that wound down in the first months of 1993 but has never fully ended. Estimates of the number of casualties have varied widely, between 20,000 and over 100,000; it appears that the war in Tajikistan has cost more lives than have been lost in the years of fighting over Nagorno-Karabakh.[1]

The civil war in Tajikistan may be ultimately attributed to the removal of Soviet-era constraints that kept regional and ethnic frictions under control; as Moscow's control weakened in the late 1980s and early 1990s, indications appeared that a political opposition was developing that might eventually pose an effective challenge to Tajikistan's Communist leadership. The first unmistakable sign that the traditional power structure was weakening was the demonstrations of February 1990.

Political Background of the Civil War: the Demonstrations of 1990 and the Growth of the Opposition

On February 12, 1990, demonstrators gathered in front of the building of the Communist Party's Central Committee in Dushanbe to protest rumoured plans to give Armenian refugees preference in receiving housing. Hundreds of Tajiks were still homeless after an earthquake in the Hissar Valley west of Dushanbe, and many young people from Hissar joined Dushanbe townsfolk in the demonstrations, which also included members of the Tajik intelligentsia protesting the unwillingness of the Republic's Communist leadership to introduce the types of liberalisation that were being felt in other parts of the USSR.

Depending on the version one accepts, the demonstrations were either accompanied by or deteriorated into riots that caused at least 22 deaths and considerable material damage in the city. The Tajik leadership barricaded itself in the Central Committee building, where during a stormy session of the Central Committee in which the top leadership blamed each other for what was happening in the streets, Communist Party chief Kakhar Makhkamov attempted to resign.[2] A handful of young officials, most notably State Planning Committee chief Buri Karimov, joined the protesters demanding a change in leadership and were reported to have set up a People's Committee that was seen by the Party and government leadership as an incipient rival government.

This first attempt to dislodge the traditional Communist leadership of Tajikistan was quickly put down after Makhkamov regained his nerve and appealed to Moscow for help, which arrived in the form of troops of the Soviet Ministry of Internal Affairs. The young officials who had sought to force perestroika through the use of what Makhkamov dismissed as 'the democracy of the streets' lost their jobs and harassment of the organised opposition, which at that time consisted largely of the Tajik nationalist movement *Rastokhez* ('Rebirth'), began.

The Rastokhez movement had begun as a group of Tajik intellectuals who wanted to restore traditional Tajik culture and revive use of the classical Tajik language. Similar small informal groups had appeared in Dushanbe in the late 1980s, but by February 1990 Rastokhez had become the most influential, as shown by the role its members played in the demonstrations in front of the Central Committee building. Although Communist Party chief Makhkamov blamed Rastokhez leaders for inciting the February disturbances, he never banned the movement, preferring to engage in harassment rather than outright repression.

The same treatment was meted out by the Communist authorities to the Democratic Party of Tajikistan, a grouping of Western-oriented intellectuals which was formally founded in August 1990. Its Chairman, Shodmon Yusupov, a researcher in the philosophy section of the republican Academy of Sciences, claimed soon after the Party

87

was created that some of the Supreme Soviet deputies elected immediately after the suppression of the February disturbances were members or at least sympathisers of the Democrats.[3] When the concept of an executive presidency was introduced in Tajikistan, the Democrats staged a hunger strike in protest at having been prevented from nominating their own presidential candidate.

The opposition group that fared the worst at the hands of the Communist authorities was the Islamic Renaissance Party.[4] When Tajik participants in the founding congress of the all-USSR Islamic Renaissance Party applied for official permission to set up a branch of the Party in Tajikistan, the authorities not only denied permission but the Supreme Soviet Presidium banned the Party before it could even be established. The ban did not prevent the growth of the organisation in the underground, and by the time Tajikistan declared its independence in 1991, the Party was estimated to be the largest after the Communist Party of Tajikistan and was particularly influential in the Garm region east of Dushanbe, the Gorny Badakhshan Autonomous Oblast in the Pamirs, and the regions in the plains of southern Tajikistan where people from the two former areas had been settled in the 1930s and 1940s to grow cotton. It was weakest in Leninabad Oblast in northern Tajikistan, which had traditionally been the home of most of the Republic's Communist leadership.

The growth of an active opposition in Dushanbe and in certain regions of the Republic set the stage for the political antagonisms that would lead to the civil war. It was the coup by Communist hardliners in Moscow in August 1991 and the abrupt decision of Tajikistan's leadership to declare independence that brought these antagonisms into the open.

Independence

Tajikistan's Supreme Soviet declared the Republic independent on September 9, 1991, as part of the republican rush to independence precipitated by the Ukraine and Uzbekistan in the wake of the August coup in Moscow. The new country was born in a state of greater internal political turmoil than affected many of the other republics that were declaring independence at the same time, for not only were major demonstrations by the opposition under way in Dushanbe, but the head of state had resigned a few days earlier.

Makhkamov had tried to preserve the power of the Communist Party of Tajikistan by severing its ties with the Communist Party of the Soviet Union, discredited after the events of August 20–22. The Tajik opposition, however, was convinced that Makhkamov, who had been President of the Republic since November 1990 in addition to heading the Communist Party, had sided with the hardliners who were seeking to restore the leading role of the Communist Party in society, and was determined to force him out. On August 23, the day after the collapse of the Moscow junta, the Democratic Party of Tajikistan organised a demonstration to demand the resignation of the republican leadership and multi-party elections to a new legislature. This time there was nothing to be gained from calling for help from Moscow, so Makhkamov chose to depart.

The resignation of the President and Communist Party chief was only the first act in a drama of confrontation between the Supreme Soviet, dominated by anti-reform Communists, and the nationalist-democratic-Islamic opposition. Whenever the Supreme Soviet resumed the special session that had begun at the end of August to deal with the emergency precipitated by the events in Moscow, opposition demonstrators would gather before the Supreme Soviet building to demand the banning of the Communist Party and the legalising of the Islamic Renaissance Party.

Apparently in response to opposition pressure, the Chairman of the Supreme Soviet and acting head of state, Kadriddin Aslonov, banned the Communist Party on September 22; his decree was rescinded the next day by the Supreme Soviet and Aslonov himself was replaced as Acting President by a former republican Communist Party chief, Makhkamov's predecessor, Rakhmon Nabiev, who had already registered as a candidate in the presidential election scheduled for October 27. By the end of September the number of opposition demonstrators in Dushanbe had reached at least 10,000, and the Minister of Internal Affairs was refusing to enforce a state of emergency voted by the Supreme Soviet.

To reduce tensions, Nabiev agreed to the legalisation of the Islamic Renaissance Party, supporters of which made up a large percentage of the demonstrators in Dushanbe, to restore the ban on the Communist Party, and to step down as Acting President during the election campaign. In the election, which had been rescheduled to the end of November, he won two thirds of the vote. The relatively poor showing of filmmaker Dawlat Khudonazarov, the candidate of the united opposition, seemed to discourage the opponents of Communist rule. Soon after his election Nabiev lifted the ban on the Communist Party, which quickly re-established itself as the country's dominant political organisation. Tajikistan's political tensions were, however, only dormant; four months after the presidential election they burst out again on an even larger scale.

The Demonstrations in Spring 1992

The immediate prelude to the civil war was a series of demonstrations that began at the end of March 1992 in Dushanbe. These protests were precipitated by supporters of Lali Badakhshan, a movement that sought greater autonomy for the Gorny Badakhshan Autonomous Oblast. The Pamiris had come to Dushanbe to protest against the threatened removal of Minister of Internal Affairs Mamadaez Navzhuvanov, the Badakhshani who had refused to enforce the state of emergency ordered by the Supreme Soviet in September. Lali Badakhshan was quickly joined by supporters of the other three opposition groups, Rastokhez, the Democratic Party and the Islamic Renaissance Party, who renewed their earlier demands for the banning of the Communist Party and added a call for the resignation of Nabiev, who was seen as the dismantler of what little the opposition had achieved the previous autumn.[5]

At the height of the protests the number of opposition demonstrators occupying Shakhidon Square in the centre of Dushanbe was estimated by eyewitnesses to have reached at least 100,000. In mid-April a demonstration by supporters of the government began in nearby Ozodi Square; according to the semi-official daily *Narodnaya gazeta*, most of the pro-government demonstrators were from Kulyab Oblast in the southern part of the country.[6] Many government officials were from Kulyab, and the protests may have had less an ideological than a regional orientation.

Nabiev's pleas to the opposition to stop the demonstrations and let the country get on with solving its acute economic problems were unheeded, and at the end of April he asked the Supreme Soviet to grant him emergency powers, which he used on May 2 to create a National Guard answerable only to himself. The arming of this group, which consisted largely of young men from Kulyab, precipitated the outbreak of violence in Dushanbe that led directly to the civil war.

After opposition supporters gained control of the Tajik Television centre on May 3, Nabiev ordered the Guard to suppress the demonstration on Shakhidon Square. Fighting began between pro- and anti-government factions on May 5, and there were a number of fatalities. Both sides seemed to have been shocked by the violence, and

Nabiev began negotiations with the leadership of the opposition that culminated on May 11 with the signing of an agreement providing for one third of the seats in a new government of National Reconciliation to be held by opposition supporters. According to Democratic Party Chairman Shodmon Yusupov, there was an informal agreement that no top leader of an opposition group would hold a government post, but Davlat Usman, an official of the Islamic Renaissance Party, was named a Deputy Prime Minister and soon began functioning as the spokesman for the new government. The opposition retained control of the state television and radio system, which quickly took on a nationalist tone. To the disappointment of the leadership of the Islamic Renaissance Party, Nabiev remained President.

The Civil War Begins

The agreement between Nabiev and the opposition was repudiated immediately by two of Tajikistan's provinces, Leninabad Oblast in the north and Kulyab Oblast in the south. Leninabad, which is more industrialised than the rest of the country except Dushanbe, and also has close ties with neighbouring Uzbekistan, threatened to secede from Tajikistan. The leadership of Kulyab Oblast demanded that Nabiev's agreement and the decisions of the new government be scrutinised by the Constitutional Oversight Committee. On May 12, supporters of two opposition groups began fighting in the town of Kulyab; apparently former members of Nabiev's short-lived National Guard joined the fray, thereby igniting the struggle that soon threatened to tear Tajikistan apart.

The fighting that raged in southern Tajikistan for the last six months of 1992 involved regional, ethnic and family disputes as well as political ones. The most savage fighting was reported from Kurgan-Tyube and Kulyab Oblasts as villagers in Kurgan-Tyube Oblast who had migrated from the Garm region fought villagers from Kulyab. Tajiks settled scores with Uzbek neighbours and thousands of Uzbeks fled into Uzbekistan. The town of Kurgan-Tyube was reported to have been nearly destroyed in attacks by Kulyabi forces. One of the most efficient, if undisciplined, armed groups was the Popular Front of Tajikistan, a troop of Kulyabis commanded by a charismatic former criminal, Sangak Safarov.

Attempts by the Dushanbe government or by democratic figures such as Khudonazarov to initiate ceasefires or merely to get the opposing sides talking to each other came to nothing, largely as a result of the intransigence of the supporters of Nabiev and a Communist restoration who immediately violated any ceasefire that was arranged. The most promising of these attempts at reconciliation was an agreement reached in July in Khorog, capital of Gorny Badakhshan, that seemed to have been accepted by all sides. It, like similar, less ambitious attempts to end the fighting, failed to go into effect when pro-Communist forces refused to begin laying down their arms.

Some Tajiks crossed into Afghanistan to buy weapons or be given them by Afghan sympathisers. Tajikistan had not had time to create its own army or border troops, and protection of the border was left in the hands of Russian border guards under an agreement reached between the two countries at the time Tajikistan became independent. There were almost daily skirmishes on the border as the Russian guards tried to stop the illegal cross-border traffic. The Tajik coalition government asked Kyrgyzstan for help in the form of a peace-keeping force, but the Kyrgyz legislature flatly refused to send Kyrgyzstani citizens into a war zone.

In addition to the Russian border guards, the 201st Motorised Division of the Russian Army was still stationed in Tajikistan. Through most of the fighting in 1992 the Russian Division attempted to stay neutral, according to the frequent assertions of its Tajik commander. Leaders of the nationalist-democratic-Islamic coalition claimed, however, that the Russians were secretly helping the pro-Nabiev forces. At the beginning of September the Presidents of Russia, Uzbekistan, Kazakhstan and Kyrgyzstan issued a warning to the government and political organisations of Tajikistan, branding the unrest in that country a danger to the Commonwealth of Independent States and announcing that the four states would intervene to stop the large-scale smuggling of arms and to prevent Tajikistan from leaving the CIS.

On September 7 an obscure group of youthful opponents of Nabiev caught the President at Dushanbe airport, apparently attempting to flee to his home in Leninabad Oblast. After several hours of argument, Nabiev agreed to resign, appearing later the same night on television to tell the population that his resignation was voluntary. He later said that he had been forced to resign at gunpoint. His departure did not, however, have a perceptible effect on the level of fighting.

Forces opposed to the coalition government entered Dushanbe on October 24, but they were forced out two days later. The attack on the capital so discouraged the acting head of state, Supreme Soviet

Chairman Akbarsho Iskandarov, that he persuaded the government to resign and called a session of the national legislature. The Supreme Soviet had refused to meet to approve Nabiev's resignation, but declared its willingness to assemble in November on condition that the session was held in Khojent in Leninabad Oblast, outside the control of the anti-Communist coalition. Among the actions taken by the Supreme Soviet was the naming of a new government which was almost entirely made up of former officials from Kulyab and Leninabad. Nabiev offered to resume the presidency, but he was not only rejected, the office of President was abolished as well.

Aftermath of the Civil War

Most of the fighting in the civil war had ended by January 1993. A new government of former Communist officials installed itself in Dushanbe at the end of December but had difficulty controlling its own armed supporters, who killed unknown numbers of the opponents of the Communist restoration, mostly Islamic Renaissance Party sympathisers from the Pamirs. Revenge killings were reported from many places in southern Tajikistan where fighting had gone on, and tens of thousands of Tajiks, mostly supporters of the Islamic Renaissance Party, fled into Afghanistan between late December 1992 and February 1993. Government spokesmen denied that atrocities were being committed by the irregular troops whose civil war successes had helped bring the new rulers of the country to power, but many foreign and Russian journalists reported having witnessed such attacks.

From the moment of its establishment in Dushanbe in December 1992, the new government determined to silence, if not physically destroy, the anti-Communist opposition that had briefly dominated the country's government the previous year. The groups that had made up the anti-Communist coalition in 1992 – the Islamic Renaissance Party, the Western-oriented Democratic Party, the Tajik nationalist Rastokhez movement and the separatist Lali Badakhshan – were first suspended and then formally banned by the Supreme Court in June. Their leaders were charged, largely *in absentia*, with armed insurrection against the constitutional order and waging civil war. Most opposition leaders fled to Afghanistan, Iran or Russia, where they attempted to continue resistance to the pro-Communist forces in power in Dushanbe. Until the creation of a People's Party in late August under the leadership of the First Deputy Chairman of the

Supreme Soviet, Abdumajid Dostiev, the only legal party in Tajikistan was the Communist Party. Government officials asserted, however, that they were not really Communists and were committed to eventual democratisation.

The opposition press was closed down in December and January and opposition control of the broadcast media was ended with the arrest in early February of Mirbobo Mirrakhimov, the Tajik nationalist who had been put in control of Tajik Television, and two of his deputies. Some liberal journalists were arrested and others went into exile. Attempts to smuggle opposition publications into Tajikistan had limited success.

Throughout the first half of 1993, the Tajik government's troops tried to mop up the continued insurgency inside Tajikistan by armed sympathisers of the Islamic Renaissance Party. Fighting continued into the summer between government troops and small groups of resistance fighters who took refuge in the mountains east of Dushanbe. Plans to create an army for Tajikistan using the troops of the Tajikistan Popular Front, the most effective of the armed groups fighting the nationalist-democratic-Islamic coalition, received a set-back at the end of March when two of the group's top leaders killed each other in a shoot-out.

The Dushanbe government had limited success in establishing control over Gorny Badakhshan. The leadership of the Autonomous Oblast continued to sympathise with the opposition, but the increasingly desperate economic situation of the Pamiri population forced local officials to appeal to Dushanbe for help. In June they formally renounced the goal of independence for the province. Fighting blocked the highway from Dushanbe to Khorog for much of the year, and by August there were reports that the population of Gorny Badakhshan was in danger of starvation.

The main threat to the regime in Dushanbe was not the insurgencies inside the country but rather the attacks on the Tajik-Afghan border by Tajik opposition sympathisers who had taken refuge in Afghanistan, and their Afghan supporters. Fighting on the border occurred almost daily throughout the year with casualties on both sides. The new Tajik government appealed for CIS help, which was promised at the CIS summit in January. Russian border troops had to take the brunt of the fighting in 1993, although troops from Uzbekistan, Kazakhstan and Kyrgyzstan were also stationed on the Tajik-Afghan frontier. Uzbekistan assumed responsibility for protecting Tajikistan's airspace.

In May, the Tajik government became convinced that a major attack from Afghanistan was imminent, but an assault on the scale expected never materialised. In mid-July Russian forces shelled several villages on the Afghan side of the border, claiming that they were being used as staging areas for assaults on Russian troops. The Afghan government protested and the Russian artillery attacks were stopped. The daily skirmishing continued. One such clash, in which 25 Russian troops were killed, was widely believed to be the reason for the firing of Russian Security Minister Viktor Barannikov. While most assaults involved small handfuls of Tajik opposition fighters and Afghan helpers, in September and October incursions by groups of up to 400 men were reported by Russian border guards.

The return of the Tajik refugees who had fled to Afghanistan at the beginning of the year became a major concern for Tajikistan's leadership, who feared with some justification that the refugees would come under the influence of Afghan Muslim fundamentalists. Tajikistan's head of state, Parliament Chairman Imomali Rakhmonòv, sought United Nations help and even courted the Kabul government in an effort to get the refugees back. By year-end, however, few had been willing to accept government assurances of their safety. Those few who did return from Afghanistan, and the refugees from southern Tajikistan who had fled to other parts of the country, often found upon return to their former places of residence that they had neither food nor shelter.

By the end of 1993, Tajikistan was the only former Soviet republic to still be using Soviet roubles as its only currency. Dependent on Russian military aid and with the Tajik economy virtually destroyed by the civil war, the country's leadership believed that it had no alternative but to join Russia in a new rouble zone that had been spurned by the other CIS states. In return, Russia promised to provide assistance to keep Tajikistan's economy from complete collapse, but it was apparent that Tajikistan was at least as dependent on Russia as it had ever been when it was part of the USSR.

Notes

1 *Le Monde*, July 17, 1993.
2 *Kommunist Tadzhikistana*, February 15, 16, 18 and 20, 1990.
3 See 'Ten Months After the Dushanbe Riots', *Report on the USSR*, January 4, 1991.

4 See 'The Islamic Renaissance Party in Central Asia', *Report on the USSR*, May 10, 1991.
5 For a detailed account of the 1992 demonstrations, see 'Whither Tajikistan?', *RFE/RL Research Report*, June 12, 1992.
6 *Narodnaya gazeta*, April 29, 1992.

THE TAJIK CONFLICT AND THE WIDER WORLD

Chapter 6

Some Reflections on Russian Involvement in the Tajik Conflict, 1992–1993

Catherine Poujol

On 25 May 1993, the Tajik President Imomali Rakhmonov declared: 'Were it not for Russia and Boris Nikolayevich Yeltsin, were it not for Uzbekistan and Islam Abduganievich Karimov, the Tajik people and the Tajik state would no longer exist.'[1] The purpose of this article is to show, particularly with the help of the appended chronology, how the situation prevailing during winter 1993 came about.

It is useful, first of all, to introduce the protagonists, as well as the main facts which affected them between spring 1992 and December 1993. We shall then examine, in a parenthesis, some ideas which motivated the intervention forces; finally, the spotlight will be turned on some of the problems that have resulted.

The *dramatis personae* are well-known: the Tajiks, the Russians of Tajikistan, the Russian Federation, Tajikistan's CIS neighbours and other powers in the region. However, the following points need to be emphasised:

1. Their opinions and interests are necessarily different, especially since there are divisions within these groups themselves.
2. The specific nature of Russian military involvement in Tajikistan is a product of the specific nature of the Soviet situation, where political withdrawal has not thus far been followed by military retreat, for reasons that are well-known, and still less by economic disengagement. There are thus 25 million Russians outside the Russian Federation, in what has come to be known today as the 'near abroad', and 200,000 soldiers who should theoretically be returning to Russia by the end of 1995.

The Protagonists

1 The Tajik people: the authorities, the opposition and the rest of the population

From the outset of the civil war on 28 June 1992, it was clear that the Tajik authorities wanted armed intervention from Russia, which was roundly condemned by the opposition from August 1992 onwards. The Tajik population itself is still reeling from the brutality of the civil war and is not yet aware of the negative implications which the Russian military presence in Tajikistan could entail, although its attitude to this question could change. As for the creation of a Tajik national army, it is scarcely on the agenda. The Republic was not as lucky as Uzbekistan, which had in Tashkent the headquarters of the Turkestan Military District (abolished on 30 June 1992), as well as three of the former USSR's military academies. The lack of military cadres was sorely felt in Tajikistan, and recourse to the Russian army seemed inevitable.

2 The Russians in Tajikistan: the military, civilians and diplomats

Even before the outbreak of armed conflict, Russian forces had been acting as mediators in Tajikistan; from July 1992 their mission also involved the protection of strategic installations. The Russian troops in Tajikistan chiefly wanted to avoid becoming involved in the conflict, though the details of this position varied. In November 1992, for example, some border guard officers demanded to be withdrawn from Central Asia, while others were happy with the relative clarity of the task in hand and the pay, which was better than they would have got in Russia.

It is difficult to know exactly how many Russian troops there were in Tajikistan in 1993. They were made up of different elements, the exact number of some of which it is impossible to ascertain, especially the forces of the Ministry of the Interior. Press communiqus constantly repeated (as did General Pyankov at the time) that Russia had about 25,000 men stationed in Tajikistan, backed up by Tajik, Kazakh, Kyrgyz and Uzbek units.[2] In reality, effective numbers seem to have been less. The Russian force consisted chiefly of the 201st Motorised Division, based in Dushanbe. This division should have had 10–12,000 men, but it had been below strength by 40% for years, leaving about 6,000 men. There was a regiment based in

Kurgan-Tyube (the 191st) and a motorised regiment in Kulyab. The Joint Peace-Keeping Forces, which had come as reinforcements to the 201st Division, together with a unit of paratroops and the 201st Division itself, probably did not exceed 6–8,000 men all told. There was also an indeterminate number of Interior Ministry (OMON) troops and 2,000–2,500 border guards.[3] A figure in *The New York Times* on 30 November 1993 overestimated by 30%, giving 15,000 in all, the majority of which were not conscripts but a new category of voluntary soldiers with three-year contracts (paid the equivalent of US$ 109 a month).

In 1989 the Russian civilian population in Tajikistan numbered 388,000: there are less than 100,000 left today, including many families who have taken refuge with Russian units.

Tajikistan plays host to a very small number of Russian diplomats, ten or so on a permanent basis, engaged in arranging humanitarian aid and managing economic problems. Their point of view does not always coincide with that of the military, whom they accuse of making Russian foreign policy themselves.

3 The Russians of the Russian Federation

With the outbreak of the Tajik conflict at the end of June 1992, a split appeared in the official stances taken in Moscow. Yeltsin on one hand refused to open a new front, while on the other Marshal Shaposhnikov was already talking of sending intervention forces. A consensus was rapidly reached: Russia took the Tajik border guards under its jurisdiction on 24 August and became more and more concerned with the Tajik situation. Marshal Shaposhnikov was sent to the scene, and on 4 September a declaration was signed with Presidents Nazarbayev, Karimov and Akayev, signalling Russia's intention to help Tajikistan re-establish peace. Russia's distinct reluctance to bear sole responsibility for the situation in the region made itself felt straight away; urgent demands were made in July to the Kazakh, Uzbek and Kyrgyz Parliaments to agree to send troops to defend the CIS's southern border, since the Russian guards (and a few locals) were complaining that the burden was falling entirely on them. At this point, Yeltsin abruptly changed his position, announcing to the Russian Parliament on 6 October 1992 that he had decided to withdraw Russian troops from Tajikistan. This was only a temporary volte-face, no doubt caused by political pressure from those in Russia who were opposed to any further sacrifice of Russian lives. He did, nevertheless, send his Minister of Foreign Affairs, Andrei Kozyrev, to Dushanbe on 6 November, to help restore calm. The process of setting up a joint force was speeded up in words, but not in deed. On 9 October, there were talks at the Eighth CIS Summit in Bishkek; on 30 November, a decision was made to send in CIS troops. However, their number was not specified, and their deployment took some time to materialise.

During his visit to Dushanbe on 16 July 1993, the Russian Defence Minister, Pavel Grachev, exhorted the Central Asian Presidents to act. An incident on 13 July at Border Post No. 12, in which 25 Russians were killed, forced a greater awareness of the gravity of the situation and of the stakes involved, and led to the internationalisation of the conflict. From now on the Russians were vigilant not to be drawn into a second Afghan war, though they still sent reinforcements to the border. They began to look to the UN for support. The tide of Russian popular opinion, however, began to turn towards disengagement. The official position was that a decision to pull out would have serious consequences. On 24 August 1993, the CIS Defence Ministers decided to set up a coalition force to control the insurrection in Tajikistan, protect the border, defend strategic installations and help in the delivery of humanitarian aid. The move came exactly fourteen months after the creation of a force was first mentioned by Marshal Shaposhnikov, and ten months after the Eighth Summit, where the decision had been passed.

4   CIS neighbours in the peace-keeping coalition

Uzbekistan, right next door to Tajikistan and keenly aware that there were at least two million Tajiks living on its territory and 1.4 million Uzbeks in Tajikistan, was alarmed by the Tajik situation. In September 1992, Islam Karimov alerted the United Nations to the bloody events in Tajikistan. Conscious of the risks of contagion for his own Republic, which had all the ingredients for political destabilisation, he repeated his warning in March 1993 and then in September of that year, at the 48th General Assembly of the Security Council of the UN. Karimov actively participated in bringing the Communists back to power in Dushanbe, loath though he was to admit it officially. He began to worry, however, that Russian forces might become established in Tajikistan in the medium to long term.

Kazakhstan was just as worried about developments on its southern borders, which is why the Kazakh press was under orders not to publish any information about the civil war throughout its duration. This did not, however, stop President Nazarbayev from signing the agreement to participate in the CIS coalition forces, at the Eighth and Ninth Summits, nor from sending, like Kyrgyzstan, a portion (500 men each) of the promised contingent, at a time when Uzbekistan had still done nothing. It should be noted that 75% of the Kazakh border troops were ethnic Russians, and that the Kyrgyz battalion arrived with only half the promised troops: 500 men, without arms or bullet-proof jackets. It was the Ninth CIS Summit in Moscow, therefore, which saw the signing on 24 September 1993 of the agreement creating the joint defence force. It stipulated the division of the border into zones of responsibility, followed by a letter to the UN from the Foreign Ministers of the four Republics which had formed the coalition.

This did not prevent Lieutenant-General Aleksandr Tymko, chief of the Russian border troops' headquarters, from criticising the Central Asian states for their inaction on 12 October 1993. In fact, this coalition force was considered not the outcome of real military cooperation, but rather a subterfuge used by Russia to mask its desire to reassert its influence, since it did not admit from the outset that it was unable to bear alone the full financial weight of military engagement.

5 Neighbouring states also involved

I will limit myself to naming them. Afghanistan has taken a leading role as the retreat base for the armed Tajik resistance, as well as for refugees; Iran has confined itself officially to the role of mediator, and Pakistan and the Arab countries are only involved through the participation of individual militants, which is beyond the scope of this article.

6 The border

The border itself is an interesting subject to consider, since it has generated actions and political and strategic positions both internally and externally, by the UN, the CSCE and NATO.

Several historical facts should be recalled here, which prove that, despite the crucial nature of this border, which has been established for almost a century, it has been crossed continually. There is no need to dwell on its geographical features: essentially mountainous, it is about 1,200 km long and follows the course of the Pyanj, the upper reaches of the Amu Darya, which at this level is very rough and difficult to cross. Nor do we need to go back to the famous division between Iran and Turan; I will plunge straight in at 1894, when the border of the Khanate of Bukhara with Afghanistan was guarded by Russian soldiers who set up customs posts (the protectorate of Bukhara was subject to the customs tariffs of the Russian empire).

Thus, this border was never watertight. In the 1920s, at the height of the civil war, numerous Uzbeks, Tajiks and Bukharan Jews, under threat of being shot as capitalists by the Bolsheviks, crossed it with the help of Afghan guides – to say nothing of the Bukharan Emir, Alim Khan, who made the journey with his harem and his treasure. At the other end of the Soviet period, infiltrations by the Afghan Mujahidin into Tajik territory were noted from 1980, as were those by Muslim preachers who carried in their knotted scarves Qurans at 1,000 roubles each (before devaluation) and cassettes of Sufi music. It should be remembered that in the stagnant Brezhnev era, there were numerous Soviet citizens in Moscow and Leningrad who dreamt of crossing the Pamir frontier, although they knew full well that the KGB border guards were extremely efficient.[4] Nowadays the situation has become much worse, but it is important to see it in a historical perspective.

This conflict zone is thus protected by border guards, formerly under the jurisdiction of the KGB, and now under that of the Russian Ministry of State Security: its commanders are Russian, its officers mixed. The assault of 13 July 1993, when Border Post No. 12 was attacked by 200 Mujahidin and 200 Tajik militants,[5] had three consequences:

1. Russia was obliged to define its geopolitical priorities more clearly.
2. Some supporters of integration, both in Russia and Central Asia, became newly determined to transform the CIS into a reconstituted USSR.
3. The question was raised of Russia's real opportunities for action or inaction in the region.

The events of 13 July therefore encouraged the development in Russia of the opinion that it has a special responsibility to end all conflicts in the former Soviet Union, that its armed forces have a special mission to protect the 25 million Russians living outside Russia. After all, did not Yeltsin declare to the military authorities on 9 June 1993 that withdrawing the Russian army from Tajikistan would mean leaving a whole nation to perish, something Russia would never allow?[6] We will not enter here into the polemics unleashed within the Russian political class by the events of 13 July. The most tangible result they produced was to strengthen support for a more aggressive, less Westernising national security policy, which generated an upsurge of Russocentric tendencies with regard to the near abroad within the Ministry of Foreign Affairs, and intangible positions at headquarters about the role of the Russian army, as the following series of opinions by Russian politicians and soldiers shows.

Russian Views

There have been several interviews with Russian political figures, and I will cite the following:

– Interview with Viktor Barannikov, Russian Minister of Security, 19 July 1993, on his return to Moscow from a visit to Tajikistan.[7] '*Question*: After the incident on 13 July which left 25 Russian soldiers dead, many politicians and journalists are wondering why Russia should be guarding the borders of a foreign country. *Answer*: Defending the Tajik section of the border is defending the backbone of Russian security. The Russian border guards hold the key to Russian and CIS security.'

– Interview with Marshal Shaposhnikov, 27 July 1993, on the role of Russia in Tajikistan.[8] According to him, Russia had five options:
   1. Complete withdrawal of Russian forces from Tajikistan, which would mean transplanting 400,000 Russians to Russia, a very costly option.
   2. Reprisals against Afghanistan, which would probably lead to another war, the outcome of which would be unpredictable for Russia.
   3. Russian soldiers could be brought in to reinforce the Tajik-Afghan border, which would be very difficult for Russia, as well as futile, since Russia was in no condition to take control of 1,400 km of border.
   4. Reinforcement and defence of the border with joint CIS forces, notably from Kazakhstan, Kyrgyzstan and Uzbekistan, accompanied by financial aid for Tajikistan to establish its own armed forces, with border guards equipped by Russia.
   5. The diplomatic option: conflict resolution by a Forum organised by the neighbouring Muslim countries, Afghanistan and Pakistan.

Marshal Shaposhnikov's choice was to combine options 4 and 5, which would require that the CIS present a united front, diplomatically, technically, politically and militarily, and that negotiations be arranged.

- Interview with Evgenii Ambartsumov, President of the Russian Federation's Committee for International Affairs, also on 27 July 1993.[9] To the question, 'Why not leave Tajikistan immediately?', his answer was, 'Where would we go? If we withdraw to the Kazakh-Kyrgyz border, Tajikistan will be sacrificed to the Islamists.'

From this point onwards, Russia's distinct reluctance to bear sole responsibility for the region could be seen through its demands to the Kazakh, Uzbek and Kyrgyz governments to take part in defending the southern borders.

The same man, interviewed by *Izvestiya* on 7 August 1992, had said: 'As the internationally recognised legal successor to the USSR, the Russian Federation must base its foreign policy on a doctrine that will make the whole geopolitical space of the former Union a sphere of vital interests ... following in this the example of the USA's Monroe Doctrine in Latin America ... Russia must be invested by the international community with the role of political and military guarantor of stability throughout the territory of the former USSR.' The publication of the Military Doctrine in October 1993 followed from this.

- Interview with Andrei Kozyrev on 25 August 1993.[10] 'We cannot leave Tajikistan because the Tajik border is in fact the border of the CIS and of the CSCE.'

The Problems

Several questions arise here. Is Russia's engagement in Central Asia going to ruin its chances of becoming a normal European country? Is there not a risk that Russian forces will be used by former-Soviet states to annihilate internal opposition, or simply to relieve their inability to bear the cost of military operations themselves? It is true that the Tajik authorities used the emotion generated by the 13 July attack to launch an offensive against the Pamiris, in which the Russians did not participate. Nonetheless, Russia's position is still ambiguous. Moreover, to what extent are the armed forces controlled by the central power in Tajikistan?

One thing is certain: the more the Russians intervene, the more difficult their situation becomes. An article published on 16 September 1993 by *Nezavisimaya Gazeta* was entitled: 'The Russian Army in the Tajik War: Aims Unclear, Preparation for Combat Weak, Strategy Lacking'. There is a huge gulf between political declarations, such as 'the Tajik border is the Russian border,' and the real situation in the region. Lack of strategy and poor circulation of information are just some of the problems besieging the Russian troops guarding the Tajik-Afghan border. It is difficult for them to make sense of the complexity of the local armed formations and the motivations for their actions. There has not so far been sufficient help from the Central Asian countries involved in the deployment of joint forces. It is also difficult to form a clear picture of the opposition forces: are there 5,000, plus 3,000 Afghan partisans? The information that has been gathered is unreliable. Preparation for combat is also a problem, for soldiers and officers alike, especially those who come from other regions and feel that they are there only temporarily, and that they are not always remunerated in proportion to the risks they run. The chief of the CIS forces, Colonel-General Boris Pyankov, stated in the newspaper *Krasnaya Zvezda* (9 November 1993) that he earns less in six months than an ordinary UN blue beret.

However, the Russian tactics are coherent: to prevent transgressions of the borders, a task which is becoming more and more difficult; to seek local agreements with Afghan chiefs who could control part of the border; to share responsibility with the other CIS members concerned; and to invoke the fundamentalist threat as a justification for the Russian presence.

Yet despite the clear declarations of the politicians, will not the Russian army in Tajikistan suffer the same troubles as elsewhere in the former Soviet Union: the same sense of uselessness, loss of purpose in life, lack of career prospects, and financial problems in supporting their families? Moreover, the CIS has no experience of establishing intervention forces, which causes numerous financial and customs problems, etc. The only thing the states involved in the intervention forces have decided is the percentage of financial participation: the rest they improvise as they go along.

It remains to be seen whether the continued presence of Russian forces or their withdrawal from Tajikistan will also be improvised.

107

Notes

1 Interfax.
2 Reuter, 1 November 1993.
3 DAS, Paris.
4 In this connection, I would like to recount a personal anecdote which occurred in 1980 in Dushanbe. I was talking to a small boy of about seven or eight, the son of a film-maker who was about to be awarded a 'KGB Prize' for a film praising the USSR's border troops, at a time when glorifying this line of work was no longer *de rigueur*. This boy innocently recounted the difficulties encountered by the film crew, who were forced to enter Afghan territory several times, attacked by 'Basmachis' with huge dogs and obliged, in self-defence, to kill several of them. (In addition, he had enjoyed the border very much because of the flares that would go off if one so much as touched a tuft of grass ...) The naïve words of a child, perhaps, but like the flares they were very illuminating of the fact that the Uzbek-Tajik-Afghan border has always been the USSR's Achilles' heel in Central Asia.
5 BBC, *Summary of World Broadcasts*, 15–16 July 1993.
6 Interfax, 10 June 1993.
7 Interfax.
8 *Ibid.*
9 *Ibid.*
10 *Ibid.*

Bibliography

BARRY, F. 'Les missions de la CEI: le bilan', *Le Courrier des pays de l'Est*, 374, November 1992, pp. 55–63.

DJALILI, M.-R. 'L'Iran face au Caucase et à l'Asie centrale', *Le Trimestre du monde*, 4, 1992, Observatoire des relations internationales, pp. 181–9.

EGGERT, K. 'Rossiya v role evraziiskogo zhandarma' ('Russia in the Role of Gendarme of Eurasia'), *Izvestiya*, 7 August 1992.

ERLANGER, S. 'In ex-Soviet Lands, Russian Army Can Be a Protector or an Occupier', *The New York Times*, 30 November 1993.

FAVRET, R. 'Tadjikistan: les soldats russes reviennent', *Le Figaro*, 21 November 1992.

FUNDER LARSEN, P. 'Le gendarme russe de la CEI', *Inprecor*, 361, 23 October to 5 November 1992, pp. 3–7.

GRIGOREV, S., 'Rossiiskaya armiya v Tadzhikskoi voine' ('The Russian Army in the Tajik War'), *Nezavisimaya Gazeta*, 1 September 1993.

GUPTA, R. 'Tadjikistan: Locked Horns for Power', *Strategic Analysis*, September 1992, pp. 519–37.

GUSEINOV, G. 'Srednyaya Aziya posle raspada imperii' ('Central Asia after the Collapse of the Empire'), *Überblick*, April 1992, p. 1 (German version).

IOUSSINE, M. 'La Russie dans l'engrenage tadjik', *La Croix*, 24 September 1992.

Some Reflections on Russian Involvement in the Tajik Conflict

KAHN, M. 'Les Russes dans les ex-républiques soviétiques', *Le Courrier des pays de l'Est* 376, January-February 1993, pp. 3–18.

KAPELIOUK, A. 'L'armée russe comme force de police', *Le Monde Diplomatique*, December 1992, p. 13.

KISELYOV, V. 'Russian border troops get a tough ride in Tadjikistan', *Moscow News*, 21 January 1993.

KRAUZE, J. 'Les troupes russes vont rester au Tadjikistan', *Le Monde*, 12 October 1992.

——— 'La Russie va accroître son engagement militaire au Tadjikistan', *Le Monde*, 10 August 1993.

——— 'Les casques bleus de Boris Eltsine', *Le Monde*, 12 August 1993.

LADIN, A. 'My obyazany utverdit' mir v Tadzhikistane' ('We Have a Duty to Impose Peace in Tajikistan'), interview with General B. Pyankov, *Krasnaya Zvezda*, 9 November 1993.

LEVINE, S. 'Afghan, Arab Militants Back Rebels in Ex-Soviet State', *Washington Post*, 27 April 1993.

LOUGH, J. B. K. *Defining Russia's Role in the Near Abroad*, Conflict Studies Research Centre, Royal Military Academy Sandhurst, April 1993.

MONIER, C. 'Forces d'interposition au sein de la CEI', *Défense nationale*, February 1993, pp. 169–71.

ORR, M. 'The Civil War in Tadjikistan', *Asia – Jane's Intelligence Review*, April 1993, pp. 181–4.

PANFILOV, O. 'Rakhmonov zayavil ob okonchanii grazhdanskoi voiny' ('Rakhmonov Announces End of Civil War'), *Nezavisimaya Gazeta*, 18 November 1993.

PATSEGINA, N. 'Bremya okhrany tadzhiksko-afganskoi granitsy Rossii nesti nelegko' ('Burden of Defending Tajik-Afghan Border is Weighty for Russia'), *Nezavisimaya Gazeta*, 12 October 1993.

PETROVSKII, V. 'Tadzhikistan vzryv eshche vozmozhen' ('Tajikistan, Explosion Still Possible'), *Rossiiskie Vesti*, 10 October 1993.

PORTNIKOV, V. 'Rossiya obratilas' litsom k Azii chtoby stat' garantom stabil'nosti v regione' ('Russia has Turned towards Asia in Order to Become a Guarantor of Stability in the Region'), *Nezavisimaya Gazeta*, 19 May 1992.

POSEN, B. 'The Security Dilemma and Ethnic Conflict', *Survival*, 35 (1), Spring 1993, pp. 26–50.

RASHID, A. 'Tournament of Shadows: Opposition Sceptical over Latest Efforts to End Tadjik War', *Far Eastern Economic Review*, 16 September 1993.

——— 'Dominion of Dominoes', *Far Eastern Economic Review*, 24 September 1992.

ROTAR', I. 'Srednyaya Aziya: Moskva vyzidaet i riskuet opozdat'' ('Central Asia: Moscow Stalls and Risks Being Late'), *Nezavisimaya Gazeta*, 29 May 1993, pp. 1–3.

ROY, O. 'La formation d'un nouvel espace stratégique en Asie centrale', *Relations internationales et stratégiques*, 5, Spring 1992, IRIS, pp. 136–44.

RUBIN, B. R. 'The Fragmentation of Tadjikistan', *Survival*, 35 (4), Winter 1993–94, pp. 71–91.

—— 'Post-Cold War State Disintegration: the Failure of International Conflict Resolution in Afghanistan', *Journal of International Affairs*, 46, Winter 1993, pp. 469–92.

SCHMEMANN, S. 'War Bleeds ex-Soviet Land at Central Asia's Heart', *The New York Times*, 21 February 1993.

SHERMATOVA, S. 'Tadjikistan Tangle Making Serious Problems for Moscow', *Moscow News*, 30 July 1993.

—— 'Russia and Afghanistan Discuss the Tajik Problem', *Moscow News*, 17 September 1993.

SHERR, J. 'Escalation of the Tajikistan Conflict', *Asia – Jane's Intelligence Review*, November 1993, pp. 514–16.

SHIHAB, S. 'Le Pamir entre deux feux', *Le Monde*, 12 August 1993.

TADJBAKHSH, S. 'Causes and Consequences of the Civil War', *Central Asia Monitor*, 2 (1), pp. 10–14.

TCHERNEGA, V. 'La Russie et les anciennes républiques de l'Asie centrale', *Le Trimestre du monde*, 4, 1992, Observatoire des relations internationales, pp. 191–8.

UMNOV, A. 'Whose Border is Guarded by Russia in Tadjikistan?', *Moscow News*, 27 August 1993.

WOFF, R. 'Independence and the Uzbek Armed Forces', *Asia – Jane's Intelligence Review*, December 1993, pp. 567–71.

ZHILIN, A. 'Russian Military Presence in Georgia, Central Asia Reaffirmed', *Moscow News*, 10 September 1993.

Chronology of Russian Involvement in the Tajik Conflict, 1992–1993

Catherine Poujol

1992

2 March   Admission of Tajikistan to the United Nations.

May   The Red Army takes a conservative turn, with the nomination of Pavel Grachev, an Afghan War veteran, to the post of Defence Minister of the Russian Federation.

11 May   Agreement signed between the President of Tajikistan, Rakhmon Nabiev, the leaders of the opposition and Qazi Turajonzoda, through the mediation of the commander of CIS forces stationed in Dushanbe, Colonel Vyacheslav Zabolotskii. Coalition government in Dushanbe.

15 May   Signing of the treaty on collective security by the Russian Federation, Kazakhstan, Uzbekistan, Kyrgyzstan, Tajikistan and Armenia.

27 June   First serious attack in Kurgan-Tyube Province, 100 dead.

28 June   Nabiev on an official visit to Iran. Increase in violations of the Tajik-Afghan border by Tajik groups going to buy arms in Afghanistan. Nabiev calls for Russian troops to intervene to restore calm. Marshal Shaposhnikov, Commander-in-Chief of CIS forces, announces that an intervention force could be sent to preserve peace.

July   The Tajik Cabinet of Ministers orders CIS troops stationed in the Republic to protect strategic sites: the Nurek hydroelectric power station, the nitrogen fertiliser plant in Vakhsh, the electrochemical complex in Yavav, the Chormagzak and Fakhrabat passes, the roads to Kulyab and Kurgan-Tyube and munitions dumps.[1]

10 July   Leaders of the democratic and religious opposition in Dushanbe accuse Nabiev of violating human rights at the CSCE conference in Helsinki. Despite the protocol on refugees recently signed by the two republics, Uzbekistan refuses to allow civilian Tajik aircraft to land at its airports.

The Tajik authorities want to create a regiment of border guards comprising 1,200 men, impossible without CIS help. Tajikistan's Russian soldiers do not want to take part in the civil war.[2]

111

24 July	Russia's Deputy Prime Minister, Aleksandr Shokhin, visits Tajikistan.
August	In Dushanbe, Major-General Mukharidin Ashurov, of the 201st Motorised Infantry Division stationed in Tajikistan, threatens legal action against Shodmon Yusuf of the Tajik Democratic Party if he does not stop his 'unfounded accusations' about 'genocide against civilians by Russian troops'.[3]

The Fatherland Salvation Front and Alliance of Democratic Forces protest to President Nabiev and the government against the despatching of 'foreign' troops to Tajikistan, which they consider an act of aggression.[4] |
24 August	Russian President Boris Yeltsin issues a decree placing border guards, formerly under the control of the KGB, under Russian jurisdiction, a decision condemned by the Tajik opposition.
27 August	The Tajik Prime Minister, Davlat Usman, condemns Yeltsin's decree placing the troops on the Tajik-Afghan border under Russian jurisdiction. The troops themselves, however, respond positively.[5]
28 August	Marshal Shaposhnikov, on a visit to the Tajik-Afghan border, does not rule out intervention by 'CIS Blue Helmets'; 180 dead in the south. Nabiev signs a preliminary agreement on the deployment of an intervention force in the south, on the condition that the warring parties accept it.
30 August	Shaposhnikov's visit interrupted after two days; confusion in both government and opposition camps; no one knows whether Russian troops will be despatched or not.
1 September	Nabiev takes refuge in the barracks of the 201st Division. He was to have left for Moscow the next day to sign bilateral agreements.
2 September	The Presidium of the Supreme Soviet and the Tajik government make an appeal to the people about the irresponsibility of Nabiev and the risks of Tajikistan disintegrating.[6] The Prime Minister, Jamshid Karimov, sends a message to Yeltsin asking him not to allow Russian troops to intervene: 'No Russians have been killed in the civil war'. The Tajik opposition also writes to Yeltsin, asking him not to let the CIS interfere in Tajik internal affairs, after a decision by four of its members to send reinforcements to the Tajik-Afghan border, officially to fight arms and drugs smuggling from Afghanistan. State of emergency in Kurgan-Tyube.[7] The Mufti of Tajikistan demands Nabiev's resignation. 'Civil war is, to all intents and purposes, here.'[8] Several thousand demonstrators in Kulyab demand CIS intervention. Russian headquarters receives instructions not to attempt anything which could be denounced by the Tajik opposition as a form of neocolonial policy.
4 September	Presidents Yeltsin, Nazarbayev, Karimov and Akayev sign a declaration, according to which all necessary measures should be taken to help the brother people of Tajikistan to stabilise the situation. The Central Asian Presidents (with the exception of

Turkmenistan) seem to have convinced Yeltsin to become involved in the Tajik conflict.

7 September In Dushanbe, Rakhmon Nabiev signs his resignation at the airport under pressure from the armed opposition.

8 September Uzbek President Islam Karimov is concerned by the situation in Tajikistan ('A time-bomb a hundred times worse than the conflict in Karabakh'), which he partly blames on events in Afghanistan; he appeals to the Secretary-General of the United Nations, Boutros Boutros-Ghali, to send a committee of enquiry to Tajikistan.

10 September Further casualties in the south of Tajikistan.[9] The Russian infantry regiment has difficulty staying neutral; Russia suffers its first casualties. Bloodshed in the Dushanbe suburb of Neftyanik, violence against Uzbeks and Russian-speakers, desecration of a church and graves in Kurgan-Tyube Province.

16 September The Provincial Committee of Kulyab calls for CIS troops to intervene.

24 September Yeltsin sends reinforcements to the Tajik-Afghan border area and orders CIS soldiers stationed in Tajikistan to take control of the border.

6 October Temporary U-turn: Yeltsin announces to the Russian Parliament that he has decided to withdraw Russian troops from Tajikistan.

9 October Eighth CIS Summit in Bishkek votes to send humanitarian aid to Tajikistan. The resolve to create a peace-keeping force, and in the meantime to keep Russian troops in Tajikistan, seems to be hardening. Kyrgyzstan is encouraged to continue its mission of mediation.

24 October The interim President, Akbarsho Iskandarov, returns from Moscow, where he had gone to ask for CIS help, and declares a state of emergency. A few hours later, Nabiev supporters from the south of Tajikistan, living in Dushanbe, launch an offensive. There is talk of a coup d'état by the deposed former President, violent clashes take place in the capital, the US Embassy is evacuated and Iskandarov appeals to CIS leaders on Tajik television 'to send an intervention force immediately'.

26 October The situation in Dushanbe is still confused. The main buildings are stormed by Nabiev supporters; Parliament has to meet in Leninabad under armed Russian protection. Several hundred dead.

6 November Russia's Minister of Foreign Affairs, Andrei Kozyrev, visits Tajikistan: Russia has chosen to help Tajikistan re-establish calm, as the country is important for Russia. One of the solutions suggested is to give power to the Russian army commander, General Ashurov; he refuses. Arrival of paratroops and fifty tanks.

14 November Some Russian officers guarding the Tajik-Afghan border appeal to Yeltsin to consider the reasonableness of keeping them in Central Asia without guarantees of social or legal protection.

113

19 November	The Tajik Parliament elects Imomali Rakhmonov, Governor of Kulyab Province, which is in Communist hands, as President. Iskandarov resigns. Between 6 June and 24 November, the Tajik civil war claims over 50,000 victims and 500,000 refugees.
27 November	Kozyrev adopts the following concept of foreign policy towards the 'near abroad': 'Russia's tasks are to end and regulate armed conflicts around Russian territory, to prevent them spreading, and to ensure the strict application of human rights, especially those of the Russians in the near abroad.'
30 November	Russia, Kazakhstan, Uzbekistan and Kyrgyzstan decide to send a peace-keeping force on behalf of the CIS. The number is not specified, but will partly comprise the 201st Motorised Division already stationed in Tajikistan.
3 December	A CIS delegation visits Tajikistan before sending a peace-keeping force.
9 December	The Uzbek Parliament votes to send a contingent to Tajikistan to participate in the CIS force.
10 December	Capture of Dushanbe by pro-Communist forces led by Safarali Kenjayev, who had been at the head of the failed coup of the previous October; the 201st Motorised Division does not interfere, but then moves into position to prevent an Islamist counter-attack. The intervention force has still not arrived.
14 December	The commander of the Russian garrison in Tajikistan, Colonel Anatolii Yevlev of the 201st Motorised Rifle Division, talks of 1,500 soldiers expected in the new year.
17 December	Terror in Dushanbe. The Democratic Mayor, Maksud Ikramov, places himself under the protection of the 201st Russian Division; Islamist leaders join the 45,000 refugees in the south of the country, and more than 50,000 cross the Amu Darya into Afghanistan.

1993

January	Creation of the Tajik People's Army. The border guards are caught in the crossfire of the Mujahidin and the Tajik opposition.
7 March	President Karimov alerts the UN to the 'violation of the territorial integrity of Uzbekistan' on the borders with Afghanistan, and to the 'Tajik and Uzbek refugees taken hostage by the Afghan Islamists'.
25 May	Agreements signed between Russia and Tajikistan, including a treaty of friendship and a treaty of military assistance for the protection of the southern border. Agreements cover regional stabilisation on CIS borders, the prevention of arms, drugs and other smuggling, and Eurasian security. At a press conference, Rakhmonov says: 'Were it not for Russia and Uzbekistan, the Tajik nation and the Tajik state would no longer exist.'

9 June	Yeltsin announces that withdrawing Russian troops from Tajikistan would mean leaving a whole nation to perish, something Russia could not accept.[10]
13 July	Attack on Post No. 12 on the Tajik-Afghan border: 25 Russians killed. Russia talks of provocation and national tragedy. The Russian Ministers of Defence and Security blame each other.
15 July	Viktor Barannikov, Minister of Security, declares that border guards will take all necessary measures to avert and repel acts of aggression on the border of Tajikistan and the CIS.
16 July	Pavel Grachev, Minister of Defence, visits Tajikistan. He hopes that the neighbouring CIS states will begin to appreciate the dangers of the situation of undeclared war.
17 July	The Afghan Minister of Foreign Affairs claims that Russia has organised a raid on the north of Afghanistan, costing 300 lives; the accusation is denied by Russia and the Tajik government. At the end of Grachev's visit, the decision is taken to form an operational group of the Russian and Tajik military departments, under the command of the Russian General Aleksandr Sokolov. Tajik rebels in Afghanistan are preparing an operation for the autumn, with the aim of forming an Islamic Republic in Gorny Badakhshan. No reinforcement of the Russian presence in Tajikistan: the border should be protected but no attacks made on Afghanistan.
19 July	Barannikov in Dushanbe. Visit to Border Post No. 12 with Rakhmonov on 20 July. The aim is to protect the border without increasing the Russian presence, to help Tajikistan form its own troops of border guards, and to protect the Russians in Tajikistan, now considered a primary objective.
20 July	Barannikov talks of Russia's moral right to invade Afghan territory and admits to carrying out operations across the border.
24 July	Kozyrev informs the UN Security Council of his decision to help Tajikistan in the event of further attacks by Afghan fighters. There is talk in Russia of a second Afghan war, but if the number of Russian casualties increased there would be pressure to withdraw the troops.
26 July	Kozyrev fears becoming embroiled in a second Afghan war.
27 July	Russia defers repayment of Tajikistan's debts until the year 2000 and offers new credit to buy Russian goods. Tajikistan is 85% dependent on Russia. Barannikov is forced to resign and a ministerial inquiry begins into corruption in Yeltsin's entourage. The events in Tajikistan become a new weapon in the power struggle in Russia.
29 July	Yeltsin decides to send additional troops to Tajikistan with the status of 'Blue Helmets' and to seek UN support. There is a growing tide of public opinion in Russia in favour of withdrawal. The official position is that such a decision would be fraught with consequences.

6 August	The Russian Prime Minister, Viktor Chernomyrdin, announces that the conflict is inter-Tajik, not between Russia and Afghanistan. Russia will not allow another Afghan war.
7 August	Meeting in Moscow between Boris Yeltsin and the leaders of the Central Asian member states of the collective security treaty, on regulation of the Tajik crisis. A representative of the Turkmen President, Saparmurat Niyazov, declares that his country will not send a single soldier to the conflict zone. The Kyrgyz President, Askar Akayev, says that none of his soldiers will participate in operations within Tajikistan, a position also held by the Russian Defence Minister.
24 August	The CIS Defence Ministers decide to set up a coalition force to control the insurrection in Tajikistan. The force, under the command of Colonel-General Boris Pyankov, will consist of Russian, Kyrgyz and Kazakh contingents, plus Tajik forces. Armenia considers participating.
25 August	The Council of CIS Defence Ministers agrees to replace the recently abolished unified CIS command with an operational body under their control, to be led by General Viktor Samsonov.
30 August	End of President Rakhmonov's visit to Kabul; the Afghan government is unable to control the regional factions.
31 August	Ismat Kittani, Special Envoy of the UN Secretary-General, arrives in Dushanbe.
End August	Tajik government forces recapture the border region of Darvaz. Yeltsin threatens to withdraw his troops if the Tajik government does not enter into negotiations with the opposition.
18 September	Kozyrev arrives in Dushanbe for talks after a visit to Kabul: Russia and Afghanistan think there can be a political solution to the Tajik conflict.
24 September	Ninth CIS Summit in Moscow: signing of the agreement to form coalition defence forces on Tajik territory. The Tajik-Afghan border is divided into zones of responsibility between Russia, Kazakhstan, Kyrgyzstan, Uzbekistan and Tajikistan. Colonel-General Boris Pyankov is proposed for this command.
30 September	The Foreign Ministers of Kazakhstan, Kyrgyzstan, Tajikistan, Uzbekistan and Russia write to the UN Secretary-General to inform him of their decision to establish a Joint Peace-Keeping Force in Tajikistan. National shares are decided for financing the coalition forces' unified command.
8 October	Rakhmonov holds a press conference on his return from a visit to the USA (26 September – 1 October), where he had attended the 48th General Assembly of the UN.
12 October	Lieutenant-General Aleksandr Tymko, Chief of Staff of the Russian border troops, criticises the Central Asian states for their lack of action. Kyrgyzstan and Kazakhstan announce that they have sent 500 men each; Uzbekistan has still done nothing. Russia holds negotiations with the Afghan authorities and several local chiefs, including General Dostom.

18 October	Iranian President Ali Akbar Hashemi-Rafsanjani visits Tashkent; Karimov asks Iran to help mediate in Tajikistan.
25 October	Letter from Rakhmonov to the UN Secretary-General, informing him that the situation on the border is deteriorating. Rakhmonov asks that Ismat Kittani's mandate be prolonged, a request that is granted, until 31 March 1994. Armed confrontation intensifies in Gorny Badakhshan and Khatlon.
27 October	According to Colonel-General Pyankov, commander of the Joint Peace-Keeping Forces, the total number of armed forces in the Republic is 25,000 men. They are meant to stay for six months, but at the request of the Republic's authorities this period could be curtailed or prolonged, according to the sociopolitical situation.
2 November	The Russian Federation's Security Council approves the country's military doctrine: the first stage, up to 1996, is to create more mobile armed forces which could enable conflicts in former Soviet republics to be stopped.
3 November	President Karimov recognises the decisive role played by his country, more even than by Russia, in Tajikistan. He hopes that elections will soon be held and that Russia will not acquire too great a military weight, which could revive tensions.
12 November	Foreign diplomats estimate that there are 5,000 armed Tajik opposition members in northern Afghanistan.
16 November	Having met Islam Karimov during a tour of Central Asia, to ask him to stop criticism of Moscow in the Uzbek media, Foreign Minister Kozyrev requests in Britain that the West should help Russia finance its peace-keeping operations in the former USSR. He states that Russia will not take part in the Tajik conflict and that it will not be able to maintain stability there in the long term.
18 November	The Russian military doctrine is published in *Izvestiya*. President Rakhmonov announces the end of the civil war. Several Russian politicians declare that, on the contrary, the situation is deteriorating and that negotiations must be opened.
19 November	Officially there is only one batallion of Kazakhstani border guards, and one unofficially confirmed batallion of paratroops (500 men), making up the coalition force with the Russians.
24 November	As part of the Russian electoral campaign, Vladimir Zhirinovskii makes a speech on the radio about the restoration of the empire. He denounces discrimination against Russians in Central Asia caused by the 'temporary presidents who have temporarily seceded ... Moscow will one day become master of those lands again ...'
29 November	Russia seeks the support of the CSCE in Rome for its self-appointed mission of settling local conflicts in the former Soviet Union.
30 November	General Pyankov denies that Russia is dictating Tajikistan's defence policy: there is no Russian dictatorship in Tajikistan. Although the army under his command is essentially Russian,

	the command is divided between Moscow and the Central Asian republics. He estimates that the number of Tajik rebels and their allies fluctuates between 7,000 and 8,000.
1 December	Preliminary conditional approval by the CSCE of Moscow's request to ratify and finance its peace-keeping activities.
6 December	The Tajik government has still not negotiated with the armed opposition, even though Russia has been asking it to for several months. Its position does nevertheless seem to be softening, and it has overcome its earlier objections to Afghan mediation. Talks will probably take place, but not clear with representatives of which factions.
End December	The situation on the Tajik-Afghan border continues to deteriorate.

Notes

1 Decree of 24 June with the agreement of the Minister of Defence of the Russian Federation – ITAR-TASS.
2 ITAR-TASS.
3 Moscow, ITAR-TASS.
4 Radio Dushanbe.
5 ITAR-TASS.
6 Radio Dushanbe.
7 ITAR-TASS.
8 Radio Dushanbe.
9 ITAR-TASS.
10 Interfax.

Chapter 7

Regional Ambitions and Interests in Tajikistan: the Role of Afghanistan, Pakistan and Iran

Mohammad-Reza Djalili and Frédéric Grare

Since it attained independence on 9 September 1991 (the sovereignty of the state having been proclaimed in June 1991), Tajikistan has been going through a very painful period of transition, marked by a series of political crises. These have resulted in the division of the Tajik people into rival and antagonistic clans; foreign intervention, essentially by Russia and Uzbekistan; and a civil war which has made the country the battlefield of choice for the political and ideological struggles of the region.

After Russia and the Central Asian republics of the former USSR, Afghanistan, Pakistan and Iran are obviously, though for different reasons, the countries most concerned by the situation in Tajikistan.

In this article, we will try to show that, apart from Russian and Uzbek interference – which seems today still to be more a question of the internal politics of the former USSR than of truly inter-state relations – the 'internationalisation' of the Tajik conflict remains limited. At the same time, this interference bears witness to the rebirth of a Central Asian space that is now no longer closed.[1]

This study will try to highlight the basis and expressions of Afghan, Pakistani and Iranian policies towards Tajikistan, and attempt to pick out in the complex mass of events the conflicting interests which exist between these three countries, as well as the development of power relationships in the region.

Afghanistan

Bordered in the east by Pakistan, in the west by Iran, and in the north for a distance of almost 2,000 kilometres by Central Asia, Afghanistan is the only one of the three states examined in this study which shares a frontier with Tajikistan. Its geographical situation makes it a necessary transit point for Iran and Pakistan, and partly – since Iran also has a common border with Turkmenistan – the key to their ambitions in Central Asia.

There is, moreover, an ethnic, cultural and religious continuity between the populations of Afghanistan and Tajikistan. The same Tajiks and Uzbeks live on either side of the border, a certain number of them driven there by the repression that followed the crushing of the Basmachis in Central Asia. (Some Tajik refugees fleeing the regime in Dushanbe have recently joined relatives who had been living on the other side of the frontier for generations.)

There are numerous similarities between the clan and tribal social structures of the two countries. Division is an attribute common to both Tajik and Afghan society. At grass-roots level, it is characterised by fragmentation into small-scale networks of solidarity. These cover many different things, from the clan and the village community to the *ethnos* or the tribe, with each group constituting a real community, living as an integrated whole, at the head of which, in Afghanistan, there is usually a traditional chief, the khan. The khan has a power of influence which rests essentially on his openhandedness, his generosity, and hence necessarily on his fortune, which creates a system of client-patron relationships, a corollary of which is endemic corruption.

In Tajikistan, seventy years of Soviet rule have partially eroded the authority of the local chiefs and reinforced the role of the central power. In Afghanistan, however, the phenomenon of fragmentation has been reinforced by nearly fifteen years of conflict. The elimination of traditional leaders by the successive regimes of Hafizullah Amin and Babrak Karmal, the choice of resistance chiefs from outside the traditional power networks, the civil war which followed the Soviet withdrawal and saw the leaders of the parties which grew out of the resistance struggling for power in Kabul, have led to the complete collapse of state structures and the proliferation of centres of power. This phenomenon, combined with all the parties' dependence on external help, has allowed them to be manipulated by the big players in the region, who have used them as so many instruments of their ambitions in Central Asia.

Afghanistan's attitude to the Tajik conflict is thus the result of external ambition and manipulation, but is also just as much a product of the internal dynamics of the Afghan civil war. To a certain extent, the Tajik conflict in turn has altered the relationship between the powers in Afghanistan itself.

The first consequence of the Tajik conflict for Afghanistan was undoubtedly the influx of refugees. Thousands of Tajiks fled Dushanbe in December 1992 and at the beginning of 1993, fearing reprisals by the new conservative government against supporters of the pro-Islamic coalition. Although estimates of the numbers of refugees vary, at least 70,000 have moved to Afghan territory.[2] Having undergone an exodus for ten years, Afghanistan has become a country of asylum, with the authorities having in their turn to build refugee camps. In fact, despite appeals to return by the Tajik government, promising a general (though dubious) amnesty, some of the refugees have still not dared to return to Tajikistan.[3]

Five years after the end of the Soviet retreat, Afghanistan is still a conflict zone. And it is no longer just the victim of external aggression. Commando operations are regularly launched from its territory against Russian and government positions in Tajikistan. As a base for the rebels, Afghanistan is exposed to Russian and Tajik reprisals. A raid in July 1993 by Tajik rebels on the border between Tajikistan and Afghanistan killed 125 people, almost 100 of them civilians. Some time later, Kabul accused Moscow and Dushanbe of having killed nearly 360 Afghan villagers with artillery fire.[4]

Unlike its neighbours, Afghanistan is not really seeking regional expansion. Its involvement in the Tajik conflict is essentially an extension of its own civil war, and follows the development of the balance of power in Kabul. The main Afghan warlords, the Uzbek General Dostom, the Tajik Ahmad Shah Massoud and the Pashtun Hekmatyar, who is the current Prime Minister, have more or less 'shared out' the refugees among themselves. With Dostom seemingly neutralised,[5] the refugees are for the moment divided between the pro-Massoud and pro-Hekmatyar camps.

Although he has denied any interference in Tajik affairs and insisted that he offered asylum only to refugees who were not involved in political activities,[6] Hekmatyar supported the rebels by providing them with arms and training camps (especially near Qunduz), in the hope of breaking the coalition between Afghan Tajiks and Uzbeks. Apparently spurred on by Pakistan and Saudi Arabia, he then attempted to isolate Tajikistan from the other Central Asian countries by launching a campaign against the Russians in the hope of making them leave the country. From this point of view, the next stage is to provoke a conflict between the Tajiks and Uzbeks in order to tip the balance of power in Kabul itself in his favour, since his position there is still precarious, to say the least.[7] In so doing, Hekmatyar was also serving the interests of his Pakistani protectors, some of whom even hoped for a while that Russia itself would disintegrate. The Russians, however, were on their guard. In their eyes, Tajikistan was a bridgehead for the extension of Islam into Central Asia and from there into Russia. A diplomat declared in 1993: 'What the activists in northern Afghanistan want is not only the return to power of the Tajik opposition, but also to penetrate the other Central Asian countries, destabilise these regions, and replace these governments with Islamist governments, and that includes Russia itself.'[8] The proposals of the Afghan Prime Minister, who within the space of a few days demanded first the holding of elections in Tajikistan[9] and then the abolition of visa restrictions for nationals of the ECO member states,[10] seemed to be a step in this direction.

The position of Ahmad Shah Massoud is more ambivalent. Although his sympathy for the Islamist fighters is beyond doubt, his motives are not. While supporting the Tajik rebels, he seemed in fact to be seeking to improve his own position, so that he could negotiate more effectively with the Russians and the Tajik government, with whose support he hoped to overthrow Hekmatyar.

The difficulty of the situation is exacerbated by the weakness of affiliations within the opposing sides. They can only count on the fairly loose affiliations of local commanders, which further multiplies the allegiances of the Tajik rebels themselves. A negotiated solution is therefore extremely unlikely. The meeting in Dushanbe during the summer of 1993 between the Afghan Minister of Foreign Affairs, Hidayat Amin Arsala, and his Tajik counterpart, Ashid Alimov, produced no concrete results.[11] The risk of the conflict eventually spilling over into another Afghan war, invoked several times that summer by the Pakistani press, thus seemed a possible outcome of the general disintegration and chaos.

Three months later, the situation had evolved significantly, and the prospect of a 'regional' conflict seemed to have receded. Massoud's policy had borne fruit. Helped by the election of Benazir Bhutto (after which Hekmatyar seems to have stopped receiving funds from Pakistan), Massoud was able to 'buy back' one by one the allegiances of the local commanders. Isolated at the end of August, he seemed several months later to be in a position to reverse the balance of power to his own advantage. However, this was still scarcely possible unless he abandoned the Tajik cause. While some Jamiati commanders still seemed ready to fight in Tajikistan, Massoud was concentrating on recapturing power in Kabul.

However, this proved difficult. From the beginning of 1994, the 'lion of the Panshir' came up against Dostom's troops, whom he had imprudently jolted out of neutrality, and who were supported by Uzbekistan.[12] Massoud had to retreat, while a Tashkent-Islamabad axis developed, through Dostom and Hekmatyar.

By summer 1994, however, the situation had become more muddled than ever. Sayyaf's change of sides, under the protection of Saudi Arabia, following Hekmatyar's alliance with Iran, made the recapture of Kabul by Massoud more likely, but hardly gave cause to expect that a strong alliance could be formed with the military capacity to guarantee the stability of the country. The continuation of the civil war in Afghanistan poses a persistent potential threat to the stability of Central Asia as a whole, and most immediately, to that of its weakest link, Tajikistan.

Pakistan

Pakistan's Central Asian diplomatic policy – of which its policy towards Tajikistan is only one feature – partly originates in the trauma caused by the secession of East Pakistan in 1971, when it became the state of Bangladesh. Situated at the intersection between South, Central and West Asia, Pakistan was brutally rejected from the subcontinent and suddenly became much more vulnerable to its powerful Indian neighbour. From then on it could only wish to reinforce its Central Asian border and develop a heightened sense of belonging to that region. This desire, however, collided with the irredentism of Afghanistan, which was allied with India and becoming more and more pro-Soviet. While the Afghan threat by itself presented problems which Pakistan could cope with, politically and militarily, it took on another dimension altogether in the scenario of a conflict with India, when Pakistan would risk having to fight on two fronts. It was against this background that the Soviet invasion of Afghanistan occurred, in December 1979, confirming the worst fears of Pakistan's decision-makers, but at the same time giving them a unique opportunity to formulate and gradually develop their ambitions and policies with regard to Central Asia. At first Afghanistan was the only stake involved, but it became, paradoxically, both the key and the main obstacle to more grandiose ambitions.

From the creation of Pakistan in 1947 to the Soviet invasion of Afghanistan in December 1979, Pashtunistan was a constant source of tension between the two countries. Afghanistan's irredentist claims on

Pashtunistan led it to oppose Pakistan's entry into the United Nations in 1947; thereafter it caused numerous other problems which culminated in the severance of diplomatic relations and the closure of Pakistani ports to Afghan goods in 1961–62, which only strengthened the already close ties between Afghanistan and the USSR. More seriously still for Pakistan, the Afghan claim on Pashtunistan was at the root of the establishment of relations between Afghanistan and India. (The events of 1961–62 are, moreover, interpreted by some authors as a signal from Moscow to Islamabad, warning it not to take advantage of the conflict brewing between China and India to settle the Kashmir problem in its favour.) From 1975 onwards, however, the promise of economic aid from Iran led President Daoud to make overtures to Islamabad. Nevertheless, the Communist coup d'état in April 1978 returned Pakistani-Afghan relations to their former state. Faced with the extension of the civil war, the successive governments of Muhammad Nur Taraki and Hafizullah Amin had no alternative but to seek a semblance of legitimacy in the reaffirmation of Afghan nationalism, and thus renewed the traditional claims on Pashtunistan. The invasion of Afghanistan by the Red Army and the war which followed therefore gave Pakistan's leaders a chance to try and prevent the renaissance of expansionist Afghan nationalism and to secure definitive recognition of the Durand Line, which Pakistan has always considered its international border.

This aim was reflected in Pakistan's policies towards the refugees as much as towards the resistance itself. Although admitting nearly 3.5 million Afghan refugees helped to create a temporary feeling of gratitude which diminished the antagonism over Pashtunistan, the Pakistani authorities did their utmost to control all aspects of the Afghan presence in Pakistan, as well as the direction of the war. Pakistan's Inter Service Intelligence (ISI) chose seven organisations from among the hundred or so Mojaheddin groups in Pakistan and compelled all the others to join them by providing only these seven with arms. Having thus cleverly divided the allegiances of the Afghan population and removed the élite of the old regime, its intellectuals and diplomats, the Pakistani government set itself up as arbitrator between the groups and monopolised the diplomatic representation of the resistance.

The leaders of the seven chosen organisations (Gaylani, Mojadeddi, Muhammadi, Rabbani, Khales, Hekmatyar and Sayyaf) had all taken refuge in Pakistan after the abortive attempt at a fundamentalist coup d'état in 1975. With the well-known exception of Khales, none of these leaders had a territorial base, and thus they also lacked any real political weight in Afghanistan. In fact, the real weight of each of their organisations (measured by the number of men each of them could effectively control) stayed relatively limited throughout the war. The more radical Islamist movements, and especially Hekmatyar, were, moreover, systematically favoured. Indeed, once the Soviet retreat was announced, Pakistan's only objective in Afghanistan was to impose the absolute dominance of Hekmatyar's Hezb-e Islami.

It was during the war with the Soviet Union that the first operations on the territory of Central Asia itself were undertaken. From 1984, at the instigation of the ISI and the CIA, propaganda operations followed by commando attacks were carried out in Uzbekistan and Tajikistan. Their aim was to increase the pressure on the Soviet Union by carrying the war into its own territory and, if possible, provoking these two republics to rebel against Moscow. They were, however, halted in 1987 for fear of an escalation of the conflict and reprisals on Pakistani territory.[13]

It was only after the collapse of the Soviet empire at the end of 1991 that Central Asia really became the object of Pakistani ambitions. The Pakistanis had no more faith than their Saudi financiers in the durability of the neo-Soviet regimes. Their goal was at once ideological and economic. Some set their sights on detaching Central Asia from the CIS, which they hoped would lead to the disintegration of the Russian Federation itself, and the emergence of a new space dominated by conservative Islamic regimes. From this point of view, the return to power of the neo-Communists in Dushanbe was a reversal for Islamabad, hence its support, through Afghanistan, for the Tajik rebels.

On the economic level, Pakistan sought to make itself Central Asia's main route of access to the Indian Ocean. It therefore launched a huge road construction programme in summer 1993, which was to link Karachi and the ports of the Indian Ocean with Central Asia via Peshawar and Afghanistan.[14] The success of this goal was, however, dependent on the pacification of Afghanistan, which was rendered highly improbable by the policies pursued in previous years. If solving the Pashtunistan question implied putting a Pashtun – in the event, Hekmatyar – in power, with Pakistan being able, if the need arose, to tolerate the partition of Afghanistan, the establishment of a road corridor to Central Asia presupposed a stable, united Afghanistan. The difficulty for Islamabad, then, was to compel the Pashtun, Tajik and Uzbek leaders to come to an agreement; hence the Peshawar

Accord in March 1993. Since Massoud remained implacable, Islamabad's policy consisted in trying to isolate him, which it at first succeeded in doing by buying off Dostom. Thereafter, Massoud incessantly denounced Pakistan's meddling in Afghan internal affairs and its support for the fundamentalist movements of Hekmatyar, Khales and Sayyaf.[15]

In banking, if not exclusively then at least primarily, on Hekmatyar, the ISI hoped to be able to conciliate the demands of Pashtun nationalism and of Pan-Islamism, which allowed him both to transcend the ethnic divisions in Afghanistan and to reach out towards Central Asia. Although Hekmatyar is a convinced fundamentalist, his political base is essentially Pashtun, and he saw himself as forced to choose between Pashtun support – and power – and his ideological convictions. The country may not actually have exploded, but it is very divided and the basis of Pakistani influence in Afghanistan remains very fragile.

This Afghan policy is also a bone of contention within the ruling élite in Islamabad. While Benazir Bhutto found herself forbidden by the military to interfere in any way in Afghan affairs during her first term of office, her election victory in autumn 1993 allowed her to relegate the more hard-line elements of the ISI to the background, along with their allies in the Jamiat-e-Islami. This new situation could only enhance Pakistan's image in the eyes of the Central Asian leaders, but Islamabad on its own no longer seemed to be in a position to impose its will in Afghanistan: it had seen its ambitions drastically curtailed, and the prospect of linking Central Asia with the outside world simultaneously made more remote.

Furthermore, there are other burdens on Pakistan's Central Asian policy. Afghanistan is not its only obstacle: Pakistan also has to cope with the rivalry of its neighbours. On the question of Persian-speaking Tajikistan, Iran is a serious contender, and its investment capabilities are far superior to those of Pakistan. The competition between the two countries to provide Central Asia with access to the sea is intensified by an economic and religious contest. Finally, thanks to its privileged relationship with the former Soviet Union, India also has a foothold in Central Asia.

Iran

Iran's Central Asian policy, unlike Pakistan's, is not compelled to realise itself primarily through Tajikistan. From a geographical point of view, Tajikistan seems very remote from Iranian territory. But despite its physical distance, Iran is very sensitive to everything to do with Tajikistan, because of the cultural, historic and above all linguistic affinities between the two countries. This sensitivity is not only felt by the Iranian state, but also by the country's population and intellectual élite (including those exiled abroad). This emotional attachment, whose roots stretch back into the distant past, combines with ideological considerations on the part of the Islamic regime. Of all the Central Asian states, Tajikistan is the only one thus far where Islamist movements have played a relatively important role, with a real capacity to influence the overall political scene. That is why the recapture of Tajikistan by the neo-Communists, the return of Russian influence, the failure of the Islamists and even to some extent that of the 'democratic' nationalists, were not regarded with pleasure in Tehran. Thus, on 23 December 1992, Iran abandoned its habitual reserve about the internal situation of the Central Asian countries to denounce foreign intervention in Tajikistan. The Tehran press even openly accused Russia and Uzbekistan of supporting the Communists who had returned to power and of helping the Dushanbe government to carry out brutal repression.[16]

Although it had not played a leading role in the rise of the Tajik Islamist movements, Iran felt their failure as a setback. Nevertheless, this did not cause a withdrawal of Iranian diplomacy from Tajikistan, Afghanistan or, indeed, the rest of the Central Asian region. Iranian policy in this part of the world is in reality dictated by far more fundamental considerations, and cannot therefore be deeply affected by circumstantial events such as those in Tajikistan.

The guiding logic of Iran's Central Asian policy lies in a double preoccupation. On the one hand, there are the geopolitical considerations of a country which is itself in some ways a Central Asian state, while on the other is Iran's need to break out of the isolation it is suffering on the international scene through active involvement in regional affairs. Tehran's policy, developed from this perspective, is reflected in completely general diplomacy which does not allow of any exclusivity towards one country or another, and where necessary even authorises some infringements of ideological constraints. In other words, Iran will not and cannot sacrifice the totality of its policy towards its new neighbours by putting an inordinate emphasis on its relations with Tajikistan.

Aside from the limits imposed by its overall diplomatic choices with regard to Central Asia, Iran's policy on Tajikistan takes into account other imperatives. From a political point of view, Iran does not wish to jeopardise its relations with Russia in any way by taking too high a profile in Tajik affairs. Tehran, perfectly aware of the pressure Moscow could still put on its borders, wants to maintain privileged links with a country which is one of its most important suppliers of arms and military materials. The Iranians are further aware that in the light of the rise of Turkish ambitions in the region, there is a community of interests between them and the Russians. On the economic level, active support for the Tajik opposition could also have negative consequences for Iran, since its potential partners in Central Asia, apart from Turkmenistan, are Uzbekistan and Kazakhstan, two countries which have thrown in their lot with the Tajik neo-Communists.

Under these conditions, it is difficult to see how Iran's ambitions concerning Dushanbe, as expressed in June 1993 by the Islamic Republic's Foreign Minister[17] (to create an axis running from Iran in the west to China, through Afghanistan and Tajikistan), can possibly get off the ground in the near future. It is all the more difficult, since, on top of these problems, there is also the Afghan dimension of Iranian policy. This policy suffers from two major handicaps: its over-emphatic support for the Shiite parties, and rivalry with the Sunnis, of whom Pakistan and Saudi Arabia are the chief supporters. The Tehran authorities' decision to send back, since the summer of 1993, some 300,000 Afghan refugees living in Iran, has also reduced the sympathy the Islamic Republic enjoyed among certain Afghan factions.[18]

President Rafsanjani's visit, in October 1993, to all the Central Asian republics except Tajikistan, where the authorities were unwilling to receive the representative of a country they suspected of supporting the Islamist movements, demonstrated the limits of Iranian policy in the region. Nevertheless, the Iranian head of state used his tour to offer his services as mediator in the Tajik conflict, a suggestion which elicited only 'cold' approval from Dushanbe.

In the final analysis, despite the undeniable cultural and historic links between Iran and Tajikistan, and regardless of Tehran's diplomatic pragmatism, the Islamic regime's sympathy for Tajik Islamism has alienated any possibility of real action or even of influence in the crisis Tajikistan is undergoing. In seeking to present itself as a regional power which must be taken into consideration and playing several different tunes, Iran seems paradoxically to have reduced its already very limited room for manoeuvre with regard to a country which means a great deal to it.

Conclusions

1. Unlike Russia and some of its Central Asian allies, these three countries in the region are only spectators. Though they are certainly attentive to and concerned by the Tajik crisis, at this stage their official role, in the case of Iran and Pakistan at least, is essentially limited to offering mediation and support, in order to try and establish a dialogue between the Tajik government and opposition: their capacity to intervene in Tajik affairs remains extremely limited.

2. The main issue at stake in the Tajik conflict today is maintaining the country's unity and strengthening the state. If the country implodes, extending to Tajikistan the present chaos and fragmentation in Afghanistan, countries like Iran and Pakistan would find themselves faced with an enormous space without any real state power, riven by clan rivalry and open to all kinds of traffic. This situation could not fail to worry Islamabad and Tehran, who would see in it threats to their own security.

3. Relations with the Afghan, Pakistani and Iranian governments are not a matter of indifference to the powers-that-be in Dushanbe. In its search for international legitimacy, the Tajik government, whose popular support base is quite narrow, will inevitably have to angle for a rapprochement with its neighbours outside the CIS. This would imply negotiations and some concessions on both sides.

4. If the government in Dushanbe chooses a real policy of national reconciliation, it will have to consider negotiating with the armed opposition based in Afghanistan. From this point of view, Kabul and the local Afghan groups who have some authority in the border regions will no doubt have their views, and a contribution to make, both to the maintenance of security on the border and to the return of refugees.

5. The Tajik Islamist refugees in Afghanistan are backed by Afghan fighters and Islamists from neigbouring countries and even from the Arab world. Afghanistan, Pakistan and Iran could therefore also manipulate and infiltrate these groups, but given that overall these groups' capacity for action is limited, the role of the three states in the conflict remains marginal.

6. Iranian, Pakistani and, to a lesser extent, Afghan ambitions bear witness to the re-emergence of a historic space which has not existed for seventy years. This re-emergence is expressed in the revival of ethnic ties and the renewal of historic and cultural links.

The chaotic way in which it has happened is not without risks for the stability of the whole region. In this respect, it is symptomatic of the contradictions which are tearing Muslim societies apart today: secular modernism versus fundamentalism, tradition versus modernity, centralising statism versus tribal and clan segmentation. Trying to find an identity, between a Soviet past which it has not yet really thrown off and its Muslim history, Tajikistan's present is ravaged at once by the temptation to retreat into itself and by the risk that its internal conflicts will tear it apart still more violently. In seeking to remove it at any price from the Russian sphere of influence without offering it any serious alternatives, the Muslim countries of the region might push it back into that sphere more permanently than could seventy years of Communism.

Notes

1 On this 'opening' of the Central Asian space, see Djalili, Mohammad-Reza, 'Caucase et Asie Centrale: entrée en scène et recomposition géostratégique de l'espace', *Central Asian Survey*, 13 (1), 1994, pp. 7–17.

2 Brown, Bess, 'Tajikistan: The Conservatives Triumph', *RFE/RL Research Report*, Vol. 2, no. 7, 12 February 1993.

3 Dorronsoro, Gilles, 'Les réfugiés tadjiks en Afghanistan', *La lettre d'Asiecentrale*, no. 1, Spring 1994, p. 4.

4 Bashkatov, Nina, 'Eltsin faces a new Afghan war', *The News International*, Islamabad/Rawalpindi, 20 August 1993.

5 Dostom assured the Tajik and Uzbek authorities that the refugees in the zones controlled by his troops would not take part in border 'provocations', and made an agreement with the Uzbek President, Islam Karimov, to create a sort of buffer state between Kabul and the Afghan border with Uzbekistan and Tajikistan. See Griffin, Keith, 'Tadjikistan: Civil War Without End', *RFE/RL Research Report*, Vol. 2, no. 33, 20 August 1993. According to other unconfirmed reports, he was then receiving 17 million rupees a month from Pakistan's Inter Service Intelligence (ISI) to stay neutral in the conflict between Massoud and Hekmatyar, in order to allow the latter to reinforce his position in Kabul.

6 'Afghanistan vows not to give in to Russian pressure. Says it will continue to offer asylum to non-political Tajiks', *The News International*, Islamabad/Rawalpindi, 3 August 1993. This did not, however, prevent it, three days later, from offering political asylum to the leader of the Tajik Muslim Brothers, Himmatzāde, who had been expelled from Pakistan. As a mark of his gratitude, Himmatzāde hastened on the same day to deny any Afghan interference in Tajik affairs. See particularly 'Afghanistan ready to grant asylum to Himmatzade' and 'Himmatzade denies Afghan interference in Tajiks affairs', *The News International*, Islamabad/Rawalpindi, 6 August 1993.

7 Appointed Prime Minister on 7 March 1993 after the Peshawar Accord, imposed by Pakistan and Saudi Arabia, Hekmatyar had still not returned to Kabul by the beginning of the summer. See particularly Barry, Michael, 'La deuxième mort de l'Afghanistan', *Politique Internationale*, no. 60, Summer 1993, pp. 279–312.

8 *The News International*, Islamabad/Rawalpindi, 7 August 1993. Arif, Jamal, 'Hekmatyar's formula to resolve Tajik crisis', *The Muslim*, 18 August 1993.

9

10 'Hekmatyar calls for the abolition of visa restrictions among ECO countries', *The News International*, Islamabad/Rawalpindi, 25 August 1993.

11 'Afghan, Tajik talks make no headway', *The Muslim*, 13 August 1993.

12 The motivations behind Uzbekistan's support for Dostom were twofold: a) the creation of a corridor across the regions controlled by Dostom and Hekmatyar, allowing the transport of Uzbek raw materials (cotton and gas) to international markets via Pakistan and the Indian Ocean; b) the fear that the struggle between the Afghan factions would cause the situation in Tajikistan to degenerate still further, to the point where it threatened Uzbekistan's own stability.

13 Yousaf, Mohammad and Adkin, Mark, *The Bear Trap*, London, Leo Cooper, 1992.

14 Samina Yasmeen distinguishes two schools of thought in Pakistani foreign policy: the 'Muslim school' sees in the emergence of Central Asia a chance gradually to create an Islamic bloc, while the 'independence school' adopts a pragmatic approach, emphasising the economic opportunities that the new situation presents for Pakistan. 'Pakistan's Cautious Foreign Policy', *Survival*, Vol. 36, no. 2, Summer 1994, pp. 115–133.

15 *Le Monde*, 8 September 1993.

16 *Le Monde*, 25 December 1992.

17 Fourth Crans Montana Forum, 18–20 June 1993.

18 *Le Monde*, 29 October 1993.

Chapter 8

Is the Conflict in Tajikistan a Model for Conflicts Throughout Central Asia?

Olivier Roy

The civil war in Tajikistan, which lasted from May to December 1992, was Central Asia's most violent conflict since the war against the *Basmachi* ('Muslim rebels') in the 1920s. What is at stake in Tajikistan today is nothing less than its continuance as a unified nation-state. Even before the civil war, which profoundly traumatised the country, Tajikistan had been approaching independence with some serious handicaps:

– it was the ex-Soviet republic with the lowest per capita GDP; it was also the one with the highest demographic growth (3.3% per year in 1988).
– the carving of borders is even more nonsensical here than elsewhere: the three large river basins that make up the country (the Syr Darya, Zarafshan and Amu Darya) all lead into Uzbekistan, whereas the north and south of Tajikistan are linked by a single road, which is often blocked in winter. This geographical fragmentation is reflected in the country's history: the north was conquered by the Russians in 1864, while the south remained in the Emirate of Bukhara, which became a People's Republic in 1920, until 1924. These factors have led to the development of strong regional identities, at the expense of very weak national feeling. Regionalism is the key to Tajik politics.

To what extent does this conflict prefigure other conflicts in Central Asia? Conflicts could potentially arise in Central Asia from four different causes, which occur to varying degrees in Tajikistan:

1. An ideological conflict, i.e. the rise of political Islam against the regimes currently in power, which are the descendants of the old nomenklatura.

2. Ethnic conflicts between the majority peoples and other groups carelessly relegated to minority status, since the dominant ideology in the new republics (and the only source of political legitimacy) is ethnic nationalism, and the delineation of territories under Stalin ignored the overlapping of ethnic groups between them. This type of conflict could spill over into inter-state conflicts if certain states (primarily Russia) are moved to intervene in the name of protecting their ethnic minority.

3. An anarchic situation in which the new republics implode. This could arise from weak national feeling and struggles between regional factions, which would hinder the establishment of a stable central state.

4. The pursuit of neo-imperialist policies by Russia, anxious to defend what it considers as its strategic frontiers and protect the Russian-speaking minorities, who have now been removed from all political and most economic power.

We will examine the Tajik conflict from these four angles.

An Ideological Conflict?

On the surface, the civil war in Tajikistan pitted an 'Islamic-democratic' coalition, whose essential component was the Islamic Rebirth Party, similar in inspiration to contemporary Sunni Islamist movements (the Muslim Brothers of the Arab world and the Pakistani Jama'at-i Islami), against the old Communist Party. It is the only case in Central Asia where the old Communist Party was overthrown: the Islamic-democratic coalition held political power from May to November 1992.

It is primarily the players, or at least the Islamists, who give an ideological reading of the conflict. During the anti-government demonstrations at the beginning of 1992, the opposition which assembled on Martyrs' Square in Dushanbe conspicuously deployed the whole vocabulary of Islamic symbolism: the green flag, a return to the Arabic-Persian alphabet, quotations from the Quran, chants and slogans borrowed from the Islamic revolution in Iran (this mimesis was more cultural than ideological, since Persian is the common language). The writings of the IRP, the sermons that we were able to hear in the mosques, interviews with the various protagonists (particularly Mullah Khodaydad Abdulghaffar, the leader of the Islamist militias) could leave no doubt as to the ideological dimension

133

of the movement: it is an Islamist movement, even if a relatively moderate one in the sense that it has never advocated the immediate establishment of an Islamic republic, and that it allied itself with democratic or nationalist parties. In the weeks when the victorious Islamic opposition occupied the television, the programmes took on a distinctly more Islamic tone. Finally, once defeated, the opposition received protection in Afghanistan from local Islamist commanders and parties (such as Hekmatyar's Hizb-i Islami, branches of Islamic 'humanitarian' organisations such as the IIRO in Kunduz and, to a lesser extent, the Jamiat-i Islami). There can be no doubt that Iran discreetly supported the Islamists, while Moscow backed the conservative camp.

Conversely, the 'conservatives' who have come back into power explicitly emphasise their secularism and descent from the Soviet heritage. They advocate a close alliance with Moscow, say nothing about the Arabic-Persian alphabet, and maintain Soviet terminology and iconography (statues of Lenin, for example).

Yet a closer study of political affiliations, on the national as well as the local level, reveals that allegiance to a particular camp is determined, not by the militants' political development, but by their membership of ethnic or inter-ethnic solidarity groups. Almost all the militants on both sides are in fact members of the old nomenklatura: in the 'Islamic-democratic' camp, Qazi Turajonzoda was the head of the official clergy during the Soviet era, while Shadman Yussof [Yusupov], leader of the Democratic Party, had been in charge of the Communist Party at the Philosophy Faculty in Dushanbe; even one of the leaders of the Islamic opposition in the Kurgan-Tyube Valley, Abdullo Nuri, came from a family of apparatchiks. On the other hand, one finds outsiders in the conservative camp: the chief of the pro-Communist militias in Kulyab, Sangak Safarov, had served 23 years in prison under the Soviet system, which hardly qualifies him as an apparatchik.

The 'ideological' reading turns out to be still more limited because it is wrong to say that mullahs in general were on the side of the IRP while 'apparatchiks' supported the regime. Furthermore, in the civil war, kolkhoz presidents and mullahs from the same kolkhoz usually found themselves in the same camp: Islamic-democratic if they were 'Garmis', conservative if they were 'Kulyabis', like the Kulyab Mullah Sharifov, and the then Mufti of the Republic, Fathullah Khan Sharifzade, a Hissari from the Naqshbandi order. The local mullahs usually followed, rather than led, the groups they belonged to. In a word, mullahs and collective farm presidents could end up together, to the extent that they joined not an ideological camp but a local faction. The mosque only opposed the Executive Committee of a kolkhoz when the kolkhoz was divided ethnically, or into local factions, and one took a secular approach while the other adopted an Islamic orientation. Numerous utterly secular, indeed atheist, democratic intellectuals joined the ranks of the Islamic-democratic opposition. In the same way, even though the stance of the conservatives now in power is clearly more secular, it would be wrong to say that they repress Islam: there is complete freedom of worship and the regime does not hesitate to use certain Islamic symbols (Muslim holy days are public holidays). It is therefore clear that ideological allegiances are completely inadequate to explain the opposing camps.

Closer study of political affiliations reveals that they are all based on ethnic or local origins.

An Ethnic Conflict?

At first glance, the ethnic explanation makes sense. It is clear that behind the Islamism of the IRP lies a strong 'Persian' nationalism: a return to classical Persian literature and to the Arabic-Persian alphabet, the expurgation of Russian words from the language and the assertion that 'Tajiki' is actually 'Farsi' (whereas the 'conservatives' uphold the distinction and speak a strongly dialectal Tajik, favouring Russian for more abstract discussions). Conversely, as a general rule the Uzbeks in Tajikistan have joined the conservative camp wherever they live: the Hissaris (west of Dushanbe) played a decisive part in the recapture of the capital and the Uzbeks from Kurgan-Tyube Province all fought against the Islamists. Along the same lines, the behaviour of the Uzbek population in Leninabad Province was indistinguishable from that of the Tajiks of the province, who were massively pro-conservative. On the other hand, the 'Pamiris', who belong to a separate linguistic group, live in the Autonomous Province of Gorny Badakhshan and mostly belong to the Ismaili sect, joined the Islamic-democratic coalition, even though they were undeniably the most secular, de-Islamised group in the whole republic. The Tajik nationalist intellectuals, who are now in exile, and especially the members of the Rastakhiz party, therefore have a tendency to present the conflict as an Uzbek plot to crush Tajik nationalism.

Yet it is wholly incorrect to say that the 'conservatives' are mainly Uzbeks or Uzbekised Tajiks. The Kulyab region, which is the bastion of conservatism, could not be more 'Tajik'. The proportion of Uzbeks in the present government is probably no more than their real number in the country, taking into account the fact that it is often difficult to make a clear distinction between Uzbeks and Tajiks because of intermarriage and widespread bilingualism. The very fact that there are many mixed marriages proves how far from categoric is the opposition between Uzbeks and Tajiks. There is a distinct tension between the 'Kulyabi' government and the Uzbek government in Tashkent.

We must therefore look for an explanation of political affiliations at a sub-ethnic level.

Localism

The key to the Tajik conflict is localism, that is to say, factions defined above all by geographical origin, reshaped and restructured as it was by the population displacements of the Soviet period. Almost all the officials of the IRP are 'Garmis' (natives of the Garm Valley, or Karategin), and almost all the current leaders of the country are 'Kulyabis' (natives of Kulyab Province) or come from Leninabad Province. Garmis and Kulyabis alike are Tajiks. The solidarities thus created have always transcended political divisions: the relative neutrality of the Russian 201st Division, based in Dushanbe, when the opposition seized power in May 1992, is explained more by the fact that its head, General Ashurov, was a Garmi (despite his 'Soviet' identity) than by instructions from Moscow. The other Russian garrisons immediately supported the ex-Communists. With one exception, the mullahs of Leninabad and Kulyab violently condemned the IRP; it was a Kulyabi mullah, Sharifov, who challenged the power of the Qazi. Moreover, from the first demonstrations, identity obtained over ideological denomination in both camps: in the sermons of the mullahs, '*Kulabi*' was equivalent to '*Kāfir*' ('infidel'). Arrests of opponents were carried out according to criteria of geographic origin; when the opposition was in power it imposed an economic blockade on Kulyab Province, while since the recapture of Dushanbe, the Kulyabis have been carrying out systematic executions of Garmis and Ismailis.

The two main solidarity groups involved in the current conflict are primarily defined by geographic origin: the Kulyab Valley and the Garm Valley. But how have such allegiances managed to acquire the political force which characterises them today? These phenomena of regional identity occur throughout Central Asian society (and many other cultural regions) without becoming the key to political conflicts. For us, these allegiances play a key role inasmuch as they are a product of the social restructuring brought about by the Soviet regime (through collectivisation and the role of the kolkhozes in the formation of community identity), rather than remnants of old clan affiliations.

There are doubtless traces of ancient segmentations to be found, often very complex, since the identity groups never define themselves along symmetrical criteria, in relation to each other. There may be names of tribes, drawn from a historical repertoire of prestigious tribe names, without necessarily any well-attested connection (Barlas, the tribe of Tamerlane, Moghol, the 'tribe' of Babur, where it is clear that this is a reconstruction after the event, since the word did not designate a tribe before Babur); ethnonyms without ethnic groups (such as the 'Turks' of Kulyab and the 'Arabs' of Kabadyan, who are Persian-speakers); solidarity groups which have chosen prestigious names with a religious resonance (the 'Ghazi Malek' Persian-speakers of Kurgan-Tyube Province), or even sometimes that relate to old social divisions reinterpreted in religious terms, unless it is the other way round (the 'Khwaje' of Ferghana as opposed to the 'Fuqarā') etc. Those who have studied these identities have tried to impose substantialist classifications on them, that is, those based on the search for a historical ethnogenesis, a quest on which the anthropological substantialism of the nineteenth century was joined by the historical 'materialism' of Soviet specialists.[1] The relationship between old segmentations and new identities remains a field open to research (with all the questions hanging: is there really an ethnogenesis, a history of the groups, or is there rather a permanent reordering, a nominalism of identities, which are redefined after the event, as dictated by social, economic and political constraints?). We will not go into this subject here, since in the course of our inquiry we have noted that the living memory of ancient identities rarely illuminates the present conflicts (even if it does play a role in matrimonial relations: people are loath to give their daughters to a group deemed 'inferior' in historical prestige).

By contrast, what does immediately explain the conflicts is the reordering of identities induced by the Soviet system, through population displacements and the reformation of groups around the kolkhozes. A kolkhoz is either the expression of a solidarity group, old or new; or the object of a power struggle between rival groups, who are thus inclined to identify themselves with ethnic or political oppositions conceptualised somewhere else.

Our hypothesis is that ethnic violence in Central Asia is less the clash of traditional 'ethnic' groups than of groups formed by restructuring within the framework of the Soviet system. This system, through collectivisation and the kolkhozes, 'territorialised' solidarities and made them depend on a single source and collective framework for the distribution of goods and access to wealth. In the Soviet system, social existence and economic survival were dependent on belonging to a 'collective' (kolkhoz, factory, trade union), which was plugged into the state apparatus. These 'collectives' transformed themselves, especially in the countryside, into 'clans'. The Soviet state, far from turning society into a collection of individuals, was, on the contrary, a powerful factor forming society into networks. But these networks only took a Soviet form (the Party, the kolkhoz, social organisations, professional organisations); ultimately, they were the vehicle for a very Central Asian re-traditionalising of the Soviet system, since they borrowed many methods of consolidating and perpetuating themselves from traditional society (nepotism, patronage, clan loyalty, even endogamy). In the countryside, the scope of these groups is the district and the kolkhoz, that is, a territory; the prize is the land. Whereas traditional groups before collectivisation had divided up the space, often after conquests and conflicts, into 'ecological niches' (Tajiks in the bazaars and foothills, artisan Jews, Uzbeks in the irrigated plains, mountain-dwelling Ismailis and Kyrgyz, and semi-nomadic groups who constituted a link in the marginal spaces, such as 'Arabs' etc.), collectivisation brought about a territorialisation of solidarity groups in the framework of the kolkhozes, and thus the end of complementarity. The homogenisation of society, far from ending differentiations between groups, made them competitors for possession of the land.

This territorialisation came in two waves: the 1930s, when lands abandoned by the Basmachis were repopulated (a phenomenon which particularly affected southern Tajikistan) and collectivisation took place; and the 1950s, when marshy and desert lands were reclaimed (which had also started in the 1930s). These development policies could only be implemented by moving people from mountainous areas, where the birth rate was high but the opportunities for development weak, that is, essentially from Tajik and Ismaili regions. These movements of population did not spring from political objectives (to punish one group or another), but from a bureaucratic vision of rural development. The groups thus displaced, by force or economic incentive, far from melting into new Soviet identities, 'solidified' themselves according to their region of origin. The mixing of populations caused the disappearance of the micro-solidarities of villages, extended families, even of pseudo-ethnic affiliations (such as the 'Turks' of Kulyab) in favour of a wider identity, based on the valley. The 'Kulyabi' identity seems thus to have been forged above all in the 1930s, when people were 'brought down' from the foothills to develop the dried-up marshes.

The province of Kurgan-Tyube was 'colonised' later, during the 1950s, by people from Garm and Kulyab. This valley was not uninhabited, but the groups that populated it (Uzbeks from the Lakay tribe in the district of Vakhsh, other Uzbcks on the Afghan border, 'Ghazi Malek' and 'Arabs' between Sharituz and Kurgan-Tyube) were sedentarised on the foothills they occupied, in relatively homogeneous kolkhozes. By contrast, the two new groups (Kulyabis and Garmis, to whom were added Ismailis from the Pamirs) were settled in the same kolkhozes. This mixture, however, far from blurring the differences, and despite the fact that both the groups spoke Persian, fixed their new, mirror-image identities. In terms of habitat, each group formed its own *mahalla* ('neighbourhoods'); there are very few intermarriages (apparently fewer than with the Uzbeks). 'Garmi' and 'Kulyabi' identities formed, above and beyond the age-old segmentations of clan, village and caste, and congealed into a mutually antagonistic relationship.

For reasons which have yet to be elucidated, the Garmis rapidly acquired a dominant position locally: their wealth is apparent from their houses (often multi-storeyed). By contrast, on the national political level, it was the Kulyabis who made a breakthrough in the 1970s by forming an alliance with the northern province of Leninabad, which provided all the First Secretaries of the Communist Party from 1937 to 1992. Well off, but excluded from Communist power, the Garmis rallied *en masse* in the 1980s around a network of fundamentalist mullahs, while the Kulyabis, although they called themselves Muslims, remained loyal to the Soviet system. This does not mean that the mullahs had supplanted the Garmi apparatchiks, nor that the Kulyabi population was more 'secular' than the Garmis. Indeed, the prominent people in each group (whether mullahs or kolkhoz directors) showed solidarity in expressing the interests of their group, even if the sources of their legitimacy differed. The Garmi apparatchiks therefore joined the

Islamist camp; thus, too, the Director of the Nowruz Sovkhoz, Shadi Kabirovich, joined the Islamists in spring 1992 and later fled to Afghanistan; the new Director was, needless to say, a Kulyabi, born in the only Kulyabi *mahalla* of the sovkhoz, where the other officers of the sovkhoz also came from. Conversely, the mullahs of Kulyab, with a few exceptions, and of Hissar (the other 'Soviet' bastion) supported the conservative camp, even though they tried to develop an Islamic rationale for this, often based on the idea of a national and traditional Islam heavily imbued with Naqshbandi Sufism, as opposed to the 'innovative' Islam imported by the 'Wahhabis' (a generic and pejorative term used for Islamists, whether or not of Saudi allegiance). It is a curious case, when Sufism is brought to the rescue of the Soviet order.

But why did the crisis erupt so late, when all its elements had been in place since the 1950s? Obviously the anaesthetising effect of the Soviet system should be borne in mind, with its techniques for social control and maintenance of order. Independence put an end to this system and opened a Pandora's box. Many protagonists will say in interviews that they believe 'localist' tensions were alive but contained during the Soviet era, while a minority denies the existence of the problems; but the way the word 'localism' (*mahalgera'y*) suddenly became very widely used in the Tajik press implies that what it referred to was very familiar). However, there is one other important dimension which explains the brutal explosion of violence: the pauperisation which resulted from the disappearance of the welfare state.

The fall of the Soviet empire immediately introduced a state of scarcity, because southern Central Asia, for strategic reasons, lived on a constant economic transfusion. As the gateway to British India before the war, then a window onto Afghanistan and the Muslim world, then in the rear of the fighting during the war in Afghanistan, Central Asia had enjoyed, not a better standard of living than Moscow, but at least a guarantee against all want, thanks to the intervention of the centre (especially in the form of petrol and fuel, but also roubles). Then, in one fell swoop, there was no more petrol and no more subventions. This impoverishment occurred against a general background of lack of social and geographical mobility. Conflicts between local groups over land and power in the kolkhoz were suddenly exacerbated. They were open to any possible ideological reading: Islam versus Communism in Tajikistan, but in the city of Osh ethnic conflict between Uzbeks and Kyrgyz.

A Unique Conflict or the Shape of Conflicts to Come?

The factors which provoked the civil war in Tajikistan – Islamism, ethnicity and localism – exist everywhere in Central Asia to varying degrees, but in Tajikistan they have been aggravated by the weakness of the state apparatus and the national identity. Elsewhere, they could set off local troubles, but do not risk leading to general conflicts. The only area of comparable fragility is Kyrgyzstan.

1 Islamic Fundamentalism

Political Islamism is in crisis throughout Central Asia. The Tajik IRP was largely discredited by proving incapable of ensuring the defence of the population after the conservative victory, and by identifying itself with the Garmis. Its officials are now in Afghanistan. Afghanistan holds no fascination for the Tajik people, and cannot serve as a bridgehead for the reconquest of Tajikistan. The training camps in Afghanistan, whose importance has been exaggerated, at most provide gathering points and maintain insecurity on the border.

Apart from this military impotence, the Islamists are divided on strategy. The Islamic Rebirth Party, which once covered the whole USSR, is today divided into national branches, frequently at logger-heads: the Russian IRP violently condemned the adventurism of its Tajik counterpart, berating its alliance with democrats and nationalists, but also, at a deeper level, its very establishment as a 'national' party.[2] What is striking is the inability of the Islamists, just as in Afghanistan, to rise above national, ethnic and localist rifts. We have seen it in Tajikistan, but the phenomenon also exists in Ferghana, that other bastion of Islamism. The Islamist *'lashkar'* of Namangan, armed militias who managed to establish a real alternative power structure in some districts of the city in 1991–92, are the expression, not of an alternative politics, but of the identity of the neighbourhood, along the lines of the *futuwwat* traditional in the Muslim world ('strong-arm' groups organised around a sports hall, a mosque and a 'patron saint' to provide 'protection' and representation for a neighbourhood or *mahalla*).

Secondly, the 'fundamentalist' label masks a more complex reality. One can roughly distinguish four categories of mullahs in Central Asia: the 'traditionalists', the Muslim Brothers (the IRP), the 'Wahhabis' and the 'Tablighis'. The first and largest group has the legitimacy of having kept Islam going during the Soviet era; sons and grandsons of mullahs, they were trained on their elders' books, heavily imbued with Sufism, philosophy and Persian literature (this was essentially the 'manual' known as *Chahar Kitab*, which can be found in almost every mosque). The 'Wahhabis', on the other hand (this term was once used to designate all fundamentalists, but today denotes those mullahs who are influenced by the Saudis, especially through the intermediary of émigrés from Ferghana who had settled in Saudi Arabia and have since returned), like the Tablighis (recently trained in India and Pakistan under the auspices of the preaching movement Jama'at ul Tabligh), violently condemn this literature as un-Islamic. The Muslim Brothers favour political action, which the other three categories reject.

These hostilities also fuel more prosaic rivalries about who should run the official mosque (*Masjid-i jama'*) of the district or town. The mullahs, whatever their personal convictions, are thus far from being an autonomous political power. This is demonstrated by the failure of the old official mullahs (the Mufti of Tashkent, the Qazi of Dushanbe) to 'clericalise' the unofficial mullahs to their own advantage, and weld them into an alternative political force. In Tajikistan as in Ferghana, the mullahs' disenchantment with politics is palpable.

The governments thus have some room to manoeuvre. They are using the framework of the official clergy to 'nationalise' Islam (all the muftis today are 'republican') and to box the big mosques into an administrative hierarchy (mufti of the republic, mufti of the province, mufti of the district, *imamkhateb* of the towns). Now they are attempting to get their candidates appointed as muftis. In Tajikistan, the High Qazi is in exile and has been replaced by a Naqshbandi Mufti. In Uzbekistan, the regime first reinstated the State Committee for Religious Affairs, whose aim was to exercise tight control over the Grand Mufti, and then nominated a new Mufti, also a Naqshbandi. Although officially the state does not finance mosques, the same cannot be said at the local level: in Ferghana, the kolkhozes and *Hakim* ('governors') finance the mosques.

Furthermore, the regimes are not averse to using some Muslim symbolism, such as the crescent and green stripe on the Uzbek flag. In the provinces, the authorities regularly attend the mosque. Foreign missionaries have been expelled, and overseas visits by mullahs are controlled. But pilgrims can travel freely to Saudi Arabia, while Saudis of Central Asian origin are allowed to return to their countries.

Finally, the Uzbek government has made attempts to revive Sufism, probably in order to combat the Muslim Brothers and Wahhabis more effectively. The 650th anniversary of the death of Bahauddin

Naqshband, who founded in Bukhara the Naqshbandi order, which is the most widespread in Uzbekistan, was ceremonially celebrated in October 1993 (thanks also to a personal gift from the late President Özal). Likewise, Ahmed Yassawi, the founder of the Yassawia, the most 'Turkic' of the Central Asian orders, is being brought back into fashion (which allows for 'Uzbek Islam' to be promoted, as against 'Arab' or 'Iranian' Islam). This operation is made all the easier since Sufism as a structure is today urbanised, thinly scattered and decentralised, and has no political weight, while the spirit of Sufism strongly permeates the traditional training of Central Asian mullahs.

2 Localism

This exists everywhere in different forms. Tribalism and clan identity are still strong in Turkmenistan and Kyrgyzstan; geographic localism in Uzbekistan. Knowing about origins and networks is essential to understanding the internal policy of all these states. Localism is equally important for understanding local crises (Ferghana, Osh etc.), but at the same time it acts as its own limit, because where there is national awareness and a state apparatus a local incident will not readily escalate into a national dynamic. In fact the state machinery manages localism by sharing out important posts or by according a degree of autonomy to the local level. Only in Kyrgyzstan are there warning signs of a stark division of the state apparatus according to the rival regions.

3 Ethnicity

Ethnicity has been deployed by the established states to give themselves legitimacy and generate national feeling. The states are founded on ethnic nationalism. The problem is therefore that the other ethnic groups living in the country suddenly find themselves cast as minorities, whereas in the Soviet era everyone was a Soviet citizen. However, the recent crises have led to a growing ethnic homogeneity, which strengthens the countries' stability. There are only two real cases of strong ethnic minorities: the Europeans on the one hand, and the Uzbeks and Tajiks on the other, since Uzbekistan has a large Tajik minority and vice versa. The Kazakh question comes down to the opposition between Russians and Kazakhs.

These two cases apart, the areas of ethnic tension nowadays are the border regions, especially the border between Uzbekistan and

143

Kyrgyzstan in the district of Osh. But, precisely for this reason, they are manageable as long as there is a consensus between the ruling regimes, as is the case at present.

Relations between Tajiks and Uzbeks are more complex. The two populations are very interwoven; the Tajiks make up both the old urban population (in Samarkand and Bukhara) and (in competition with the Kyrgyz) that of the foothills and mountains, while the Uzbeks live on the plains, including those of south and north Tajikistan. The Tajik-Uzbek tension is not on the same level as the others in cultural terms: nothing but language separates them; there are many mixed kolkhozes and no conflict between the two groups for control of land has been reported. In fact all the Tajiks in Uzbekistan and many of those in Tajikistan are bilingual in Tajik and Uzbek, and inter-marriages are frequent.

The strong Tajik minority in Uzbekistan are certainly frustrated by the marginalisation of their language in favour of Uzbek (which they consider unliterary), but one could not say that they are repressed: there is no ethnic discrimination, in the sense that a Tajik can gain a management position if he speaks Uzbek (and all are bilingual). The Tajiks of Uzbekistan can study in Dushanbe or in the Tajik universities of Samarkand, they have their own national newspaper (*Awaz-i Tajik*, published in Tashkent), and Tajik schools in areas where they form the majority.

The civil war in Tajikistan paradoxically contributed to reining in the emerging ethnic antagonism between Tajiks and Uzbeks. In Tajikistan, the ideological rifts and 'localist' hatreds which set Tajiks against each other prevented the emergence of a Tajik nationalism, defining itself primarily against the Uzbeks. On the contrary, the mass of Tajik apparatchiks (including those in Uzbekistan, who are even more 'Soviet' than their Uzbek colleagues), were the first to seek help from their Uzbek 'big brother'. Dushanbe has therefore not become a pole of identity or nationalist mobilisation against Tashkent.

Similarly, in order to play its role of 'big brother' to Tajikistan to the full, Tashkent has an interest in handling its own Tajiks carefully, especially as it is no longer afraid of hostile propaganda from Dushanbe. Tajiks opposed to the Uzbek protectorate therefore cannot have recourse to Tajik nationalism, which because of the civil war is in crisis, but must look to Islam. This ideological polarisation contributes to masking the ethnic antagonism.

In any case, whatever the reading, ethnic or ideological, of violent confrontations, the key to these micro-conflicts is the struggle for land in the context of harsh impoverishment. That is why it is impossible to talk of generalised ethnic conflicts. In fact the groups which have established themselves in economic niches where they do not compete with others are not the object of any vendetta. The Russians and Europeans are generally workers or technicians, never peasants. There are two exceptions: the Koreans and the Germans, who have kolkhozes. The latter have left; the former have installed themselves in very specialised economic roles (for instance, the Koreans of Tashkent rent out land to Tajik kolkhozes for intensive onion farming).

The ethnic juxtapositions which have evolved over the course of history through adaptation to environmental or economic niches have also been bypassed by the conflict: in this category are the ancient cohabitation of Tajiks and Uzbeks, that of Jews and Muslims, even that of Gypsies (the Jogis) and Muslims, although in the last two cases there is no intermarriage. Recent juxtapositions, implying absolute otherness (Russians, Germans, Koreans) do not entail conflict either. This does not mean that Russians and Jews feel perfectly at ease, but it is the change in the environment and the poverty which make them leave, rather than ethnic pressure.

As is so often the case, the question of ethnicity hides complex social realignments which neither the protagonists nor the states can control, and which give rise to various ideological readings which, when they do not definitively cloud the issue, end up producing real effects.

Finally, the ethnic question arises in cases which do not involve conflict between Central Asian ethnic groups, inasmuch as Russia could use the question of the Russian minorities for its own ends.

4 National Identity and the State Apparatus

In Uzbekistan and Turkmenistan, one can see stable state apparatuses emerging, with a strong national identity; but these things are not happening in Tajikistan and Kyrgyzstan. Why is there a weak state and weak identity in Tajikistan?

There is a Tajik identity crisis. What, indeed, is a Tajik? Tajiks waver between several identities. Perhaps they are the entire Sunni, Persian-speaking community of the former USSR; but in that case, half the territory of the Republic and 30% of its population are not Tajik, and the historic cultural centres of Samarkand and Bukhara are outside the Republic. If they are the whole Sunni, Persian-speaking community of Central Asia then a large number of Afghans are Tajiks; finally, if they are all 'Persians', then Tajiks are Iranians. The losers in the Stalinist carve-up of Central Asia in the 1920s, ruralised, dialectised, cut off from their literary and historical roots, Tajiks have withdrawn into localist solidarities.

Why a weak state? Because at the end of the Soviet period, Moscow, probably wittingly, had divided the apparatus of the state between different groups. If the people of Khojent (Leninabad) were in charge of the Party, the security organs were largely in the hands of the Ismailis, who were considered more trustworthy in the Afghan conflict, since the Afghan Ismailis were in favour of the Communist regime. Whereas in Turkmenistan and Uzbekistan, despite the existence of tribalism and localism, the apparatchiks managed to maintain sufficient consensus to control and preserve the state apparatus, in Tajikistan ethnic and localist affiliations immediately predominated.

Of the other Central Asian states, Kyrgyzstan probably has the most tribal and clan divisions, but it lacks the ideological element which could allow factionalism to become radicalised. The peculiar situation of Tajikistan is the stark ideologisation of a localist conflict in a state with a weak identity. This combination of factors is not found anywhere else.

Economic Interests

As we have emphasised, one of the key factors in post-civil war Tajikistan is sudden impoverishment and the scarcity of goods for the state to distribute, caused by the end of subsidies from Russia. This has given rise to a bitter struggle to appropriate what remains. The situation is exacerbated by Tajikistan's galloping birth rate and the low proportion of land which is cultivable. The beginnings of a form of privatisation of agricultural production (sharecropping contracts) have heightened the feeling among the population that there is a shortage of land. The peasants are therefore less concerned about taking over land individually than about seeing that 'their' kolkhoz does better than the neighbouring one (especially when it is inhabited by a different clan or ethnic group).

The kolkhozes are also surviving on credit, borrowing money from the state: there is a danger that the monetary crisis of the rouble (with the withdrawal of old notes) could make it impossible for the state to give credit, which would paralyse the whole system. The shortage of fuel has also brought about a fall in agricultural production. These blockages aggravate the struggle for land between kolkhozes: each kolkhoz expresses the interests of a local population group (clans, ethnic groups, factions) and takes sides at the national level according to local conflicts and systems of alliances. The kolkhozes are the new tribes, and as such play the leading part in political and armed mobilisation, through the creation of kolkhoz militias. However, unlike under the Soviet regime, this mobilisation is not masterminded by the state.

Thus, the threat today comes from an economic crisis which might once again mobilise the kolkhozes and local clans against each other, and possibly for or against one or another minister or government faction. Throughout Central Asia, the essential factor in conflicts today is the economic and social crisis, which could delegitimise the existing regimes.

Notes

1 For example, on the Kulyabis, read B. Kh. Karmysheva, 'On the history of population formation in the southern areas of Uzbekistān and Tadjikistān', *VII International Congress of Anthropological and Ethnological Sciences*, Nauka, Moscow, 1964.

2 *Al Wahdat* newspaper, December 1992, published in Moscow.

PEACE-MAKING AND
PEACE-KEEPING

Chapter 9

The Russian Army and the War in Tajikistan

Michael Orr

'Intervention' is too strong a word to describe the process by which the Russian army found itself involved in the war in Tajikistan. The former Soviet Army garrison force has gradually changed its role from bystander via kingmaker to main combatant largely in response to the developments within Tajikistan and without any clear plan on the part of Russia's political leadership. Just as it is difficult to define the start of Russia's involvement in the Tajik war, it is almost impossible to forecast how this involvement might be brought to an end.

When Tajikistan declared its independence from the crumbling USSR in September 1991 the Soviet armed forces in the country were composed of three elements: 201st Motor Rifle Division (MRD), a regiment of the Air Defence Forces (PVO) and KGB Border Guards along the Afghan and Chinese borders. In addition the traditional military commissariat system existed throughout the country, to mobilise conscripts and reserves. The 201st MRD formed part of the 40th Army in Afghanistan during the Soviet intervention; it was deployed in the Kunduz area, just south of the Tajik border. With the Soviet withdrawal from Afghanistan in February 1989 the division returned to its pre-war garrison area in the Tajik Republic. After the collapse of the Soviet Union some of the constituent republics took the armed forces stationed on their territory under their own jurisdiction; this was the case in most of the Central Asian republics. Tajikistan was one of those who were unable to do this, leaving the armed forces there in limbo, from which they passed under CIS and eventually Russian control. Thus the Russian General Staff in Moscow never had to make a strategic assessment of the positive reasons for stationing troops in Tajikistan. The strategic justifications for their presence there were basically negative. Russia was happy to retain responsibility for guarding Tajik (and other former Soviet) borders rather than pay for a new system of frontier protection along its own national boundaries. If Russian border troops were to be left on the border with so unstable a state as Afghanistan they might require support from heavily-equipped combined-arms units. In any case, Russia was already swamped by the burden of relocating forces from Eastern Europe and did not want to increase the number of homeless military families. 201st MRD, therefore, remained in Tajikistan, recruiting its conscript soldiers largely from Tajikistan, but with an overwhelmingly Russian professional cadre of officers and warrant officers. The newly independent Republic of Tajikistan had no armed forces of its own, other than a Presidential Guard of about 1,000 men and some weak Interior Ministry forces.

Without a national army the Tajik government had no means of controlling the growing political instability within the country. When Dushanbe was blocked by rival demonstrations in April 1992, President Nabiev tried to compensate for his lack of an army by supplying weapons to his supporters among the demonstrators. This, however, led to the commander of the Presidential Guard, Major-General Rakhmonov, declaring his support for the anti-Nabiev group. Serious bloodshed was averted by the appearance of armoured vehicles from 201st MRD to separate the two factions. The divisional commander, Colonel Vyacheslav Zabolotnyy, then brought Nabiev and other government and opposition leaders together in his office in a barracks in Dushanbe on 10 May. He is reported to have said, 'There's enough blood-letting. Authorised as garrison commander, I will arrest all of you and no one will leave this office until you finally resolve all the disputes between you'.[1] It is remarkable that all parties accepted his authority and did work out an agreement by which a coalition government was formed. Zabolotnyy, a Belorussian by birth, seems to have acted on his own initiative, without instructions from his superiors in CIS headquarters or elsewhere in Moscow, but backed by a resolution of the 201st MRD's officers' assembly.

The truce arranged in Dushanbe did not last long outside the capital. In June fighting broke out in the southern provinces of Kulyab and Kurgan-Tyube in which current political disputes cloaked the settling of long-standing ethnic grievances. Tajikistan still had no armed forces to check the outbreak of civil war. Although 201st MRD had regiments in Kurgan-Tyube and Kulyab they took no official action other than protecting refugees (mostly Russian) and guarding key sites and communications at the Tajik government's request. The summer of 1992 was the time when a peace-keeping force was most urgently required in Tajikistan and could have prevented the loss of thousands of lives and the displacement of hundreds of thousands of refugees. The 201st MRD declared its neutrality and an attempt to create a peace-keeping force under the CIS aegis was still-born when Marshal Shaposhnikov, Commander-in-Chief of the CIS Armed Forces, cut short a visit to Tajikistan at the end of August. There were accusations that 201st MRD supported the Kulyabis and supplied them with arms. This was strongly denied by the divisional command, although it is possible that some Tajik nationals within its ranks did try to help fellow-members of Kulyabi clans. This was clearly without official sanction and when some armoured vehicles were stolen from the barracks in Kulyab and moved towards Kurgan-Tyube, they were destroyed by helicopters on the divisional commander's orders. No doubt there was a great deal of political confusion in Moscow as to whether their forces in Tajikistan should intervene, but it is likely that there were also practical reasons for the division's inaction. In June, when fighting started in the southern provinces, most of the Tajik conscripts deserted and returned home. The Kurgan-Tyube regiment was reduced to a strength of about fifty men, in effect its Russian officers. In these circumstances units of 201st MRD could do little more than try to defend their own barracks, in which they were effectively besieged. Colonel Merkulov, commander of the Kurgan-Tyube regiment, was told by a mob trying to break into his barracks, 'You are no more than fifty and there are thousands of us'. 'We're professionals,' he replied. 'Start something and you'll only find my men under mountains of your own dead. Any one of my subordinates is worth a hundred of your fighters.'[2]

While 201st MRD was just managing to protect its own barracks and the Russian refugees who fled to them, it could not stop the war itself. Much of Kurgan-Tyube Province was destroyed in bitter inter-clan fighting. Neither side had the military expertise or the equipment to win a clear victory. Instead, using small arms and armoured vehicles improvised out of tractors and lorries they ground their way through collective farms, villages and towns. Civilians fled from their ruined homes across the border to Afghanistan; many men, having seen their families into refugee camps, acquired arms and began infiltrating back into Tajikistan. The Russian Border Guards were too weak to stop them.

In early October 1,200 troops were sent from the Siberian and Volga-Urals Military Districts to reinforce 201st MRD and in the same month some of its troops helped to defend Dushanbe against a force of irregulars from Hissar, calling themselves the 'Popular Front of Tajikistan'. Meanwhile, the idea of a CIS peace-keeping force was again being discussed. On 30 November the Russian, Kazakh, Uzbek, Kyrgyz and Tajik Defence Ministers, meeting in Termez, agreed to create a peace-keeping force from units of the first four states. It may be that they came to a further, unpublicised, understanding about the situation in Tajikistan. It has been suggested that the other Central Asian states persuaded Russia that order must be restored and the incipient Islamic fundamentalist threat in the region, the supposed cause of the disorders in Tajikistan, defeated. It can hardly be coincidence that within days a force loyal to Safarali Kenjayev, a former Communist leader and a Nabiev supporter, began a new attack on Dushanbe. It was led by a 'special forces battalion' of the Ministry of Internal Security, which had been trained and equipped in Uzbekistan and was provided with air support from Uzbekistan. This time 201st MRD did not intervene and Kenjayev's troops occupied Dushanbe, followed by much of Kurgan-Tyube Province. However, the fighting continued in the east of the country, where the Pamiris were able to check the new government's poorly-trained troops.[3]

The Popular Front drove the opposition's representatives out of government and their military forces were responsible for a harsh campaign against opposition supporters and rival ethnic groups in the countryside. The exodus of refugees to Afghanistan grew. By the early summer of 1993 most of the country was under some form of Popular Front control, though resistance continued, particularly in Gorny Badakhshan. The nature of the conflict changed from a civil war to a guerrilla war, with anti-government forces concentrated in the refugee camps across the Afghan border. With help from various Afghan groups they launched hit-and-run attacks across the border, particularly in the Pyanj and Moskovskiy areas. Inevitably, the Border Guards, under Russian jurisdiction, were often the target for these raids.

The culmination of this phase of the war came on 13 July 1993, when Border Post No. 12 in the Moskovskiy sector was attacked by mortar fire from across the Afghan border and assaulted by guerrillas. The post's defences were totally inadequate; the garrison was armed only with small arms, had no reliable communications or effective fortifications and its ammunition dump was destroyed at the start of the attack. Twenty-five men, about half the garrison, were killed and several others wounded. The shock of this attack was immediately felt in Russia. First the commander of the border troops, V. I. Shlyakhtin, and then the Security Minister, Viktor Barannikov, were relieved of their posts. The Defence Minister, General Pavel Grachev, was ordered to coordinate measures to secure the Tajik-Afghan border. Grachev, an experienced Afghan War field commander, was angered by the tactical slackness of the Border Guards, and brought in students from the Kuybyshev Military Engineering Academy to plan border defences. Over 43,000 mines had been laid by the beginning of September, obstacles built and border posts fortified. Mortars and heavy artillery covered the fortifications and coordination between the border posts and 201st MRD's quick-reaction forces was improved. These measures could not prevent attacks on the border posts completely but they have ensured that the 13 July debacle was not repeated.

More significantly, that incident ensured that action was finally taken on the deployment of a CIS force to Tajikistan. On 24 August, at a meeting of CIS Foreign and Defence Ministers in Moscow, Russia, Kazakhstan, Kyrgyzstan, Uzbekistan and Tajikistan agreed to set up a Joint Peace-Keeping Force with the mission of 'stabilising the situation in Tajikistan and supporting peace'. Its commander was Russian Colonel-General Boris Pyankov[4] and its total strength 25,000 men. Deployment began in October. Since then the force's mandate from the CIS has been renewed every six months and it can claim that the situation has become stable enough for peace talks to begin.

However, there is still no sign of an effective agreement and Russian servicemen continue to be the target of guerrilla attacks, both along the border and in the interior of the country. To follow the detailed history of these attacks would try the reader's patience unnecessarily but it is worth describing the general character of operations in Tajikistan and assessing the effectiveness of the CIS force there. The CIS Joint Peace-Keeping Force has always been a basically Russian organisation. The battalions or companies sent by the three Central Asian partners have varied in strength and effectiveness. At one time the Kyrgyz contingent refused duty when its pay fell into arrears and the Kazakh battalion was withdrawn when the Kazakh Parliament refused to approve its deployment. The Joint Force has never approached its declared strength of 25,000 men, unless by sleight of hand the Russian Border Guards are included in the figures. The 201st MRD, even after reinforcement, had a total strength of about 6,000 men.[5] Two of its regiments were stationed close to the Afghan border in Kulyab (149th Motor Rifle Regiment)[6] and Kurgan-Tyube (191st Motor Rifle Regiment) and bore the brunt of the fighting. Two more regiments (92nd Motor Rifle and 401st Tank), together with divisional headquarters and most of the combat and service support units, were deployed in Dushanbe (see map). Air support, including Su-25 ground attack aircraft, was apparently provided by the Russian air force on short tours from bases in Russia. In early 1995, for instance, a helicopter sub-unit from Stavropol in the North Caucasus Military District was operating in Tajikistan.[7]

The Group of Russian Border Guards in Tajikistan has (as of 1996) five subordinate detachments on the border, with their command posts at Pyanj, Moskovskiy, Kalay-Khumb, Khorog and Murgab. The Group's headquarters are in Dushanbe, from where an air regiment and a reserve force, including air assault troops, also operate. The reserve includes part of the Commander of the Russian Border Guards' own reserve, which is permanently stationed in Tajikistan. The total strength of the Border Guards is hard to estimate but may be about 10–12,000 men. Attempts to form a Tajik Border Guards force have had only limited success. Recruitment is hampered by the fact that Tajiks can serve with the Russian border troops, where a private earns as much as the Commander-in-Chief of the Tajik Border Guards.[8]

Little more success has been achieved in creating a Tajik army. Russia and some of the Central Asian states are providing training for personnel and there are many Russians, including the Minister of Defence, General Shishlyannikov, within the command structure. The rank and file, however, are chiefly drawn from disbanded units of the Popular Front, who have not learnt much about military discipline. In September 1995, for example, fighting broke out in Kurgan-Tyube between the 1st and 11th Brigades and lasted a week before the brigades were separated. The 1st Brigade was also involved in the more serious mutinies of January and February 1996. Russian soldiers have little regard for Tajik fighting qualities, whether among their allies or their enemies. There is a general respect for Afghan Mujahidin, but the common view is that the Tajiks on either side will run away at the first shot. Clearly there is no possibility that Tajik forces could take over responsibility for guarding the border in the foreseeable future.

The burden of the war in Tajikistan therefore falls upon the Russian Border Guards and the soldiers of 201st MRD. After more than three years of fighting they have developed a military culture which would be familiar to the garrisons of imperial frontiers throughout history, from the French Foreign Legion or the British Army on the North-West Frontier or the American Army in the West, back to the Roman legions on Hadrian's Wall. They see themselves as professional soldiers, defending civilisation against a fanatical enemy. Regimental commanders have built up considerable *esprit de corps*, especially in 149th and 191st Motor Rifle Regiments. This unit loyalty is essential if their regiments are to be kept at anything like effective strength, given the hardships of service in Tajikistan. Overcoming those hardships, in fact, already forms part of regimental mythology. Conditions may have improved since the siege days of 1992, when Colonel Loktionov travelled around his barracks in Kulyab by motor-bike because there was not enough petrol for a staff car, but pay and post from home are often in arrears and lack of funds restricts vehicle maintenance and unit training. The hasty reinforcement of the division in 1993 overstretched its support capabilities, particularly in the medical field. Poor sanitation and hygiene led to serious problems with hepatitis, malaria and intestinal disorders, which seriously reduced units' combat strength.

The stress of service in Tajikistan is obviously very great. The forward regiments normally have up to half their strength on the border at any one time. Life back in the garrisons is far from restful, with a steady sequence of attacks on Russian servicemen. Military families in Tajikistan can never move about towns unescorted and many officers prefer to leave their families in Russia. Many marriages break up under the strain of separation. Units are still generally undermanned; regiments may be about 1,000 men strong, whereas their full wartime strength would number over 2,000. The rank and file are either conscripts drawn from Tajikistan or contract servicemen from Russia. The quality of both elements is open to question. This increases the stress on the officer cadre who, as elsewhere in the Russian Army, are constantly involved in supervising their subordinates and often in doing the jobs of ordinary soldiers. It is not surprising that a large proportion of officers seek release in heavy drinking or that it is increasingly difficult to find replacements for officers who move back to Russia. In 1994, 74 officers left and only 58 replacements were posted in. Surveys and common report agree that many soldiers serve basically either for the higher pay, or because they have been promised a flat in Russia at the end of a two-year tour.[9]

Nevertheless, whatever the shortcomings of the Russian Army, there is no reason to doubt its continuing ability to hold the ring in Tajikistan, as long as the Russian government maintains its present policy. The opposition forces are not strong enough to defeat the Russian forces in open battle. Russian casualties have averaged about thirty deaths a year,[10] which is tolerable, especially when compared with the 2,000 dead in one year's fighting in Chechnya. It is equally certain that a CIS military victory is not in prospect. In fact the CIS force is not set up to win a victory. It is deployed to support the Border Guards and interdict rebel infiltration from Afghanistan. It is trained for, and conducts, a basically linear defence of the border strip. The type of operations for which it is prepared was illustrated by the first joint exercise held by the CIS Peace-Keeping Force in March 1994. A mechanised infantry force, consisting of two Russian battalions, a Tajik battalion and an Uzbek company, was deployed to a border area and prepared a defensive position. The position was then held against an 'enemy' cross-border incursion, which was halted and destroyed by a counter-attack. They were supported by Uragan multiple rocket launchers, helicopters, fixed-wing aircraft and a company of paratroopers. Later exercises have followed the same pattern. Such tactics may ensure that the guerrillas based in Afghanistan cannot build up the strength to overthrow the Tajik government, but they will not bring internal stability to the country. The Tajik army is not capable of conducting an effective counter-insurgency campaign; moreover, counter-insurgency is outside the mandate of the CIS Joint Force. There is certainly no political will for such a role among Russia's partners in the Tajik intervention, nor, probably, within Russia itself. At the same time, the CIS force is not carrying out a traditional peace-keeping mission, which implies impartiality and very limited combat action. Thus Russia is leading a CIS intervention which falls between two stools: it is too compromised by its support for one party in the dispute to be accepted as a peace-keeping force, but not sufficiently committed to fight a counter-insurgency campaign.

The war in Tajikistan is at a stalemate; Russia's only exit strategy at the present is to hope that the warring parties will work out some sort of peace formula between themselves. So far there is little sign of such a deal, but there are indications that Russia's patience is wearing thin. At the January 1996 CIS Summit the Tajik government was warned that the Peace-Keeping Force's mandate would not be extended indefinitely. Its sponsors wanted an agreement at the peace talks and were bringing pressure on President Rakhmonov to find a compromise with the opposition leaders. This was before a series of armed revolts began in late January, in which local leaders demanded (and obtained) changes in the Tajik government.[11] Russian policy has been based on support for Rakhmonov. If he is losing what authority he had in the country and new inter-clan conflicts are starting then the Russian position may become untenable. If there should be no central government in Tajikistan Russia would be faced with a stark choice between full-scale intervention and complete withdrawal. It is hard to imagine Russia reimposing colonial status on Tajikistan and so withdrawal would seem the only option if there is no early peace settlement. The costs in human and financial terms of the Tajik commitment are not intolerable in themselves, but given the state of Russia's national finances and the army's requirements for the Chechen war, they are an increasing burden. There are political dangers in withdrawal if, as at the end of the Afghan War, the Russian Army feels that, although undefeated in the field, it has been betrayed by the politicians.

Note: The author is a Senior Lecturer at the Conflict Studies Research Centre, Royal Military Academy, Sandhurst, UK; however, the opinions expressed in this chapter are those of the author and do not necessarily represent those of the United Kingdom Ministry of Defence.

Notes

1 BBC *Summary of World Broadcasts*, SU 1380 C1/3, 14 May 1992.
2 L. Sarin, 'In the Epicentre of a Civil War', *Voyennyye Znaniya*, 8, 1993.
3 For a detailed account of the war up to this point see Michael Orr, 'The Civil War in Tajikistan', *Jane's Intelligence Review*, April 1993.
4 Pyankov was succeeded by Colonel-General V. Patrikeyev in April 1994, who was in turn replaced by Lieutenant-General V. S. Bobryshev in May 1995.
5 Data supplied by Peace-Keeping Directorate of Russian General Staff, June 1995.
6 149th MRR's regimental history includes service in Hungary in 1956, Czechoslovakia in 1968 and Afghanistan from 1980 to 1987. See V. Zhitarenko, 'Loktionov, Whose Son Threatened To Kill Him', *Krasnaya Zvezda*, 29 March 1993.
7 V. Berezko, 'A Trip To The War', *Armeyskiy Sbornik*, 2, 1995.
8 V. Strugovets, 'The Southern Borders of the CIS: Who Is Protecting Them and How', *Krasnaya Zvezda*, 4 August 1994.
9 This picture of army life in Tajikistan is based on several sources. *Krasnaya Zvezda* has published a series of personal sketches of individual officers; see, for example, the articles by V. Zhitarenko, 'Loktionov, Whose Son Threatened To Kill Him' (29 March 1993), 'What is Obvious From "Merkulov's Hill"' (21 April 1995), 'Pedant Kirillov' (26 April 1994), 'Judging an Officer's Honour' (11 June 1994) and 'The Recce Company's Godsend' (25 May 1994). See also: *Armiya*, 8, 1994; I. Konyshev and A. Grib, 'A Lesson From Which Nobody Learnt', *Armeyskiy Sbornik*, August 1994; and V. Bobryshev, 'Military Victory by the Opposition Is Impossible', *Krasnaya Zvezda*, 23 September 1995.
10 V. Strugovets, 'Far From Russia', *Krasnaya Zvezda*, 19 January 1996.
11 B. Pannier, 'Weathering Another Storm of Violence', *Transition*, 8 March 1996.

Russian Military Deployment in Tajikistan

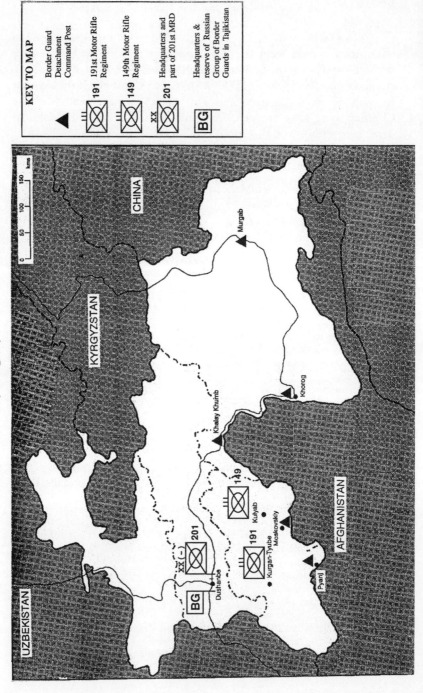

KEY TO MAP

▲ Border Guard Detachment Command Post

191 191st Motor Rifle Regiment

149 149th Motor Rifle Regiment

201 Headquarters and part of 201st MRD

BG Headquarters & reserve of Russian Group of Border Guards in Tajikistan

UZBEKISTAN

KYRGYZSTAN

CHINA

AFGHANISTAN

Dushanbe

Khaley Khumb

Murgab

Khorog

Kulyab

Moskovskiy

Kurgan-Tyube

Pyanj

0 50 100 150 Kms

Chapter 10

The Tajik Conflict: Problems of Regulation

Irina Zviagelskaya

Introduction

The civil war in Tajikistan was caused by a variety of factors. Among these were the collapse of the USSR, which revealed how unprepared the country was to exist independently; the traditional structure of society, in which a crucial role is played by local, regional and clan ties, with old and new élites fighting for power; the ideological dimension, with attempts to mobilise the population around Communist, Islamist and nationalist slogans; and the rapid internationalisation of the conflict. All these factors taken together define the highly complex structure and dynamics of the conflict, as well as the problems connected with its de-escalation.

In theory, civil wars obey the logic of settlement to a significantly lesser extent than international conflicts. Although there is an established axiom that in a civil war there can be no winners or losers, since the supporters of both sides, as well as the state itself, are victims of the conflict, in reality the side which manages to break its opponents by military force and gain power inevitably sees itself as the victor. In such conditions, the incentives prompting the regime to begin negotiations are extremely weak, if not entirely non-existent.

In other words, one of the main conditions for de-escalation, according to experts in conflict resolution, was lacking in Tajikistan, at least in the first stages after the end of the war: 'A major influence in bringing about de-escalation is the prospect that the alternatives now and in the future will be worse if the conflict continues unabated.'[1] As far as the present government was concerned, the conflict was, to all intents and purposes, over, and consequently there was no need to make concessions to an enemy whose activities hampered the establishment of total control but did not pose a direct threat to the survival of the regime.

161

A particular difficulty in settling this conflict is that, in the specific circumstances of Tajikistan, settlement would presuppose not only some sort of division of power with the opposition, but a restructuring of the whole system of regional representation in the organs of power. It is well known that in Soviet times the chief posts in the government were occupied by natives of northern Tajikistan, from Leninabad Province. The regions of the Republic were represented in government in a form of coalition, which was held together by a strong central authority, but in which the southern regions of the country were significantly less well represented.

The civil conflict, the origin of which was a struggle for political influence between regions, led to the victory of the Leninabad-Kulyab bloc. In summer 1992 they drove their opponents out of Dushanbe and forced them to retreat to the inaccessible mountain regions of Tajikistan and to Afghanistan, taking with them a wave of refugees. On 16 November the Supreme Soviet of Tajikistan met in Khojent, where President Rakhmon Nabiev's resignation was passed and Imomali Rakhmonov was elected Chairman of the Supreme Soviet. A new government came to power. Later, however, the Kulyabis consolidated their gains by forcing out the Leninabad faction and monopolising state power themselves. These events definitively destroyed the inter-regional balance of power, which is so vital to the maintenance of stability in Tajikistan, especially since the sense of national identity is extremely weak, and Tajiks define themselves primarily according to the area or region they come from. The differences between Tajiks are extremely marked, and in a number of cases there are grounds for believing that there is even a quasi-ethnic dimension to the conflict.

Both the government side, and, to an even greater extent, the opposition, are politically disunited. Within the ruling group, conflicts periodically flare up as factions compete for influence. For example, a very sinister role was played in the Tajik establishment by Yakub Salimov, who created his own, notoriously lawless, armed detachments.

As for the opposition, despite frequent assertions to the contrary, there is no real unity within its ranks. The appearance on the Tajik political scene of the Islamic-democratic bloc (now known as the United Tajik Opposition) was chiefly dictated by tactical considerations. Its representatives, uniting in the fight against the old élite, put forward their own candidate, Dawlat Khudonazarov, in the December 1991 elections for the post of President. They counted on the fact that the Islamists had relatively strong backing in the villages, while the Democratic party could claim support from the urban intelligentsia. Later, confrontation with the Leninabad-Kulyab faction, and then with the official authorities in Dushanbe, strengthened the alliance. At the same time, not all its political leaders have control over the armed opposition. The Deputy Chairman of the Islamic Rebirth Party (IRP), Haji Akbar Turajonzoda, clearly does not have that kind of control, although he regularly represents the opposition in official negotiations and at the international level. His relationship with Said Abdullo Nuri, the Chairman of the IRP and the head of the United Tajik Opposition (UTO), who controls some of the armed detachments, seems beset with rivalry. The Democratic Party has no levers of influence in the military sphere at all, and furthermore, in December 1994, it underwent a change of leadership after the departure of its leader, Shodmon Yusuf [Yusupov]. In July 1995, Yusuf's supporters re-registered the party in Dushanbe. Yusuf's attempts to appropriate the role of constructive critic of the regime within the country and at the same time to maintain his own distinct approach to the problems among the opposition have proved unproductive. The secular opposition forces treat him as a schismatic, in other words, with hostility.[2] On the other hand, neither has there been any proper dialogue between Shodmon Yusuf and the government: mutual mistrust has proved stronger than pragmatic considerations.

This article will try to explore the dynamics of the peace negotiations which have taken place, and to reveal the factors complicating the search for political resolution and stabilisation in the country.

The Organisation of Negotiations

Talks between the government and the opposition began only after heavy pressure from external forces, primarily Russia and the Central Asian states.

Russia, which had armed forces stationed in Tajikistan and whose only defended borders were those of the former USSR, could not but get drawn into the bloody conflict in Tajikistan. Its official neutrality has more often than not failed to apply to the military units in Tajikistan. During the war, they frequently acted autonomously, without waiting for orders from Moscow. The Government of National Unity, which used nationalist slogans to justify taking up arms, was perceived by the army officers, who had many ties with the former regime, as an enemy which was violating the *status quo*. The main help for the Leninabad-Kulyab faction came from Uzbekistan, to whom political Islam posed a particular threat. The Russian establishment, too, came to the conclusion that only the 'old guard' could maintain stability in the region, and actually cooperated in the decimation of opposition forces. At the same time, however, the Russian Ministry of Foreign Affairs was trying to find a political formula which could ensure a more enduring and reliable stabilisation of the situation than a military victory could provide.

Hopes that stabilisation would occur once the opposition was removed from power proved illusory. The new regime continued to use exclusively military methods of pressure, terror and repression. The arbitrariness of the authorities and their inability to resolve the country's cardinal problems, chiefly the need to improve the economic situation, did nothing to relieve the general tension.

In August 1993, at the Moscow Summit of Central Asian Heads of State, attempts were made, albeit unsuccessfully, to convince the Tajik leaders to enter into negotiations with the opposition. At this period, President Rakhmonov and his followers were utterly unamenable to the idea of negotiations. Partly this was a psychological response: too much blood had been shed for the two sides to be easily reconciled. However, there was a weightier reason as well: the government refused to accept that the opposition was a political force with which it had, however reluctantly, to reckon. According to a high-ranking Tajik official, Rakhmonov refused even to use the word 'opposition', considering it practically a swear-word. It took a great deal of work to convince him to include, in a speech he made to the United Nations, words to the effect that he was willing to enter into a dialogue with leaders of various political orientations.

In November 1993, the Russian Foreign Minister, Andrei Kozyrev, went to Dushanbe to persuade the Tajik leadership to negotiate with the opposition. He was given a warm welcome, but no progress was made whatsoever. However, the ever-worsening situation on the border, guarded almost exclusively by Russian soldiers, and armed provocation within the country forced the interested parties to act more decisively, especially as collective peace-keeping forces, again chiefly composed of Russian troops, were now stationed inside Tajikistan.

The first round of Inter-Tajik Talks opened in Moscow in April 1994, under the aegis of the United Nations, with the participation of Russia, Kyrgyzstan, Kazakhstan, Uzbekistan, Iran, Pakistan and

Afghanistan. Thus from the very first the conflict settlement process was placed in a broad international context, which gave the negotiations a higher status. The organisers hoped that this would prompt the two sides to greater mutual concessions. The talks were organised around three blocks of questions which required joint decisions: disarmament and the cessation of armed conflict; refugees; and the future structure of government. All these issues were subject to bitter disputes. It was therefore important to maintain momentum in the peace process, by moving towards a settlement step by step, reaching agreement first on those measures that would arouse relatively less controversy between the parties.

The second round of talks, held in Tehran in summer 1994, produced no substantial results. The two sides managed to develop a plan for a ceasefire and the cessation of other hostilities, as well as to agree upon temporary parameters for the application of the agreement, but in practice the meeting did not achieve any real progress. The third round took place in Islamabad in October-November 1994, the fourth in Almaty in May 1995, the fifth in Ashghabat in January-February 1996 and the sixth in Tehran in January 1997.

Since the start of negotiations, significant changes have taken place in the attitudes of a number of neighbouring states. Firstly, the evolution of Uzbekistan's position is noteworthy: chiefly, Tashkent has become disillusioned with the current Tajik leadership. It was believed in Uzbekistan that when the Leninabad-Kulyab faction came to power, it would be politically dependent on Uzbekistan and open to recommendations from its neighbour. However, the monopolisation of state positions by Kulyabis and gradual dismissal of Leninabadis, traditionally closely allied with Uzbekistan, and the increasingly hostile attitude of the Tajik leaders towards the country's Uzbek minority, in retaliation for their support for Abdumalik Abdullojonov, the Leninabad candidate in the November 1994 presidential elections, have led Tashkent to exert economic and political pressure on Dushanbe. One of the most important elements of this pressure was President Islam Karimov's meeting with Otakhon Latifi, Chairman of the Coordinating Centre of the Democratic Forces of Tajikistan, Khudoberdy Khaliknazarov, the former Minister of Foreign Affairs, and Turajonzoda, in Tashkent in April 1995.[3] Karimov had already accused Rakhmonov, at the CIS leaders' summit, of not wanting to compromise on any point at the Inter-Tajik Talks. In the course of his meeting with the opposition, the Uzbek President, overcoming his hostility towards Islamists and democrats, promised that he would recommend the Kazak and Kyrgyz Presidents to meet Turajonzoda, clearly so as to exercise more concerted pressure on the Tajik authorities.

Secondly, the Central Asian states began using the Inter-Tajik Talks to consolidate their own positions in the CIS and in relation to Russia. Thus, the fourth round of talks was held in Almaty: President Nazarbayev obviously wanted to demonstrate that Kazakhstan's active participation could lead to a breakthrough. Moreover, the deaths of Kazak soldiers in the peace-keeping forces had forced him to take more active political measures. Finally, it would seem that he was motivated by a desire to put pressure on Russia, since it was then busy with the war in Chechnya. The results, however, were not encouraging.

Unexpectedly, Turkmenistan took the mission of mediation upon itself. It is well known that its involvement in CIS discussions and agreements had always been passive. Turkmenistan did not send a single soldier to the Collective Peace-Keeping Force in Tajikistan. The situation changed after a visit to Moscow by President Niyazov in May 1995, during which 23 inter-state agreements were signed, and the Russian President emphasised 'strategic and economic cooperation with Turkmenistan': 'Turkmenia is the first country in the Commonwealth with which Russia has embarked on this level of relations.'[4] This abrupt turn-around in bilateral relations was due particularly to Moscow's attempts to put pressure on Kazakhstan: friction between the two countries was increasing steadily at the time on a number of issues, including the Caspian Sea. Whatever the reason, the status of strategic partner was conferred on Turkmenistan, which had formerly occupied one of the lowliest places in the scale of Russia's foreign policy priorities in the 'near abroad'. The question of the situation in Tajikistan and on the Tajik-Afghan border was placed within the framework of the new Russian-Turkmen relationship. The Turkmen President let it be understood that he was willing to contribute to the stabilisation of the situation and facilitate an amelioration in Russian-Afghan relations; he proposed holding the fifth round of Inter-Tajik Talks in Ashghabat.

A new stage in the talks process was the raising of their level. At the preliminary stage, the parties had been represented by fairly low-ranking leaders. The government delegation was headed by the Minister of Labour and Employment, Shukur Zukhurov, and the opposition by Otakhon Latifi. Later, the government was represented by Abdumajid Dostiev, First Deputy to Rakhmonov, and the opposition by the First Deputy Chairman of the IRP, Turajonzoda. From May 1995, Rakhmonov and Nuri entered the arena in person. They decided that a continuous round of talks should be held. This approach had its advantages. First and foremost, it precluded the possibility of one party breaking off talks, or threatening to break them off, as a means of putting pressure on their opponent. On the other hand, a 'continuous round' could lead to the parties becoming too accustomed to talks, which might make it more difficult to take important decisions. If the decision-making process on fundamental issues of regulation were to be dragged out indefinitely, there was a danger that the talks would degenerate into a mere formality. The margin for compromise was still narrow.

Military Matters

This category includes the problem of the disarmament of illegal forces, the ceasefire agreement and the exchange of detainees and prisoners-of-war.

An important aspect of the ever-worsening situation in Tajikistan since the end of the civil war has been the activity of a variety of armed groups. On the one hand, there are the so-called self-defence detachments, which, because of the legal vacuum and direct threats to people's safety in certain areas, have been the only means of protecting the civilian population. The availability of arms to ordinary people is also increased by the criminalisation of society, which is a direct result of the economic crisis and the incapacity of the law-enforcement agencies to do their job. On the other hand, the infiltration of the organs of the MVD ('Ministry of Internal Affairs') by criminals and the partial autonomisation of armed forces affiliated to the Ministry under Yakub Salimov has led to their activities also becoming a threat to public safety. The purging of the power structures by the new regime not only destroyed the regional balance, but also led to the resignation of many professionals. They were replaced by incompetent individuals, motivated by self-gain, who happened to come from the right regions. The fight against the remnants of the opposition was accompanied by ethnic cleansing, arbitrary rule and lawlessness.

During the talks, heated debates broke out on the issue of disarmament. While the government side put its main emphasis on the disarmament of the opposition, their opponents demanded the simultaneous disarmament and disbanding of the militarised subdepartments of the MVD, the Ministry of Security and the Ministry of Defence. Bearing in mind the tense situation in the Republic and on the border, and the authorities' natural interest in self-preservation, it was impossible for them to agree to this. Similarly, the opposition was not ready to disarm, since it considered military action the most effective method of putting pressure on the Dushanbe authorities.

The only compromise which was possible was on the issue of a ceasefire, although from the beginning the government demanded a permanent ceasefire, while the opposition was only prepared to accept temporary agreements. At the second round of Inter-Tajik Talks, held in Tehran in June 1994, the parties, with the active help of Ramiro Piriz-Ballon, the United Nations Secretary-General's Special Envoy, agreed to concentrate their attention on reaching an agreement on a ceasefire and the cessation of other hostilities. A draft agreement was drawn up, and the two sides managed to agree on a mechanism for ensuring its fulfilment. However, arguments about the time-scale for the activation of the agreement prevented it from being implemented.[5]

The 'Agreement on a Temporary Ceasefire and Cessation of Other Hostilities on the Tajik-Afghan Border and in the Country for the Duration of the Talks' was passed later in the Tehran talks and took effect in October 1994; it has periodically been extended. The very signing of the agreement by the warring sides seemed a positive sign, but the practical realisation of the ceasefire proved extremely difficult. Regardless of the assurances of the two sides, armed conflict continued and, as the snow began to melt in the mountain passes in the spring of 1995, intensified.

The opposition forces in Afghanistan number around 12,000 men. Moreover, in Afghan Badakhshan there are up to 14,000 Afghan Mujahidin, as well as the large detachments of a number of Afghan field commanders. Apart from the Mujahidin, the Tajik opposition is supported by fighters from radical Islamist groups. In Tajikistan itself, there are self-defence detachments in the regions of Gorny Badakhshan and Garm; these have several thousand men. The population in these areas is hostile to the authorities in Dushanbe, but traditionally well-disposed towards Russia.[6] The difficulty in making the ceasefire hold lies, firstly, in the fact that by no means all the armed detachments are controlled by the opposition leaders. The field commanders involved in military action on the border have their own aims. Secondly, the government considers the self-defence detachments in the mountainous regions of Tajikistan as part of the armed opposition. It has consequently transferred troops to these regions.

However, this was seen by the opposition as a violation of the Tehran temporary ceasefire conditions, according to which the redeployment of armed forces was prohibited. It was the Russian Border Guards who found themselves in the most awkward situation when fighting flared up again. By that time Russian soldiers had to a great extent been replaced by Tajiks on contract service in the Russian Border Guards. The Guards had to fight not only detachments making incursions from Afghanistan, but also the self-defence groups; the latter blocked the passage of motor columns, fearing the strengthening of government forces in the region. As a result, the Border Guards had the unaccustomed task of entering into negotiations with local rebel field commanders to improve relations. The increasing pressure meant that Russia took a harsher stand. In political talks in Moscow in April 1995, soon after the new battles on the border, Kozyrev announced: 'Such acts will be met with a decisive repulse ... We will not tolerate the death of our people.'[7] Russian pressure produced some results. The scale of armed clashes diminished, although attempts to cross the border, which had also become a corridor for drug trafficking, did not cease. As a measure of trust, the warring Tajik sides periodically exchanged prisoners-of-war and detainees. Here, too, frictions arose: either the government would not publish full lists of prisoners or would free only some of them, or the field commanders would refuse to hand over their prisoners-of-war. However, the process, though slow, did persist.

At a meeting between Rakhmonov and Said Abdullo Nuri in Tehran on 19 July 1995,[8] a decision was taken for the first time to consider the question of a permanent ceasefire.[9] The political significance of this step was certainly very great, although its practical realisation was problematic.

While the government and the opposition were engaged in slow and uneasy negotiations, the situation on the ground was also changing. On 15–16 September, field commanders from the Karategin area and a specially assembled State Commission met to discuss calling a ceasefire in the Komsomolabad, Garm, Tajikabad and Jirgatal areas. Staff from the United Nations Mission of Observers in Tajikistan (UNMOT) acted as mediators. The results of the talks seemed promising: the two sides agreed to eliminate a number of checkpoints, to ease transportation between Dushanbe and Jirgatal, and to solve differences by political means.[10] The agreement did not hold for long. In a new assault, opposition armed groups managed to occupy a large part of Karategin, undermining the fragile stability in the region. However, the agreement, though violated, pointed up the fact that some field commanders had got tired of the conflict and were trying to carve out spheres of influence. Such efforts to settle problems on the ground are laudable in principle, but in the absence of an overall settlement they might result in Tajikistan being split into 'semi-feudal principalities' controlled by this or that armed formation.

If the opposition and the government do eventually manage to sign a final peace settlement, they will be faced with the challenge of how to reduce the power of armed groups which are practically independent of their authority. Yet they must achieve this if they are to increase their control over the military and political situation.

Refugees

One of the problems which has aroused comparatively less disagreement between government and opposition is that of the return of refugees and displaced persons. Apart from those who left the country because of the war in 1992, there is also a number of so-called internal refugees, who, fearing for their life and safety, were forced to leave their homes and flee to other regions. The overall number of refugees is not known, and widely differing figures are given. The government deliberately lowers them, claiming, for example, that in the border regions of Afghanistan there are now no more than 6–8,000 refugees. The opposition blatantly exaggerates the numbers, putting the total at around 1 million (including all those who emigrated or were displaced), with 126,000 in Afghanistan. According to estimates by the leader of the mission from the Directorate of the UN High Commissioner for Refugees, in the first half of 1995 there were less than 7,000 registered refugees left in the Sakhi camp in Afghanistan, and about 14,000 in Kunduz. By 1 December 1994 over 26,000 refugees had returned to Tajikistan from Afghanistan through the UNHCR, while another 14,000 had returned independently.[11]

The government has taken measures to return both the internal refugees and those living in Afghanistan. However, the problem remains acute. Firstly, by no means everyone can return to the areas where they formerly lived. Some of their houses have been destroyed, some seized by others. There is a lack of trust towards those returning home, which occasionally escalates into clashes. The refugees are often held responsible for all the sins of the opposition, and, with the increasing pressure on the border and inside the country, resentment towards them is increasing. Moreover, they are often seen as unwanted competitors whose presence increases the general economic strain. It should be noted that to a certain extent the authorities themselves help to create a climate of distrust towards refugees, especially those returning from Afghanistan. Secondly, the deep economic crisis in the Republic does not allow for the rehabilitation of refugees. There is no work; there are no funds for building houses; social divisions are growing. On 5 July 1992, a Department for Refugee Affairs was set up in the Ministry of Labour. In 1993, according to the Department's Director Kh. Davlatov, the government allocated 3 billion roubles for housing reconstruction and 2 billion for the payment of compensation to each returning family. The following year, compensation payments were stopped because of the economic crisis, and the financing of housing reconstruction was replaced by credit for the purchase of products in state shops.[12]

The necessary legal framework is also lacking. For example, those who returned to Dushanbe were told that their flats would be vacated. In practice it has been impossible to achieve this. Straight after the war, crowds of people surged into Dushanbe, mainly from Kulyab, to take the place of the Russians, Garmis and Leninabadis who were leaving. Some of them came in the hope of finding food, some arrived with the conquerors to take up vacant jobs. There has been a precipitate provincialisation of the capital and the number of inhabitants has swelled sharply. Under these circumstances, there is no way that large numbers of people can be accommodated.

An even more difficult situation faces the refugees in Afghanistan, Iran and Pakistan. In Afghanistan, the local authorities have frequently hindered the refugees' return, since they are trying to benefit from the international organisations who provide aid to the refugees. Men are conscripted into local Mujahidin detachments, while the youth are taken under the wing of Islamist organisations. The radical activists in the opposition also have no interest in the repatriation of refugees, whose existence serves not only to swell the ranks of armed fighters, but also to uphold their political claims. Human Rights Watch gives numerous examples of such pressure. They range from verbal persuasion to the planting of a mine under a bus full of refugees (fortunately defused in time).[13] Finally, the refugees themselves, hearing how difficult life has become at home, are afraid to go back. The question of refugees has been raised at every round of the Inter-Tajik Talks. Only the concerted efforts of the government and opposition, supported by help from international organisations and neighbouring states, can alleviate the problem.

171

Political Issues

The main stumbling blocks in the peace negotiations are the reconciling of the political roles of the opposition and the governing regime in Tajikistan, and the determining of the future structure of the state. It is precisely on these matters that the stances of the government and opposition have always been diametrically opposed; the possibility of their rapprochement still seems extremely problematic.

At the first round of talks in Moscow the opposition's main protest was against the violation of the regional principle in personnel selection. Indeed, by then the Chairman of the Supreme Soviet, his First Deputy, the Deputy Chairman of the Council of Ministers, the Procurator-General, the Minister of Security, and many others (in all, up to 80% of state officials) were natives of Kulyab Province. At the heart of the opposition's suggestions was the idea of a State Soviet, or Council of National Agreement, to be formed by the conflicting sides on a parity basis and given the right to make legislative proposals for no more than two years. The Council of National Agreement (SNS) would form a temporary government of competent, neutral people; it would then pass a new constitution and organise democratic, multi-party elections.

The idea of an interim period had a certain logic. Theoretically, it could provide for a relatively smooth transition to participation by a wider range of political forces and regions in the running of the country, leaving enough time for drawing up and ratifying a new constitution, the necessity of which was recognised by both parties. However, in practical terms the proposal was extremely sensitive: it required the dismissal of the existing government from the political arena and its replacement with a very amorphous structure.

The idea of a Council for National Agreement was itself not a new one. In November 1992, when the country was being ravaged by civil war, Andrei Kozyrev had come up with a proposal for a State Soviet, in which representatives of all regions would be included on a parity basis.[14] The suggestion reflected a search for a mechanism under which all regions could be represented in the state structure, but the climate was not receptive to the promotion of such initiatives. It is possible that the Russian Foreign Ministry hoped that while the question of power was not yet definitively decided it would be easier to reach a compromise. In fact, the Leninabad-Kulyab bloc was not interested in any form of power-sharing: it was striving for complete annihilation of the opposition.

In 1994 the State Soviet plan was even less likely to succeed. The government indicated that a fundamental change in the organs of power would, in the prevailing conditions, only bring about a further destabilisation of the situation, by depriving the Republic of a strong central power. And although the existing situation was justly condemned both within Tajikistan and abroad, it was clear that complete restructuring of the state might lead to a bloody new round of civil strife. This was especially so since there were still large numbers of arms and semi-legal and illegal groups of fighters in the country. The Kulyabis' fears about the intentions of their political opponents also had deeper roots. During the period of the Government of National Unity (in which opposition representatives had participated), Kulyab, which had refused to recognise this government, had been subjected to an economic blockade. The vulnerability of the region, which depends on supplies from other regions of Tajikistan, was one of the reasons for its coalition with Kurgan-Tyube, which had formerly been an Islamist bastion. The experience of economic and military pressure had left its mark on the Kulyabis, who were trying to exclude the recurrence of any attempt to strangle their region.

The Tajik leadership was counting on the speedy legitimisation of the regime. At the Nineteenth Session of the Supreme Soviet of Tajikistan, which took place on 20–21 July 1994, the question of the Inter-Tajik Talks was not even raised. Instead, the Supreme Soviet approved the holding of a referendum on the new Constitution and of presidential elections in September 1994. Such measures threatened to force the opposition out of Tajik political life once and for all. It initiated armed action on the border, as well as acts of terrorism and sabotage within the country. Prompted by the deterioration of the situation, the UN Secretary-General, Boutros Boutros-Ghali, presented a report to the Security Council, in which he noted: 'Because this situation has arisen, I have been forced to review the expediency of continuing with preparations for the third round of talks in Islamabad at this stage.'[15]

International pressure produced some results. The elections and the referendum were postponed to November 1994, and the talks went ahead in Islamabad in October. During this round, a protocol was signed on a Joint Commission to implement the 'Agreement about a Temporary Ceasefire', and the two sides issued a joint communiqué, but disagreements about political questions merely increased. According to the opposition, the conditions for its participation in the referendum and elections had not been met. It considered that elections could only be held after national reconciliation. Indeed, opposition political parties were banned, and the opposition had no access to the media, while thousands of refugees remained outside the country. However, the government was not able to put off the referendum and elections indefinitely. The jurisdiction of the old Soviet Parliament ran out at the end of March 1995;[16] in the event of a further postponement of elections, the country might be left, legally and actually, without a legislative body.

Presidential elections were held in November 1994. Rakhmonov's rival was Tajikistan's Ambassador to Russia and former Prime Minister, Abdumalik Abdullojonov, a native of Leninabad Province. His candidacy was denied registration for a long time, and the day after the elections Abdullojonov's campaign team issued a protest about 'numerous cases of falsification'. Rakhmonov triumphed. Moscow considered him a safer bet, since he could ensure the continuity of the leadership, whereas if Abdullojonov, who did not control any military and security structures, had been elected, a new military crisis would have seemed inevitable. In turn, Rakhmonov gave assurances that after the election he would get rid of the more abhorrent figures in the country's leadership at various levels. His pre-election leaflet stated that as President he would 'purge the local and central organs of power, courts, public prosecutors' offices, police stations, customs and tax offices and other structures, of individuals who compromised the authorities in the eyes of the people'.[17] Rakhmonov's scope for action in this respect should not be overestimated: he obviously could not encroach upon his allies in the Popular Front, who had brought him to power and then taken up posts in many state bodies. However, many politicians did not hide their hopes that Rakhmonov would at least be able to get rid of Yakub Salimov, as indeed he eventually succeeded in doing.

Parliamentary elections followed in February 1995. Despite the announcement by Zafar Saidov, a head of department in the Ministry of Foreign Affairs, that the authorities could have postponed the elections for a few months if the opposition had expressed any interest in them,[18] the mechanism allowing the opposition leaders to participate in them remained unclear. Moreover, the opposition itself showed no desire to join in the election process, holding that a primary condition should be the restoration of legality to all prohibited parties (especially the Democratic Party and the IRP of Tajikistan) and a free press. The suggestion of re-registering the

Democratic Party evoked no response from its leaders at the time. Apart from distrust towards the regime, there were obviously fears that re-registration could lead to a schism in the opposition.

On the eve of the parliamentary elections, the active parties were the Communist Party, whose leader had become a Member of Parliament, the People's Party, the Party of National Unity and the Party of Political and Economic Revival. Some of them were the puppet parties of individual leaders. Thus, the People's Party had been formed by the First Deputy Chairman of the Supreme Soviet, Abdumajid Dostiev, on the basis of a group of people from his district, and in many respects duplicates the structure, aims and objectives of the Communist Party. The Party of National Unity was organised by Abdullojonov, and was basically a collection of his supporters from the northern regions of Tajikistan. The authorities, however, had not forgiven Abdullojonov for his presidential challenge, and obstructed his registration and that of his party representatives. On 23 February, the Supreme Court rejected the party's appeal for justice in the registration of candidates.

The ruling circles made an attempt to give the elections and the referendum on the Constitution a more democratic flavour by giving some refugees the chance to vote. Polling stations were set up in Moscow, Minsk, Almaty, Tashkent, Bishkek, Ashghabat and a number of towns in Iran and Afghanistan. In all, according to official figures, 2,179 people living outside Tajikistan took part in the referendum. The Tajik leadership also decided, in light of the widespread anger at the 'Kulyab domination', that it must balance out the regional representation in the *Majlisi Oli* ('Supreme Soviet'). Safarali Rajabov, a native of the Garm group of districts, was elected to its Chairmanship.[19]

The opposition, which had recognised neither the presidential and parliamentary elections, nor the new Constitution passed by the referendum, continued to demand the creation of a new body. At the fourth round of Inter-Tajik Talks in Almaty in May 1995, the opposition again tabled a proposal for a Council for National Agreement (CNA), to sit for a transitional period. It was to consist of 31 members: twelve from each side, taking into account regional representation, six to represent the different ethnic communities and one neutral member, by mutual agreement of the sides, who would be its head. The armed forces, the Radio and Television Committee and the Public Prosecutor's Office would all be placed under the direct jurisdiction of this CNA. The Ministry of Foreign Affairs and Foreign

Economic Relations would be controlled jointly by the CNA and the government. As is apparent from the opposition's proposals, it had not swerved from its intention to depose the present regime. The CNA, it was proposed, would take on itself all the most important state functions, leaving almost nothing to the government. However, to achieve compromise through the creation of a body which would replace the existing government was unthinkable. Such a decision was completely unacceptable to the Dushanbe authorities, whose legitimacy had been recognised by many states.

Some cautious moves towards a way out of the deadlock appear to have been made during the meeting between Rakhmonov and Nuri in Iran in July 1995. The two sides instructed their representatives to review the question of creating a Consultative People's Forum of Tajikistan, in which the opposition would participate, during the fifth round of Inter-Tajik Talks.[20] However, the results of the meeting in Ashghabat were minimal. A Protocol for the calling of a Consultative Forum was worked out but not signed, and the sides also failed to reach agreement on the date of its creation or its membership. Negotiations on extending the ceasefire likewise came to nothing. The Russian side commented on the government delegation's 'flexible, constructive approach' to the discussions, which did not meet with understanding from the opposition side. The Russian representatives in general began to speak of the opposition in a far harsher way than formerly, no doubt encouraged by the wave of opposition attacks on the eve of the fifth round. As for the government, its drive to ease relations with the political opposition can be explained by the ever-worsening situation in the country.

On 23 December 1996 Imomali Rakhmonov and Said Abdullo Nuri made an important step towards a settlement. They signed a political agreement in Moscow which papered over their differences and deferred their resolution to follow-up negotiations on the powers and composition of a National Reconciliation Commission. Its mandate was to include: boosting the opposition's representation in central and local government bodies; drafting constitutional amendments and laws; calling elections and referenda jointly with the existing Parliament and government; overseeing jointly with the government a general exchange of prisoners and detainees, the repatriation of refugees, the disarmament and disbanding of irregular forces, and their integration into society; and cooperating with the UN and the Organisation for Security and Cooperation in Europe in pacifying the country. The Commission was to function for a transitional period of 12 to 18 months pending the election of a new Parliament in internationally-supervised elections.[21] The summit was followed by the next round of Inter-Tajik Talks in Tehran in January 1997. The Foreign Minister, Talbak Nazarov, stated that the National Reconciliation Commission could only have a consultative role; the opposition delegation leader, Turajonzoda, on the other hand, called for real powers to be conferred on the Commission and, among other demands, insisted on the inclusion of the 'third force' National Revival Bloc in the negotiations.[22]

The National Revival Bloc had been set up by Abdullojonov, who, as of now, remains in opposition to the government. For tactical reasons he has entered into an alliance with the United Tajik Opposition, trying to secure a place of his own at the negotiating table. The presence of the 'Revivalists' would provide additional leverage on the government. At the same time, it is clear that Abdullojonov and the UTO leaders have different aims: each side is striving to get the upper hand in the future government. The idea of such an alliance has been supported by Uzbekistan, which is interested in bringing the Leninabad clan back to power. Obviously, this aim cannot be reached soon, but the presence of Abdullojonov's team would have balanced the Islamists in any official body.

In Tehran the UTO's demand that the National Revival Bloc be included in the National Reconciliation Commission was rejected by the government delegation, which denied the existence of any 'third force' in the country. The position of Russia was more balanced but still closer to the Dushanbe government. The Russian representatives recognised that internal opposition to the regime really existed, but they stressed that Abdullojonov's party was not the only internal opposition force.[23] It would appear that the Russian stand is dictated not so much by its support for the Tajik government as by its differences with Tashkent.

The Tehran round of negotiations produced several important results. The size of the National Reconciliation Commission was decided; likewise, the level of representation of the opposition on the Central Election Committee (25%). Military matters and the issue of quotas of seats on the National Reconciliation Commission were postponed until the next round of negotiations.[24] The opposition, dissatisfied (as usual) with the Russian position and wanting to irritate Moscow, demanded that 1,000 UN peace-keepers should be introduced into the Republic, thus questioning the role of the Russian peace-keeping forces in the country.[25] The summit in Moscow and negotiations in Tehran did not result in a breakthrough, but what has been achieved might serve as a start towards an overall political settlement.

While the government and opposition are initiating a debate about a National Reconciliation Commission, the situation in the Republic is deteriorating. The conflict has been acquiring an inter-ethnic dimension, since relations between the government and the local Uzbeks are going from bad to worse. The Uzbeks make up the largest national minority in the Republic: 24–25% of the population. They have repeatedly demanded that Uzbek be given the status of a state language, that Uzbeks be more fairly represented in government structures, and that their own culture be promoted: Tajikistan has only a few Uzbek schools. However, there are few signs that the government will accede to these requests, particularly since the Uzbeks voted for Abdullojonov in the presidential elections of November 1994. The conflict also pertains to the division of economic control. This was proved once again by government's efforts to establish control over the aluminium plant in Tursunzade, a city mostly populated by Uzbeks. The government brigade sent to the city was denied entrance by the local population. The inter-ethnic dimension of the Tajik conflict could make it even more dangerous and less manageable.

Conclusion

At the time of writing, the talks between the government and the opposition have not led to a breakthrough which could allow one to hope for a firm stabilisation of the situation in Tajikistan. The aims of the opposing parties are still too different and compromise would probably not mean mutual gain, but more likely, highly unpleasant concessions. The issue of regional representation has not been resolved; the state does not provide either legal or social protection to its citizens; the economic situation is worsening and the criminalisation of society is accelerating. All these problems, taken together, are resulting in dissatisfaction with the regime and the creation of internal opposition. Moreover, in the time which has elapsed since the end of the civil war, neither the government nor the opposition has been able significantly to strengthen its position in a way which would give it a definite advantage over the other side. Only the concerted efforts of international organisations and external powers, including Russia, the Central Asian states, Iran, Afghanistan and Pakistan, can preserve and sustain the negotiation process. The possibility of reaching a settlement at the present stage is problematic, since the Tajik conflict is directly connected with the situation in neighbouring Afghanistan. At the same time, measures for diminishing military tension should not be discounted. The most important precondition for stabilisation, apart from military and political measures, is the improvement of the economic situation in the country. The economic crisis and unemployment create a fertile climate for the development of extremely destructive tendencies in society, including separatism in various regions and the search for illegal funds, for example from the drug trade. They complicate the configuration of the conflict, since, alongside confrontation between the government and the opposition, there are growing contradictions within the country between the authorities and other influential groups.

Notes

1 Louis Kriesberg and Stuart J. Thorson (eds), *Timing the De-escalation of International Conflicts*, Syracuse University Press, Syracuse, N. Y., 1991, p. 15.
2 *Segodnya*, 10 June 1995.
3 *Nezavisimaya gazeta*, 5 April 1995.
4 *Nezavisimaya gazeta*, 19 May 1995.
5 United Nations document S/1994/893.
6 'Rossiya i musul'manskii mir' ('Russia and the Muslim World'), *Moskva*, no. 6 (36), 1995, pp. 47–8.
7 *Nezavisimaya gazeta*, 20 April 1995.
8 *Sadoi Mardum*, 19 July 1995.
9 ITAR-TASS, 20 July 1995.
10 *Sadoi Mardum*, 21 September 1996.
11 Human Rights Watch document. See *Charogi Ruz*, no. 8 (86), 1995, pp. 10–11.
12 *Ibid.*, p. 12.
13 *Ibid.*, p. 11.
14 *Nezavisimaya gazeta*, 19 March 1994.
15 United Nations document S/1994/893, official translation, cited in *Nezavisimaya gazeta*, 14 September 1994.
16 *Nezavisimaya gazeta*, 22 February 1995.
17 *Nezavisimaya gazeta*, 9 November 1994.
18 *Nezavisimaya gazeta*, 22 February 1995.
19 *Sadoi Mardum*, 12 April 1995.
20 ITAR-TASS, 20 July 1995.
21 Jamestown Foundation, *Monitor*, Vol. 2, no. 240, 24 December 1996.
22 Jamestown Foundation, *Monitor*, Vol. 3, no. 5, 8 January 1997.
23 *Nezavisimaya gazeta*, 14 January 1997.
24 *Nezavisimaya gazeta*, 21 January 1997.
25 *Nezavisimaya gazeta*, 14 January 1997.

Chapter 11

International Concern for Tajikistan: UN and OSCE Efforts to Promote Peace-Building and Democratisation

Olivier A. J. Brenninkmeijer[1]

The following study presents multilateral diplomatic efforts to end the ongoing violent conflict in Tajikistan and encourage peace-building. Conflict resolution and promoting government reforms are offered by the United Nations (UN) and the Organisation for Security and Cooperation in Europe (OSCE).[2] They work to mediate a political solution to the Tajik conflict and encourage the development of democratic institutions. Both organisations have tried, with mixed results, to advance a peace-building process and influence the political and military authorities in Tajikistan. Other participants in this diplomatic effort are Russia, Uzbekistan, Kazakhstan, Kyrgyzstan and members of the Iranian, Afghan and Pakistani governments.

Obstacles to peace-building are discussed here to highlight the challenges which the two international organisations confront. These are greatest with regard to two principal objectives: bringing the parties to agree on an end to the violence, and facilitating pan-Tajik political reconciliation. These objectives constitute peace-building, which both international organisations promote according to their respective mandates and capacities. The United Nations Secretary-General mandated a Special Envoy along with a Mission in Tajikistan to provide good offices for the parties to the conflict and mediate a ceasefire agreement supported by appropriate monitoring facilities. Furthermore, the UN Mission has the task of searching for methods by which to find a political solution to the conflict. The OSCE's Mission in Tajikistan complements the UN efforts: it has a mandate to facilitate dialogue among the parties in the conflict, to recommend democratisation of government institutions, to advise on constitutional provisions that guarantee fundamental freedoms, and to promote respect for human rights.

180

The challenges which the two international organisations face are principally: the neo-Communist Tajik regime's unbending position, the opposition coalition's demands for government reform, and the continued fighting. Another major challenge concerns the problem of interpreting commonly used concepts. For example, the Western ideals of constitutional democracy, human rights, free and fair multi-party elections and political reconciliation are worthy objectives, but they do not necessarily fit within the Tajiks' own conceptions of their future.

The divergence of concepts and objectives on what the government in Tajikistan ought to look like are visible in the contrasting positions taken by the parties in the conflict and by the two international organisations. For example, the Tajik neo-Communist regime does everything it can to maintain its position in government, the opposition groups do whatever they can to see it disappear from the centre, and the Russians do all they can to establish and maintain military security at almost any cost in the hope of seeing Central Asia become a stable buffer zone between their homeland and the Islamic world to the south. For their part, the two multilateral organisations observe very different objectives: they hope to influence all parties in Tajikistan to adopt liberal democratic principles of governance, with the conviction that only multi-party democracy will provide long-term political stability.

Leaving ideals aside, the priority for the UN and the OSCE is to help prevent a renewed outbreak of large-scale violence. A second necessity in the peace process is for the two organisations to promote dialogue and confidence-building, so as to dispel perceptions and rumours of imminent danger from ethnic warfare or Islamic militancy. Third, the two Missions need to offer their good offices and mediate among the Tajik parties to improve the understanding of the diverse positions and objectives in the conflict so that possibilities for dispute resolution can be formulated. The international mediation effort must then, as a fourth requisite, advance methods of gradual accommodation through which the incumbent Tajik regime can realise new benefits as it includes representatives of the opposition in national affairs. At the same time, opposition groups need to agree and understand that democratic reforms take a long time to be identified, developed, and agreed upon by all parties to the conflict. The neo-Communist politicians in Dushanbe will not unlearn Soviet-style rule quickly, and the Republic's opposition leaders are not in a position to introduce democratic principles merely through pan-Tajik elections.

For this reason, the fifth requirement for the international organisations is to familiarise and instruct, by means of disseminating information, holding conferences and organising seminars, on the management of a democratic system in which political disputes are resolved without violence and in which an independent judiciary can operate to guarantee basic human rights and freedoms.

A further challenge for the UN and the OSCE is to pursue their work with the limited funding at their disposal and make use of the influence which Russia, Uzbekistan, and Islamic countries can contribute. In the peace negotiations, Russia's influence is crucial because the Tajik parties to the conflict – the government and opposition groups – are not in a position to pursue a war if Russian forces make a stand to obstruct it. The Russian and CIS military have supported the present Tajik government, and, being in a position to keep the regime in power, they are also in a position to press for political reform. For their part, influential political leaders in Iran, Afghanistan and Pakistan can, through their inclusion in the peace process, contribute to ending the conflict. This process is essentially one of searching for realisable agreements that end the worst of the violence, provide institutionalised means by which to resolve disputes, and integrate Russian/CIS and Islamic influence in the reform of the country's political institutions as well as in the reconstruction of its economy.

So far, the UN and the OSCE have brought the Tajik parties to agree to the peace-building process and their good offices have facilitated dialogue. The UN Mission was able, with Russian and Iranian backing, to bring about a ceasefire agreement, and the OSCE has worked to influence the drafting of the new Constitution, to introduce principles of democratic governance, and to amplify international disapproval of undemocratic electoral methods and human rights violations.

International Concern: the UN and the CSCE

The two international organisations, the UN and the CSCE,[3] admitted Tajikistan as a member in early 1992.[4] Following their initial reconnaissance missions to Tajikistan, it did not take long for both organisations to concern themselves with the humanitarian demands of a war-stricken population and the obvious need to establish a process of conflict resolution and mediation.

The first CSCE Mission was sent in March 1992 just before the major violent clashes began.[5] Its purpose was to assess whether the

Tajik government could abide by the CSCE's 'Community of Values', such as democratic governance, the rule of law enshrined in a constitution, an independent judiciary, and respect for human rights. The Mission's staff recognised that it will take time before Tajikistan and its political leadership can abide by the principles of the CSCE; they wrote optimistically that political developments appeared to be advancing towards a multi-party system and that the Constitution was being redrawn to incorporate internationally recognised principles of pluralism and a free market economy. However, the delegation also reported that 'Tajikistan is going through a delicate stage of transition, marked by growing nationalistic and religious feelings'.[6] The CSCE Mission also expressed its concern about drug trafficking and the economic difficulties which are believed to trigger regional discontent and political instability.

In the same vein, the UN brought the dismal situation in Tajikistan to international attention following a UN fact-finding mission of September 13 to 23, 1992.[7] The Security Council deplored the conflict and the great loss of human lives in the disintegrating political situation. Responding to the information from this mission, Secretary-General Boutros Boutros-Ghali announced that a Good-Offices Mission would be dispatched to Tajikistan in November 1992, the purpose being to encourage dialogue and find avenues for political reconciliation among the parties in the conflict.[8]

Diplomatic pressure for political change in Tajikistan was also attempted by the United States Ambassador to the CSCE in Vienna. He reminded the Tajikistan government in a letter that 'countries which engage in consistent patterns of gross violations of internationally recognised human rights or of international law are ineligible for US governmental assistance'.[9] In response to international criticism about the suffering caused in the civil war and human rights abuses, the Foreign Minister of Tajikistan wrote to the CSCE Chairperson-in-Office in Vienna that during the summer and autumn of 1992, his country had approached a chaotic situation in which the constitutional structures were paralysed and the government was rendered impotent in its attempts at state-building.[10] Blaming armed opposition groups for the acts of terror, he declared his government's commitment to the principles and provisions of the CSCE Helsinki Final Act, to the Charter of Paris, and to other CSCE documents that oblige member states to observe principles of human rights and democratic governance.

At their Third Meeting of the Council (December 14–15, 1992), the CSCE ministers 'urged all the conflicting parties to cease fighting and to start a constructive dialogue to find a political settlement'.[11] In the hope that the organisations could help to ameliorate the situation, the CSCE Council asked that the crisis be 'studied' by its Committee of Senior Officials in light of a possible 'close cooperation with the efforts of the United Nations', implying that a long-term peace-building mission parallel to the UN's engagement should be considered.[12]

Earlier expressions about the possible benefits of coordinating the work of the two international organisations were made in the 1992 CSCE Helsinki Meeting. Chapter IV, Paragraph 2 of the Helsinki Document declared that the CSCE should be seen as a regional arrangement in accordance with Chapter VIII of the UN Charter. On 28 October 1992, the relationship between the UN and the CSCE was officially recognised by the UN General Assembly, which recommended enhanced coordination.[13] This was followed by an arrangement of 26 May 1993[14] and a General Assembly Resolution on 22 October 1993 that gave the CSCE Observer Status in the General Assembly.[15] This was subsequently confirmed along with proposals for cooperation on November 16 of the same year.[16] The two organisations agreed to work together in matters of observation, assistance to victims of war and advice to government ministries and representatives, and to consult with each other on a regular basis so as to operate in concert when missions are sent to the same countries.

However, how cooperation between the two organisations was to function was not clarified; in the case of their parallel missions in Tajikistan, they gradually assumed a division of labour that appears to have worked well. It is remarkable that the CSCE delegation in Dushanbe recommended that the UN Mission take the lead in conflict resolution and mediation. Even though the CSCE is mandated to engage in conflict-preventive work and crisis management according to its Helsinki Document of July 1992, the CSCE Rapporteur suggested that the UN Mission in Tajikistan would be in a better position to begin the peace process.[17] The CSCE took a secondary role in diplomatic efforts to begin peace-building because not all states which are concerned with the Tajik situation, such as Pakistan and Iran, are members of the CSCE.

Cooperation occurs most visibly in the form of regular meetings in which the UN and CSCE Missions discuss their work with representatives of the Tajik government, as well as with Tajik opposition leaders, the governments of neighbouring states and with Russia. Questions concerning security and humanitarian issues are discussed at regular intervals with the UNHCR, the UN Department of Humanitarian Affairs, the UN Development Programme, the ICRC, and the Tajik government, to coordinate relief work, food aid, and the repatriation of refugees from Afghanistan and Uzbekistan.[18] The combined efforts of the two international organisations have met with positive results regarding refugee repatriation and establishing contacts with all the parties to the conflict, but questions remain regarding an end to sporadic violence, the advancement of the peace process, democratic governance and human rights.

Russia and the CIS: Possible Cooperation for Peace-Building?

The greatest concern for all political leaders, Russian and Central Asian, is to re-establish and maintain military security and political stability in Tajikistan. But such stability has its price; the payment comes in the form of a repressive Soviet-style regime under President Rakhmonov,[19] which restricts sociocultural expression, inhibits economic development and violates fundamental freedoms and human rights to deter political opposition. Tajik and Russian fear of instability and chaos is high: it could be argued that this is a valid fear, given the scenario in Afghanistan and ethnic-religious conflicts elsewhere. Should the worst of intractable conflicts threaten the present military stability, it could happen that Russia decides that its engagement is too costly and abandons Tajikistan, just as it left Afghanistan.

At present, however, a disintegration of the situation is unlikely. Tight control on government and infrastructure by the Tajik regime and the Russian/CIS military provides some degree of stability, enough to see a gradual resumption of social and economic activities. Nevertheless, this situation is not tenable for the long term, as neither Russians nor Tajiks can live in a permanent state of military alertness and fear of unpredictable opposition insurgencies. The present situation is still the kind in which an authoritarian regime limits potential regional and political interests from being expressed for fear of renewed instability. The result is that nationalist and anti-Russian feelings are high among those Tajiks who are excluded from government. What must be avoided at all costs is the alienation of opposition groups from central decision-making, for this will encourage continued militant opposition. The consequence would be that the opposition came to view all forms of Russian involvement as undesirable; this danger is another obstacle to overcome in the peace-building process. Such an attitude towards Russia neglects the possible positive aspects of Moscow's influence, which may favour democratic reforms. As Moscow is primarily interested in long-term political stability, it could be a motor for change if it decides to support some form of pan-Tajik political reconciliation.

While Russian military methods and foreign policy are not necessarily to everyone's liking, we need to ask whether there is an alternative to Moscow's engagement in Tajikistan. No other country or organisation can provide the degree of military stability necessary to prevent another civil war. Even though the political problems which underlie the Tajik conflict are not addressed at the moment, they could hardly be addressed if military stability did not exist to begin with. But Russia also needs a solution to the Tajik conflict and the political deadlock, and it must find a way to end the attacks against its troops. This need represents an opportunity for the international mediators.

To advance the peace-building programme, the UN and the OSCE need to encourage Russia to pursue its Tajikistan policy on four fronts at the same time: first, to assist the Tajik leadership in stabilising the situation in the country through existing methods (for the simple reason that no alternative exists to maintain military stability); second, to promote Tajik cooperation with the other CIS states in establishing a common border protection regime along the old external border of the Soviet Union (to serve primarily Russian and Central Asian strategic interests); third, to apply gradual pressure on the Tajik Communist Party to open its government to moderate opposition leaders who are willing to engage in incremental reforms that do not upset the present modicum of stability; and fourth, to promote dialogue among Tajik politicians under the auspices of the UN and the OSCE, not only to discuss the maintenance of the ceasefire, but also to recommend alternative methods of governance that accommodate the clan-groups to some degree through the introduction of new administrative methods.

In response, the most effective Western policy would be: 'to help stabilise the situation around Russia's borders and to encourage Russia's search for a new, constructive role in both Eurasia and global affairs'.[20] The UN and the OSCE can, in closer cooperation with CIS-related initiatives, find avenues to encourage the institutionalisation of a pan-Tajik programme of conflict management to find suitable methods of governance.[21]

The UN Mission of Observers in Tajikistan[22]

On 21 January 1993, the UN Secretary-General established the UN Mission of Observers in Tajikistan (UNMOT). On April 29, he reported to the Security Council that his Special Envoy had received the following mandate:

a) To obtain agreement on a cease-fire and make recommendations on such international monitoring mechanisms as may be appropriate;
b) To ascertain the positions of all the concerned parties and make good offices available to assist the establishment of a process of negotiations for a political solution;
c) To enlist the help of neighbouring countries and others concerned in achieving the above objectives.[23]

Ambassador Ismat Kittani arrived in Dushanbe on May 14 as the first Special Envoy. He began meeting with government and military authorities, Tajik opposition leaders and politicians in Iran, Pakistan and Saudi Arabia. Most of his interlocutors agreed on the need to establish a ceasefire and promote a political solution to the civil conflict. However, they also believed that the conflict was far from over and that more fighting was imminent, especially on the Afghan border. In later reports, the UN Secretary-General outlines UNMOT's work and Mr Kittani's initial efforts to bring the Tajik parties to agree to negotiations for a political resolution of the conflict.[24]

While all parties, including Russians and Afghans, expressed their support for the UN initiative, diverging objectives also came to light. On the one hand, the opposition leaders whom the UN Special Envoy met in Tajikistan, Russia, Afghanistan and Iran demanded to hold discussions with the Russian authorities under UN auspices first. They believed that without Moscow's influence and pressure for reform, the Kulyab-dominated regime would not come to an agreement with them on a ceasefire or on democratisation of the government. On the other hand, the Tajik regime wanted negotiations only with those opposition leaders 'who accepted the existence and structures of the State of Tajikistan', i.e. who would be willing to work within the present Kulyab-dominated government. Furthermore, the regime refused to meet with those opposition leaders who wanted to establish an Islamic state or with those whom the government charged with crimes against the state.[25] This left little room for negotiations with the opposition, as the government gradually accused most opposition leaders of being criminals.

This was later confirmed by the Head of the CSCE Mission, who reported that the Dushanbe regime wanted to avoid confronting opposition leaders and that its 'General Prosecutor ... issued arrest warrants for most of the key opposition leaders who were planning to participate in the UN-sponsored negotiations with the government'.[26] The first UN-led Inter-Tajik Talks planned for March were not certain to begin, because not only were several of the opposition leaders to be arrested by the Dushanbe regime, but the government's authoritarian policy was supported in Tajikistan by Russia's military division, led by General Pyankov, who viewed the UN mediation efforts unfavourably. At the same time, the opposition leader, Mr Turajonzoda,[27] warned that his coalition would not give up its military activities, rendering the ceasefire discussions still more difficult.

Still, on April 5, 1994, the UN-sponsored talks did begin in Moscow and a working agenda for refugee repatriation as well as for future rounds of Inter-Tajik Talks was agreed upon.[28] The new UN Special Envoy, Ambassador Ramiro Piriz-Ballon, acted as Chairman. The greatest obstacles he faced concerned the negotiations on a ceasefire agreement and on defining concepts, values and objectives for the future shape of a pan-Tajik government that could facilitate national reconciliation. It goes without saying that a peace process which includes conflict resolution and state-building is possible only if the parties concerned are willing to cooperate, to make concessions, to compromise and to develop non-violent methods by which to resolve their differences.

The CSCE Rapporteur Mission: A Conflict of Values?

Following its initial visits to Tajikistan, the CSCE reported on the human and social costs which the Tajik civil war had inflicted upon the Republic and on the obstacles to national reconciliation.[29] Doubts were expressed about the present regime's willingness to contemplate moderation and some form of reconciliation with the country's regional opposition groups. Criticising the Rakhmonov government for the hard-line measures by which it enforced political stability, the second CSCE report touches upon a central dilemma: how far and by what means can military stability be obtained and enforced, and when is the situation 'stable' enough to embark on reforms for political reconciliation with the opposition parties?[30]

This dilemma also came to light in the report of the CSCE Rapporteur Mission. On 22 April 1993, the Chairperson-in-Office

(CIO), Baroness Margaretha Af Ugglas, met with Tajik government ministers, as well as with Mr Rakhmonov, who was then Chairman of the Supreme Soviet.[31] The purpose was to explore Tajikistan's capacity to participate in the work and activities of the CSCE and to introduce its leaders to the principles and values of the Vienna-based organisation. A clash of values concerning political change and militarily-imposed stability became clear in the meeting with Mr Rakhmonov. He told the CIO about his government's efforts to 'normalise the situation' in Tajikistan and made it clear that he had 'no inclination to open up the political process and pursue a policy of reconciliation'.[32] This was confirmed to the Mission's Rapporteur when she attempted in vain to meet representatives of opposition groups. Upon her questioning about the fate of several individuals who were considered political opponents, such as the popular anti-Communist Mayor of Dushanbe, the CIO received only negative responses. The Mission's Rapporteur attempted to impart an under-standing among her interlocutors of the importance of the CSCE's Community of Values and the organisation's expectation that Tajikistan 'move in the right direction on issues related to democracy, the rule of law and human rights'. She mentioned that 'the CSCE community had full understanding of the extremely complicated process of political and economic transition', and that in the short term, it was unrealistic for her organisation to expect that new member states such as Tajikistan could comply with all the provisions of the Helsinki documents and the Charter of Paris.[33]

According to the CIO, all the good will shown by Central Asian politicians towards CSCE principles and values was in direct contradiction with their actions. True, the Tajik government was not justified in its campaigns to eliminate opposition from the political arena as ruthlessly as it did, but one must also appreciate that Central Asian politicians knew no alternative but to rule by authoritarian methods and call for Russia to back them up with military means. These leaders criticised the CSCE for being 'insufficiently focused on problems that are crucial for participating states in Central Asia', meaning that the organisation was promoting idealistic concepts which overlooked local priorities for military and political stability.[34] The CIO quoted one politician as saying that: 'laudable as the values of the CSCE were, they would not be allowed to stand in the way of the determined policies of the states concerned to prevent ethnic hatred, complications in relations with important neighbours or a general slide into chaos and permissiveness'.[35]

Unfortunately, the CSCE report did not question whether the Tajik politicians' misgivings concerning Western concepts of democracy could be regarded as legitimate in light of the volatile situation and the local perceptions of imminent chaos. The Mission's Rapporteur did not give an assessment of why government leaders in Central Asia dealt with opposition as they did and why these same nomenklatura were reluctant or unwilling to adopt political reforms. Did these politicians have a valid argument? With their fear of chaos, and probably with equal fear for their own positions, most Central Asian leaders have not hesitated to persecute opposition leaders in their republics. Members of the Tajik Communist Party are no doubt also aware that in a democratic system they would have to give way to new political institutions and share their decision-making and the resources which they presently control with opposition groups. And given the recent history of the unsuccessful Tajik experiment with the Government of National Reconciliation in early 1992, along with the violence which followed, democracy must seem an undesirable option to most established Tajik politicians.

Nevertheless, the CIO's visit did end with an agreement for the CSCE, namely that the Office for Democratic Institutions and Human Rights (ODIHR)[36] would provide technical legal assistance for the drafting of the new Tajik Constitution, that it would consider bringing election monitors when national elections were to be held, and that seminars on legal aspects of democratic governance could be arranged for Central Asian government staff.[37]

The dilemma between militarily enforced stability and democratic reforms appears to be a deadlock; i.e. the Tajik politicians perceive their authoritarian rule as the only means to prevent political chaos, Islamic fundamentalism and the loss of their own positions. This is the 'reality' which this and later CSCE reports fail to present. This is not necessarily the reality which Tajik opposition leaders saw, but it is the situation which the leading Kulyab politicians defined. With Russian military backing, these same politicians knew that they had the best chance of winning the war against the opposition militia, and that therefore their interpretation of the situation could not be contested. However, this does not mean that the present status quo should be endorsed by the CSCE and the UN, or that nothing can be done to ameliorate the political as well as the social situation in Tajikistan.

It should not be forgotten that Tajikistan was a war-torn country in 1993, that it is poverty-stricken, and that its people long for political and economic change. This was reported by a CSCE Representative several months after the Rapporteur Mission.[38] The conditions of human rights had not improved, the press was tightly controlled, and the imprisonment of even moderate opposition leaders who had not already fled the country was common. There was no attempt to reconcile the differences between the four main regions of the country, i.e. the industrial north and the central region around Dushanbe with either the south (Kurgan-Tyube) or with the eastern Pamir and Badakhshan regions. Tajikistan's economy was in a shambles and the frequency of violent skirmishes on the Afghan border was depressing. UNHCR was at pains to help thousands of refugees to re-enter Tajikistan from temporary settlements in Afghanistan. A report from its office stated that as a consequence of the 'inter-ethnic and inter-clan' violence, approximately 60,000 Tajiks had fled over the border to Afghanistan, and approximately 5,000 had travelled to Uzbekistan. In addition to the cross-border refugees, about 600,000 Tajiks were forced to leave their homes and flee to other areas within the country.[39]

The Long-Term Mission of the CSCE/OSCE

The CSCE Long-Term Mission to Tajikistan was established at the Council Meeting of the CSCE Foreign Ministers in Rome on 1 December 1993.[40] It was provided with the following mandate: 1) maintain contact with and facilitate dialogue and confidence-building between regionalist and political forces in the country; 2) actively promote respect for human rights; 3) promote and monitor adherence to CSCE norms and principles (Community of Values); 4) promote ways and means for the CSCE to assist in the development of legal and democratic political institutions and processes; and 5) keep the CSCE informed about further developments.[41]

The Council members also 'expressed their determination to help stabilise the situation within Tajikistan in close cooperation with the United Nations and to create favourable conditions for progress towards democracy'. The shape which this mandate received was intended to complement the UN Mission mandate and not either contradict or duplicate it. Furthermore, because Tajikistan's participation in the CSCE was uneven and unrepresented in Vienna, the CSCE-ODIHR began to organise seminars and conferences for members of the Tajik government on, for example, norms of international relations, constitutional law, state-building, humanitarian law, crime prevention, and print media management. Since 1994, numerous seminars have been held in various cities in Central Asia, the Caucasus and Eastern Europe, to which Tajik government staff have been invited.

When the CSCE Long-Term Mission began its work on 19 February 1994, it soon found that the Russian armed forces in Tajikistan under General Pyankov appeared far less willing to encourage the Inter-Tajik Talks and peace process than was Moscow's Minister of Foreign Affairs, Andrei Kozyrev. Here, the Head of the Mission, Olivier Roy, hinted at a contradictory divergence between political and military objectives on the part of the Russians.[42] Cooperation with the Russian forces, as well as with the Ministry of Foreign Affairs in Moscow, is thus crucial for the eventual success of the peace-building process; however, the lack of it proved a considerable obstacle in the observance of the ceasefire that was agreed to later in the year.

In its division of labour with the UN Mission, the CSCE concerned itself with conflict resolution only in so far as it could support inter-Tajik dialogue. Its mandate gave the Mission several complementary objectives which, together with the UN, are intended to provide broad peace-building that ranges from facilitating confidence-building methods to promoting the Community of Values of the CSCE. Hence, the Mission has occupied itself with advising the Tajik government on legal matters for the new Constitution and on advancing its Human Dimension principles.[43] It also supports the UNHCR in conferences with government officials from Uzbekistan, Afghanistan and Tajikistan, and its staff have visited refugee camps in Afghanistan to speak to refugees and support UNHCR with repatriation. One problem was that many political opposition members in Afghanistan discouraged the return of Tajik refugees. They did not trust the Tajik government and their demands slowed down the repatriation process; meanwhile, however, the CSCE Mission and UNHCR hoped that the return of the refugees would help stabilise social conditions in the Republic. At the same time, the Tajik regime wished to see refugees return quickly to prevent opposition militia from recruiting them.[44]

A major obstacle for the CSCE in the fulfilment of its mandate appeared as the Tajik Constitution was drafted by the regime in Dushanbe, before being put to a public referendum. Draft proposals were expected to be made available in advance for public discussion and for commentary and recommendations by the CSCE and ODIHR. But the Tajik government did not show any interest in obtaining outside guidance, making real debate about the contents of the Constitution very difficult. The CSCE and the UN discussed the draft Constitution with the Tajik Minister of Foreign Affairs, especially its lack of guarantees of freedom of association, the right to form political parties and the independence of the judiciary.[45] The electoral law had not been improved as recommended by the CSCE, and the Tajik regime's political agenda seemed to jeopardise the UN-sponsored Inter-Tajik Talks. The UN and CSCE Missions feared that a situation akin to a political deadlock would jeopardise efforts at peace-building.

There seemed little doubt that the Dushanbe regime avoided democratising the election regulations and insisted on rapid presidential elections with a referendum on the new Constitution in the fall of 1994 so as to reinforce the position of its leadership. Both the CSCE and UN Missions recommended that the elections be postponed and that more work be done first to advance the peace talks, so that opposition parties could join in more open and fair elections. This required changes to the draft Constitution to allow opposition groups to present their candidates for President – precisely what the Rakhmonov regime wished to avoid. And although the Tajik Minister of Foreign Affairs officially supported the CSCE's work, the Tajik government ignored it – something which it could permit itself to do because Russia had not spoken against the proposed elections.

Why did the CSCE have little success in presenting its case for electoral and constitutional reform? It became clear that the Dushanbe regime avoided any suggestion of democratic reform and saw no benefit for itself in accommodating the opposition parties. Also, Russia's interests in 1994 favoured military stability and regional security above all else. But there is possibly also another reason why the CSCE did not manage to encourage the incumbent Tajik government to take another look at political and constitutional reforms. From the Mission reports, there appears to have been a problem of conflicting perceptions and values about the need for free and fair elections and how far Russia's interest in stability could be challenged. The CSCE insisted on its Community of Values, to which Moscow, as a founding member of the CSCE, had agreed to in theory, but which were chiefly Western principles of liberal democratic governance. The challenge for the CSCE was and still is twofold: first, how to assess the activities of the Tajik government and of the Russian military in the Republic in light of locally perceived needs, political and social insecurity, and the political ambitions of the ruling clans; and second, how to reconcile these Tajik and Russian perceptions with the CSCE's own interests and objectives. The reality is that the Western goals of democratic governance are unattainable given present circumstances, that they threaten the Tajik leaders' positions and are perhaps incomprehensible to them; this may apply to both the clan leaders in government and those in opposition.

What is lacking in the CSCE/OSCE reports is an emphasis on the need to learn – for all the Tajik leaders as well as for the Missions and the organisation itself – to propose methods by which the present situation, with all its political and constitutional shortcomings, can be managed in a non-violent manner. This does not mean that democratic principles and respect for human rights should not be promoted. In fact, promoting the democratisation of the Tajik government and liberalisation of its social and economic structures is essential, but how to go about it is what OSCE staff should discuss in their reports. For only such a discussion will sensitise the OSCE member countries (who fund the Mission) to the obstacles and challenges which the organisation must confront.

The Inter-Tajik Talks and the Ceasefire Agreement

The political deadlock in 1994 was apparent once the two principal opportunities for political reform – the drafting of electoral/constitutional laws and the inter-Tajik negotiations – had become contradictory to each other. The election law excluded all real opposition groups from participating, while at the same time, the UN-sponsored talks and the CSCE's work aimed at recognition and integration of the opposition. The fear expressed by the Missions was that if the negotiations were to produce positive results, they would be cancelled out by the presidential elections and the public referendum on the Constitution (scheduled for September 1994), by the mere fact that opposition groups were excluded from these. And if the talks produced no results and the elections and referendum went ahead as planned, more violent conflicts could be expected to follow.[46] And this is precisely what occurred, but not at the scale of violence which had existed during the civil war.

Still, the first Inter-Tajik Talks of April 1994 in Moscow produced some positive results. While no substantive agreements for a peace settlement were reached, it was the first time that the principal opposition groups came face to face with the Dushanbe regime. Also present at the talks were Russian Foreign Minister Kozyrev and observers from Kazakhstan, Kyrgyzstan, Uzbekistan, Iran, Afghanistan,

Pakistan and the United States. During this conference, which lasted until April 19, a discussion programme for national reconciliation was agreed, to include three clusters:

a) Measures aimed at a political settlement in Tajikistan;
b) Solution of the problem of refugees and internally displaced persons; and
c) Fundamental institutional issues and consolidation of the statehood of Tajikistan.[47]

The greatest difficulties at these first talks concerned the cessation of violence, within the first cluster. Proposals for disbanding and disarming irregular military formations and instituting confidence-building measures fell far short of objectives, and the in-depth discussions on the third cluster could not even be pursued because of the parties' differences in conceptions and values about the Republic's future political shape. Significantly, however, the delegates agreed on an agenda for the next meetings – a considerable step forward given the animosity between the two Tajik parties. Also, an agreement was reached on UN/UNHCR/ICRC assistance for refugees and internally displaced persons.[48]

The second round of UN-sponsored Inter-Tajik Talks was held in Tehran from June 18 to 28, 1994. Uzbekistan did not participate, while a CSCE representative now took part as an observer.[49] This conference produced a tentative concept for a temporary ceasefire, along with a strategy for UN monitoring of the agreement through a Joint Commission office, but dates could not be agreed upon.

At this time, Moscow's support for the talks was still unclear, as it was, like the Uzbek government, highly sceptical of any agreements with Tajik opposition leaders. The Russian Foreign Ministry assumed a similar position to the government in Dushanbe, namely that the opposition leaders at the talks represented some factions only among a large range of forces with diverging objectives which could never come to a concerted agreement at the talks. However, Moscow did support one opposition group, namely the Khojent clan from Leninabad Oblast, which had always supplied the majority of politicians during the Soviet period. Its presidential candidate was Abdumalik Abdullojonov,[50] who had taken over where former President Nabiev had left off.[51] Moscow's policy was thus two-sided. It supported the Kulyab-dominated government with its National Security Committee forces and gave the Khojent élite a helping hand in the hope that Tajikistan's two principal clans would rule the

Republic together as they had done before. In this respect, the UN Special Envoy, Ramiro Piriz-Ballon, reported that he 'failed to win Russian agreement from the Russian Ministry of Foreign Affairs in Moscow to pressure the Tajik government to postpone the Presidential Elections'.[52] He had tried again, like the CSCE Mission, to get the Dushanbe regime to agree to a postponement of both the referendum and the elections, but without result. The divergence of perceptions and priorities became obvious between the Russians, who favoured political stability founded on traditional Soviet-style military rule, and the international organisations' insistence on pan-Tajik democracy in a reformed government.

The only convergence of objectives occurred in regard to the need to end the violence. Thus, the UN Special Envoy was able, with Tehran's cooperation, to facilitate high-level consultations from 12 to 17 September 1994 in Iran's capital, to discuss prospects for a third round of Inter-Tajik Talks, to be held later in Islamabad. On the last day of this conference, an Iranian-brokered ceasefire was finally agreed to and signed by the Tajik government and the opposition.[53] The parties agreed that from October 20 onwards, they would halt all hostilities on the Tajik-Afghan border and within the country until the day of the national referendum on the draft Constitution and the presidential election. (The referendum and the elections were at first scheduled to be on September 25, but were postponed by the Tajik regime to November 6, 1994).

In the UN Secretary-General's report, the impression is given that the Special Envoy was responsible for the Tehran high-level discussions and the ceasefire agreement.[54] True, Mr Piriz-Ballon certainly did most of the organisational foot-work by holding meetings with all the participants and persuading them to attend the meeting. Nevertheless, each party to the conflict also had its individual motivations for attending the meeting and signing the ceasefire. The CSCE report of October 1 sheds some light on the underlying political motivations. Russia had apparently been the principal force behind the ceasefire agreement.[55] With the necessary cooperation from its military command in Tajikistan and from the Uzbek government, Moscow's Ministry of Foreign Affairs had decided already in July to support the Tajik presidential election regardless of its undemocratic nature. In this manner, Moscow could rely on the Dushanbe regime's future cooperation to enforce and maintain military stability.

However, Moscow also supported the Khojent clan's leader in the hope that a 'divide-and-influence' policy would offer more room to manoeuvre should conflicts arise between these two clan-groups. The Russian military command in Tajikistan was apparently 'reluctant to take the government side in [a possible] inter-Tajik armed conflict. In case of confrontation between Kulyabis and Leninabadis, Russian diplomacy might encourage the Leninabad [Khojent] faction'.[56] Since no other candidate besides the Kulyab and Khojent leaders could campaign to win the election, Moscow felt safe with either one as President. Furthermore, such a policy could be interpreted as promoting reconciliation between two important communities without which Tajikistan's government would never be able to manage the Republic's future economic recovery. Thus, as Moscow assisted the Kulyabis with massive military support, it could pressure them to send a high-level representative to the talks in Tehran. And indeed, at the high-level consultations, the ceasefire agreement was signed by Mr A. Dostiev, First Deputy Chairman of the Supreme Soviet of Tajikistan.[57] Previously, at the first two rounds of Inter-Tajik Talks, the government had sent only its Minister of Labour and Employment.[58]

A third round of Inter-Tajik Talks was organised by the UN Special Envoy in conjunction with the Russian, Pakistani, and Iranian governments. This time, it took place in Islamabad from October 20 to November 1, 1994. The CSCE and the Organisation of the Islamic Conference were present as observers. With high-level representatives now attending from all sides, the parties agreed on an extension of the ceasefire until February 6, 1995,[59] and they concurred furthermore on the establishment and implementation of a Joint Commission to monitor the agreement. On November 14, this Commission held its first meeting in Dushanbe with the assistance of UN military observers. The Protocol of this Commission contains the provisions for its operation (composition, mandate, funding, security for its observers and duration).

The Security Council endorsed the Joint Commission, and provided the UNMOT office in Dushanbe with the following mandate to supplement the earlier one for the Secretary-General's Special Envoy:

a) To assist the Joint Commission to monitor the implementation of the Agreement of 17 September 1994 [the ceasefire agreement];
b) To investigate reports of cease-fire violations and to report on them to the United Nations and to the Joint Commission;
c) To provide its good offices as stipulated in the Agreement of 17 September 1994; d) To maintain close contacts with the parties to

the conflict, as well as close liaison with the CSCE Mission in Tajikistan and with the Collective Peace-Keeping Forces of the Commonwealth of Independent States in Tajikistan and with the border forces; e) To provide support for the efforts of the Secretary-General's Special Envoy; and f) To provide political liaison and coordination services, which could facilitate expeditious humanitarian assistance by the international community.[60]

This mandate and the UNMOT are to remain valid only if the Tajik parties abide by the agreement and show their commitment to national reconciliation and the promotion of democracy.

Both the Tajik government and the opposition based in northern Afghanistan pledged to provide logistical and material support (vehicles, drivers, shelter, etc.) for the Joint Commission. In compliance with the suggestions of the ICRC, the two Tajik parties also agreed to exchange equal numbers of prisoners and consented to discuss further releases of prisoners-of-war during future talks.[61] The next round of Inter-Tajik Talks was planned to be held in Moscow in December 1994; however, as the opposition later refused to meet in the capital city of its military enemy, the meeting was postponed until spring 1995.

Obstacles to Pan-Tajik Cooperation

For all the painstaking work by the UN to get the peace talks off the ground again, the political conflict has presented numerous obstacles, which can be summarised as the diverging demands, objectives and values of the Tajik government and the opposition coalition. The Kulyab-led regime did not want to meet opposition leaders at the international level because this implied that it was itself incapable of taking care of domestic affairs, and the opposition demanded to pursue inter-Tajik negotiations at the highest level under UN auspices because in such a forum it hoped to obtain international recognition and legitimacy. And as the Tajik regime argued that the opposition parties and their militias in the south and east of the Republic and in northern Afghanistan are illegal, the latter maintained that the government is illegitimate and must be replaced with a neutral interim body until UN/OSCE-sponsored elections could be organised and a new democratic government established.

Looking ahead, though, one must ask whether the armed groups of the opposition would in fact participate in democratic elections, and be able to end all military activities regardless of the outcome. It appears that not all groups who oppose the neo-Communist regime agree on the future shape of the Tajik state. One might thus also ask whether the opposition could even come to a unified position on its participation in democratic elections. At elections, the opposition coalition would obtain an estimated 25% of the vote if it could present itself as a single party. While its enemy, the Kulyab-dominated government, might lose some power in a future multi-party government, the opposition groups could interpret their share as insufficient to obtain meaningful leverage in national decision-making.[62] Even if the opposition won a large proportion of votes, it is not certain that the coalition could maintain a common agenda on political reforms and avoid breaking into different factions in conflict with each other. An indication that such a scenario might be possible is provided by the frequent ceasefire violations: perhaps not all opposition groups agree with their leaders at the UN-sponsored negotiations.[63]

Another complicating aspect is that no organised opposition armies are mentioned in the OSCE and UN reports. Diverse groups appear to profess loyalties to different ideals, and are commonly referred to as the Islamic, the Islamic-democratic, or simply the opposition coalition. From the first days of the civil war there have been at least four major opposition parties. The lack of specific reporting on these parties' positions implies either that within the CSCE and UN Missions there is a lack of understanding about the composition of these groups, or that the opposition hides its internal differences to pursue a united struggle against the common enemy – the Communist government and the Russian military.

Still, Mr Turajonzoda managed to present the opposition coalition as a solid body when, in early February 1995, he met in New York with Mr Piriz-Ballon, UN staff, and concerned individuals in the US government. The purpose was to solicit international support to pressure Russia, and in particular the Russian border troops under General A. Chechulin, to accept the ceasefire agreement of September 1994 and participate in the next round of talks. The opposition spokesperson expressed the feeling of his compatriots that the West was letting Russia do as it pleased in the near abroad even while all could see that Moscow was not a neutral third party. This Western indifference is more 'inflaming' than the rumours of a fanatical Islamic threat, according to Mr Turajonzoda.[64]

For all the talk about an end to hostilities, however, the conflict on the Tajik-Afghan border increased after the September agreement; the

OSCE, UNHCR and ICRC have reported violence and border skirmishes that are clearly not only the work of Russian forces. Opposition armed groups attacked Russian military camps and border troops at various times and using guerrilla tactics managed to gain control of various territories in the Garm Valley and the Tavildara region.[65] Illegal border crossings are reported every day and violent skirmishes have been reported almost every week along the 1,400-kilometre Tajik-Afghan border; reports tell of drug trafficking, sporadic attacks and land-mine laying in Gorny Badakhshan and the border regions. And fighting is not restricted to border skirmishes and sporadic violence alone: even in Dushanbe presumed terrorists have killed civilians, government staff and Russian residents.[66] While the ceasefire agreement forbids all parties in the conflict to deploy new troops or move troop divisions to new areas for combat, both sides have done so in 1995 and 1996. The Tajik government sent several hundred soldiers with Russian material support to the Kalaikhumb region.[67] In early 1996, fighting resumed at numerous locations, especially in the strategic valley that links eastern Tajikistan with the central region. The opposition took Vanj to the south-east and seized local government offices. By the middle of May 1996, its fighters had managed to destroy government headquarters near Sayod and take control of the single domestic road which links Dushanbe with Tavildara and Gorny Badakhshan. On May 12 Tavildara fell to the opposition and the government suffered heavy losses of soldiers and equipment. During the intense fighting, the UN repeatedly called on both parties to cease hostilities and protested against the opposition's shelling of the town, which was putting civilians at risk. The UNMOT team at Tavildara had to withdraw from its post for its own safety. After the fall of Tavildara, the government reinforced its forces along the road from Dushanbe to Garm and Jirgatal. These troops are under constant attack from opposition fighters, leaving little doubt that the conflict in this region is bound to continue. However, along the border with Afghanistan, the situation has become relatively calm.[68]

Clearly, the parties only partially apply the ceasefire restrictions. The most problematic aspect of the ceasefire agreement is that it was signed by the Tajik government and the opposition, while the Russian border forces did not participate or agree to anything. The opposition accuses the Tajik government of weakness in not bringing the Russian ground forces to support the agreement, since it is incapable of supplying large numbers of troops or transporting them without Russian help.

In the same vein, the Joint Commission established by the Tajik parties to oversee the ceasefire agreement and enforce mutual adherence relies on Russian logistical and material support. While UNMOT chairs the Commission's work and meetings and sends military observers into the field, it has fewer members than initially agreed on by the parties, rendering the office incapable of performing as the UN Secretary-General expected:

According to the Protocol to the Tehran Agreement (see: S/1994/ 1253, Annex), logistic support for the Joint Commission, ... is to be provided on the territory of Tajikistan by the Government of Tajikistan and on the territory of Afghanistan by the Tajik opposition.[69]

The parties did appeal to the Russian-led CIS Collective Peace-Keeping Forces and to the 'international community' for financial and logistic support. However, little has been contributed by the parties themselves or by the international community. The Russians did supply some vehicles and the Tajik government offered accommodation, but 'the members of the Commission lack funds for their basic subsistence and the Commission as a whole has not received the means needed to carry out its tasks'.[70] The Joint Commission has not been able to function properly and by spring 1996 it had failed to investigate most of the ceasefire violations. The work of the UNMOT military observers has been hampered by both government and opposition parties on numerous occasions as well as by local bandits. The observers were once shot at on the Tavildara-Garm road and robbed and detained for more than three hours on another occasion in an area dominated by the opposition. While the opposition denied responsibility – citing the existence of criminal groups – they did promise to provide better protection in the future.[71]

Mr Boutros-Ghali reminded the Tajiks and Russians of their responsibilities and deplored the fact that other UN member states did not contribute to his special trust fund for Tajikistan. This leaves the bitter impression that there exists only a half-hearted commitment to UNMOT, to the Commission, and by extension, to the ceasefire agreement, on the part of the Russian military, the Russian Ministry of Foreign Affairs, the government of Tajikistan, and the international community. How much the opposition is committed to the ceasefire and the Joint Commission must also be questioned as some groups continue their armed struggle from Afghan territory and from strongholds in Badakhshan. Still, Mr Turajonzoda has expressed his desire to see the UN Mission stay in Tajikistan for a long time, in view of the stabilising effect which it provides.[72]

The Elections and Referendum

Shortly before the presidential election and the referendum on the draft Constitution on November 6, 1994, the CSCE and UNMOT decided not to send election monitors. They agreed that constitutional restrictions on the participation of opposition parties were in contradiction with democratic principles.[73] To send international monitors would amount to showing support for the incumbent Tajik government and would alienate moderate opposition politicians. Still, a 'technical mission' was sent by the ODIHR to study the elections in light of future monitoring possibilities.

The elections and referendum were a major challenge: most opposition groups had announced their boycott, the ceasefire was fragile and often breached, and military control of the country's infrastructure remained extensive, which intimidated many voters. The election process was far from free and fair. The problems of the election and referendum were further accentuated by the fact that about one fifth of Tajikistan's population remained in neighbouring countries as refugees, and most opposition groups and their leaders could not and dared not move about freely in Tajikistan. By a margin of 60% of the collected votes, Rakhmonov won the election against his only rival Mr Abdullojonov, who received support mostly from his home region of Khojent in Leninabad Oblast. Their contest was not about political ideologies, as they are both pro-Moscow conservatives; rather, it was for the country's highest office and the resources which it offered.

The scenario of preparations for the parliamentary elections of February 26, 1995 was similar to the above-mentioned period. Again, the Tajik government refused to accept OSCE/ODIHR and UN recommendations for changes to the electoral law, and again the elections went ahead with the Kulyab Communist Party as the predictable winner. Only this party had the necessary administrative and organisational capacity to prepare for the election and it did everything in its power to dominate the administrative machinery. International attempts to pressure the Dushanbe regime to change its position and postpone the elections were to no avail. Last-minute attempts by the two Missions to bring the Tajik regime to comply with Western demands seemed unfitting; here, perceptions of needs and values undoubtedly clashed.

After the parliamentary election, the OSCE reported that the government's Electoral Commission had interfered with the internal affairs of individual parties with the result that the nomination of candidates resembled an appointment process from above. The OSCE Mission also suspected that election manipulations had taken place, such as ballot-box stuffing and box substitution.[74] Three political parties contested 161 districts out of a total of 181; the other twenty districts were contested on March 12. Being composed of officially registered parties allied to varying degrees with President Rakhmonov, the new Parliament is sure to remain as conservative towards political reform as the one before – that is, unless the local balance of power, together with external influence, force change upon the regime.

And change is coming. The two largest political forces, the Kulyab and Khojent clans, have entered a new phase of competition for central power. Although these two groups had allied to capture the country's political centre from the interim administration in 1992, this latest election 'resulted in a deep political conflict between the ruling regime and broad circles of the society and is the main reason for the more and more obvious alienation between the former allies: Kulyab and Leninabad regions'.[75] Furthermore, the Tajik government, composed of the Kulyab and Uzbek clans that won the civil war in 1993, has been weakened by internal factionalism. Severe shortages of food, natural resources, water, electricity and fuel have almost paralysed the Tajik economy and the government has become completely dependent economically and militarily on Russia. One result is that, to maintain control over resources, President Rakhmonov has tried to consolidate power by narrowing the ethnic (Kulyabi) base in his administration. In doing so, he has alienated many former allies with the consequence that Uzbek commanders in the Tajik army rebelled. They staged an uprising and demanded the resignation of several ministers, to which the President conceded.[76] Another consequence of the shortage of resources is that military brigades have clashed violently in their competition for control of remaining state enterprises, such as cotton production. These internal crises indicate that the government cannot operate without a degree of power- and resource-sharing among the leading ethnic and clan groups.

In Pursuit of Pan-Tajik Dialogue

In February 1995, Mr Boutros-Ghali discussed developments on the Inter-Tajik Talks, which had been stalled since October 1994.[77] The opposition claimed that because Russian border troops repeatedly attacked opposition posts and confiscated their military hardware, they refused to meet in Moscow for the fourth round of talks. They demanded that the Russian Federation and its border troops officially recognise the Tehran ceasefire and that the Russian border forces attend the next negotiations. As the fighting on the Afghan border continued and even worsened in the spring of 1995, it was clear that the Russian forces and the Tajik government were refusing to satisfy the opposition's demands and withdraw newly deployed troops from the south and east of the Republic.

After great efforts, the UN Special Envoy managed to organise a fourth round of Inter-Tajik Talks, which was held from May 22 to June 1, 1995 in Almaty, Kazakhstan. It was preceded by two preparatory meetings, in Moscow and in Kabul. This round of the Inter-Tajik Talks was attended by Mr Ubaidulloyev, First Deputy Prime Minister in the Tajik government, and Mr Turajonzoda of the opposition. They were supposed to discuss the third cluster of objectives, the fundamental issues relating to institutions and the consolidation of the statehood of the Republic, as had been agreed to in the first Inter-Tajik meeting almost a year earlier. The government delegation presented issues for negotiation that included an indefinite extension of the ceasefire agreement, the return of all refugees, the creation of political parties, and an amnesty law for opposition leaders. The opposition coalition maintained its demand for the establishment of a transitional period of up to two years during which the government should be managed by an interim administration composed of appointed representatives from all the Republic's regions, along with a joint commission to work out amendments to the Constitution and determine a new structure for a future Tajik government. After such an interim period, elections should be held, in which all regional groups would participate, based on new electoral laws and under the supervision of the international organisations. Also, the opposition demanded that security zones be established under UN military observance, and that prisoners-of-war from the civil war and opposition members in Tajik jails would not be sentenced until thorough investigations had been done in accordance with the practice of the ICRC.

The divergence in demands, and the fact that no agreement was reached concerning the agenda for discussion or the opposition's wish to see the newly deployed Tajik troops withdrawn from Gorny Badakhshan, leaves the impression that the two parties have not managed to agree even on the most basic question: whether the Tajik conflict is over. The government appears to assume that the only issues left for discussion concern the normalisation of social and economic conditions. It argues that no reforms need to be made to its political institutions and that only small remaining issues from the civil war need to be cleared up since the present government and its Constitution were established according to proper procedures. The opposition's demands, however, are clearly formulated to advance a redesigning of the institutions of government, together with a return to the military status quo of September 1994 when the ceasefire was signed in Tehran.

It was clear that the differences in demands and attitudes between the two Tajik parties were too wide for any constructive discussions to take place during the fourth round of Inter-Tajik Talks. Mr Piriz-Ballon thus conducted minor discussions with each side individually so as to reach agreement on smaller issues, and establish an agenda for future discussions, along with confidence-building proposals. In this regard, the opposition stated its readiness to recognise the Presidency of Mr Rakhmonov if the government agreed to the formula proposed by the opposition for the transitional period. However, the Tajik government delegation was not ready to make even small concessions or to include opposition leaders in national decision-making.

A new aspect in the international mediation, however, is that Uzbekistan, Kazakhstan and Kyrgyzstan have taken a more personal role in trying to influence the Tajik government. The Kazakh President proposed a compromise plan which he had previously discussed with the opposition leader. The concern which neighbouring Central Asian governments are showing towards the peace-building process in Tajikistan is encouraging.[78]

Hope for change is expressed in the reports of the two international Missions in Dushanbe. There are still possibilities which should be explored to find methods by which to manage future political changes in Tajikistan. The ruling Communist Party will not be able to maintain its present authority, given that national political and economic policy-making necessitates – at a minimum – cooperation with the Uzbek and Khojent groups. Signs that hope for gradual political stability should not be given up are visible in the continued pronouncements by the Tajik parties that they will pursue negotiations with the other side, in their willingness to meet because they must find solutions to the current deadlock, in the other Central Asian governments' increasing impatience with the Kulyab-led regime in

Dushanbe, and in the Russians' desire to see an end to the violence against their CIS troops. Another sign that the situation can be developed in a positive manner even while sporadic skirmishes are still reported was given by the visit of Prince Aga Khan IV, the spiritual leader of the Ismailis, to Gorny Badakhshan and Dushanbe from May 22 to 29, 1995. He came on the invitation of President Rakhmonov and was enthusiastically met by his followers in the eastern region of the Republic, where he offered to provide food aid and agricultural and economic assistance. This visit led to a decrease in tension and violence on the border, according to the Deputy Director of the Russian border patrol.[79] Other signs of hope are the concern shown by Iran and Pakistan for a resolution of the conflict, new meetings 1995 and 1996 between President Rakhmonov and the opposition to pursue a dialogue to resolve the conflict, and the gradual return of most refugees, which has led the UNHCR to reduce its activities in Tajikistan, letting the OSCE take over the work that remains.

Conclusion: Possibilities for Peace-Building?

The obstacles to peace-building – finding an end to the violence and promoting the democratisation of the state – are enormous, but their existence does not mean that they should not be challenged with creativity and skilful diplomacy. The UN and the OSCE are fulfilling their mandates to the extent that they have been able to; however, their influence has not yet produced the results hoped for. While both organisations have promoted dialogue and facilitated the establishment and maintenance of the ceasefire agreement, their Missions have worked on the assumption that solutions to the conflict can best be found through Western-style democratic and constitutional reforms. These goals must not be lost for the very long term, but on their own they are not necessarily appropriate. For example, none of the states directly concerned with Tajikistan have liberal-democratic governments. Is it therefore correct to expect that Tajikistan should become a democracy through the present peace-building process?

Since the UN mandate gives its Mission the task of enlisting the help of neighbouring countries to search for methods by which a political solution to the conflict can be found, its staff in Tajikistan should, together with the OSCE, encourage neighbouring states to engage in a search for solutions. Such a search has already begun under a different rubric, namely through the information distributed and the meetings and seminars offered on legal issues and democratic state-building by the OSCE-ODIHR and the UN. However, this is a Western-led effort that still excludes Central Asian members from incumbent governments as well as from opposition parties. On their own, the UN and OSCE can only try to influence and instruct the Tajik government through inter-Tajik meetings and seminars. So far, they are fulfilling this mandate. Unfortunately, these two organisations do not have sufficient weight to bring pressure to bear upon the Tajik regime to recognise that it has no alternative but to compromise with its own ambitions and accept gradual political and legal reforms. The same is true for the UN and the OSCE's influence over the opposition parties. Without active cooperation with neighbouring Central Asian states, Russia and the Islamic states to the south, conflict mediation is bound for another deadlock. It remains, then, for the UN Special Envoy to present regionally coordinated proposals to the Tajik regime and use the political clout of the neighbouring states to advance the peace-building process. Attractive incentives, such as negotiated agreements with the opposition parties for an end to militancy, regional development support, or international economic aid and loans, could be added to move the Tajik regime to recognise the long-term advantages it can obtain through compromise and reform.

However, the standards by which the Tajik government's reforms are to be measured and rewarded should not only be Western concepts and values of democratic governance, but modifications of these principles, previously established and agreed to by all concerned neighbouring countries. Such a coordinated effort could then produce more realistic proposals which might fit better into the cultural and sociopolitical conditions in Tajikistan; but it is also necessary to recognise that nationwide political stability will take a long time to be realised. One reason is the violence in Afghanistan. As long as the civil war to the south does not end, it will invariably filter north across the border and influence militant groups in Tajikistan. This implies that peace-building must be promoted even while Russian/CIS forces continue to control the southern border and those regions which are prone to skirmishes. It is thus unrealistic to expect that fundamental reforms can be introduced rapidly; rather, changes in the structure of the central government and the judiciary will have to be introduced gradually so as to maintain the modicum of stability which exists today.

One might now suppose that it was perhaps premature of the OSCE and the UN to insist on 'free and fair' elections in 1994 and

1995. Given the Tajik and Russian perception that chaos threatened if they loosened their grip on the Republic, political reforms are not going to be accepted merely because they are called for. The question is not so much how a democracy can be established, but how reforms can be made palatable to the ruling regime so that it will want to introduce them. Rapid democratisation, promoted by outsiders (opposition groups as well as international mediators) who are not intimately familiar with the culture and society in the region and with the internal workings of the Tajik government, raises a different sort of worry: once free and fair elections are held at some time in the future, and all Tajik parties win some seats in a liberal, multi-party assembly or parliament, will these groups be willing and able to cooperate with each other? Given the structure of clan affiliations in Tajikistan, trust must first be established among these groups that all disputes can be resolved without resorting to violence. Then, under the auspices of the UN and the OSCE, institutionalised debate and bargaining may lead to meaningful pan-Tajik dialogue and to building peace.

Notes

1 The author wishes to thank Dr Jean A. Laponce and Dr Ivan L. Head of the University of British Columbia for their inspiration and support.
2 The OSCE was established in 1975 by 35 participating states in Helsinki, under the name of Conference on Security and Cooperation in Europe (CSCE). It became a multilateral forum for dialogue and negotiation between East and West and managed to establish confidence-building measures and reduce Cold War tensions between the military establishments in eastern and western Europe. Since 1990, the CSCE has been enlarged to include not only a forum for dialogue and negotiations, but also operational structures to assist in international and internal conflict resolution and the establishment of democratic institutions.
3 At the Budapest Conference of December 1994, the CSCE was renamed OSCE; in this essay, the old name is used when the period before December 1994 is referred to.
4 UN General Assembly Resolution A/RES/46/1992, 2 March 1992. The CSCE Committee of Senior Officials (the central operating body in Vienna) admitted Tajikistan on January 30, 1992, after its government had complied with the following condition: Tajikistan, along with all new republics of the former Soviet Union, had to sign a letter accepting all CSCE principles and commitments, and accept at least one CSCE Rapporteur Mission to investigate its capacity to abide by the CSCE Community of Values.
5 *Report of the CSCE Rapporteur Mission to Turkmenistan, Uzbekistan and Tajikistan*, CSCE Communication No. 127, Prague, 7 April 1992.

6 *Ibid.*, paragraph 7.
7 UN Security Council 3131st Session, 30 October 1992.
8 'Letter Dated 29 October 1992 from the Secretary-General addressed to the President of the Security Council', Security Council, S/24739, 29 October 1992. The UN Mission visited Tajikistan in November 1992, accompanied by staff from the UN Department of Humanitarian Affairs, to assess the humanitarian situation.
9 *Human Rights situation in Tajikistan*, letter from Ambassador Kornblum dated 21 December 1992, CSCE Communication No. 426, Prague, 22 December 1992.
10 R. Alimov, *Letter of the Foreign Minister of Tajikistan on Human Rights Situation in Tajikistan*, addressed to the CIO, Vienna, 30 December 1992, reproduced in CSCE Communication No. 14, Prague, 15 January 1993. The CSCE Chairperson-in-office (CIO) is vested with overall responsibility for executive action. He/she is the Foreign Minister of the member state which last arranged the Ministerial Council Sessions.
11 *Third Meeting of the Council: Summary of Conclusions. 14–15 December 1992*, CSCE, Stockholm, 1992, p. 12.
12 *Ibid.* The text of the Third Meeting of the CSCE Council was forwarded to the UN General Assembly and Security Council on 18 December 1992. See A/47/808 and S/24986.
13 'Cooperation between the United Nations and the Conference on Security and Cooperation in Europe', UN GA Res. A/47/10, 28 October 1992.
14 Romain Yakemtchouk, 'The New Security Data for Europe and the Role of the International Organizations', *Studia Diplomatica*, Vol. 47, no. 4, 1994, p. 19.
15 UN GA Res. A/RES/48/2, 22 October 1993.
16 56th Plenary Session, 16 November 1993; *Coopération entre l'Organisation des Nations Unies et la Conférence sur la sécurité et la coopération en Europe*, UN GA Res. A/RES/48/19, 24 November 1993. See also Walter Kemp, 'The OSCE and the UN: A Closer Relationship', *Helsinki Monitor*, Vol. 6, no. 1, 1995, pp. 22–31.
17 'Mission Report to the Republic of Tajikistan', *Report of the Personal Representative of the Chairman-in-Office to the Republic of Tajikistan*, CSCE Communication No. 126, written by Ambassador Ali Hikmet Alp, 25 April 1993, p. 5. See also 'Letter Dated 26 April 1993 from the UN Secretary General Addressed to the President of the Security Council', Security Council, S/25697, 29 April 1993.
18 OSCE Mission to Tajikistan, 'Activity Report No. 1/95', 1–15 January 1995, section 1; UN Department of Humanitarian Affairs, Geneva, 'Humanitarian Assistance in Complex Emergencies: Tajikistan' in *DHA News*, Geneva, September-December 1994, pp. 31–2; UNHCR, *Report on Tajikistan: January 1993-March 1996*, Geneva, May 1996.
19 Imomali Rakhmonov rose to the post of Supreme Soviet Chairman (and head of state) on November 19, 1992, after having been helped into government positions by his mentor, the Kulyabi military commander Sangak Safarov. Rakhmonov greatly benefitted from Safarov's irregular combatants during the civil war, as they pursued some of the fiercest battles against Pamiri civilians and militants. In return, Rakhmonov

integrated these mostly Kulyabi armed men into the new Tajik National Security Committee forces and prevented the inclusion of other clan-groups such as the Khojent clan. Rakhmonov was elected President of Tajikistan on 6 November 1994.

20 Maxim Shashenkov, 'Russian Peacekeeping in the "Near Abroad"', *Survival*, Vol. 36, no. 3, Autumn 1994, p. 63.

21 For discussions on Russian policies towards the near abroad with possibilities for conflict resolution, see, in *Survival*, Vol. 36, no. 3, Autumn 1994, the articles by John W. R. Lepingwell, 'The Russian Military and Security Policy in the "Near Abroad"' (pp. 70–92) and Shashenkov, *op. cit.* (pp. 46–69). See also Pavel K. Baev, 'Russia's Experiments and Experience in Conflict Management and Peacekeeping', in *International Peacekeeping*, Vol. 1, no. 3, Autumn 1994, pp. 245–60.

22 Other UN agencies, such as the UNHCR, Food and Agriculture Organisation (FAO), World Food Programme (WFP) and Department of Humanitarian Affairs (DHA), also established Missions in that same year and in 1994. Discussions are ongoing with UNDP, UNV and non-governmental organisations for a gradual transfer of management of the aid and development projects in 1996, as the emergency comes to an end.

23 'Letter Dated 26 April 1993 from the Secretary-General Addressed to the President of the Security Council', Security Council, S/25697, 29 April 1993. See also Security Council, S/RES/968, 16 December 1994, which includes the extended mandate for UNMOT (discussed below in this text).

24 Security Council, S/26311, 16 August 1993; S/26743, 14 November 1993; and S/26744, 15 November 1993.

25 Security Council, S/26744, 15 November 1993, p. 2.

26 CSCE Mission to Tajikistan, 'Update report: Tadjikistan Briefing Paper',written by Olivier Roy, 1 March 1994.

27 Ali Akbar Turajonzoda is the leader of the Islamic-democratic bloc. He was educated in the Soviet Union's official Islamic college in Tashkent and attended the University of Jordan in Amman. He was appointed *Kazi* ('official supreme religious authority') in Tajikistan and became known in politics when he appealed for reconciliation following the riots in Dushanbe in 1990. He was elected to the Supreme Soviet in the same year and campaigned to incorporate Islamic principles into the Republic's legal code. Strong Communist opposition to his ideas pushed him to side with the democratic-Islamic coalition, of which he became a leader. Living in exile today, he is regarded as an influential politician who represents a moderate Islamic voice for democratic reforms. (Keith Martin, 'Tajikistan: Civil War Without End?', *RFE/RL Research Report*, Vol. 2, no. 33, 1993, p. 21.)

28 Security Council, S/1994/542, 5 May 1994; CSCE Mission to Tajikistan, 'Biweekly Activity Report, April 13, 1994', written by Daria Fane, Acting Head of Mission.

29 'Mission Report to the Republic of Tajikistan', *Report of the Personal Representative of the Chairman-in-Office to the Republic of Tajikistan*, CSCE Communication No. 126, Prague, 25 April 1993.

30 *Ibid.*, pp. 4 and 9.

31 *Report by the Chairman-in-Office on her visit to the participating States of Central Asia*, CSCE Communication No. 159, Prague, 25 May 1993, p. 1. Baroness Margaretha Af Ugglas, from Sweden, was CIO in 1993.

32 *Ibid.*, p. 5.

33 *Ibid.*, p. 2.

34 *Ibid.*, p. 4.

35 *Ibid.*, p. 4.

36 ODIHR, based in Warsaw, is the OSCE institution responsible for furthering human rights, democracy, and the rule of law, as these elements of governance are seen as the building blocks of political stability. It organises conferences and seminars for government staff on the establishment of democratic institutions, drafting legal texts, and organising elections and their monitoring.

37 *Report by the Chairperson-in-Office on her visit to the participating States of Central Asia*, CSCE Communication No. 159, Prague, 25 May 1993, p. 8.

38 'CSCE Mission of October 1993', *Final Report of the CSCE Representative in Tajikistan*, CSCE Communication No. 293, Prague, 11 November, 1993. This was the first report from Olivier Roy.

39 UNHCR Regional Office, 'Protection Report', 1993; answer to question 1.1.1, REFPRO, UNHCR/CDR Databases. By the end of 1995, over 43,000 of the estimated 60,000 refugees in Afghanistan had been repatriated and approximately 98% of the 600,000 internally displaced people reintegrated into the areas of return. See further: UNHCR, *Report on Tajikistan: January 1993 March 1996*, Geneva, May 1996.

40 The OSCE presently conducts eleven Missions and Assistance Offices, in Chechnya, Croatia (Zagreb), Estonia, the Former Yugoslav Republic of Macedonia (Skopje), Georgia (Tbilisi), Latvia, Moldova, Sarajevo, Tajikistan, Ukraine and Uzbekistan (Tashkent).

41 The duration of this CSCE Long-Term Mission was initially foreseen as from February 1994 to the end of the first budget (June 30, 1994), and was subsequently prolonged.

42 CSCE Mission to Tajikistan, 'Update report: Tadjikistan Briefing Paper', 1 March 1994, p. 2.

43 All the documents which represent the Community of Values of the OSCE are founded on the Ten Principles which guide relations between states as enumerated in the 1975 CSCE Helsinki Final Act. They represent the outer limits of consensus on fundamental issues such as state sovereignty, refraining from the use of force, and the peaceful settlement of disputes. The principles which concern human rights, fundamental freedoms and self-determination are known as the 'Human Dimension'; they are seen as the basis for political reform in non-democratic countries. See Commission on Security and Cooperation in Europe, 'Human Rights and Democratization in the newly independent States of the former Soviet Union', compiled by the Staff of the Commission on Security and Cooperation in Europe, Washington, D. C., January 1993.

44 CSCE Mission to Tajikistan, 'Bi-weekly Activity Report, 13 April 1994', p. 3.

45 'Letter of the Chairman of the P. C. to the Minister of Foreign Affairs of Tajikistan, Vienna, 20 July 1994', Doc. 529, written by Mario Sica of the Italian Delegation, 18 July 1994, pp. 1–2.
46 CSCE Mission to Tajikistan, 'Political Report', Doc. 866/94, written by Olivier Roy, Vienna, 6 October 1994, p. 2.
47 Security Council, S/1994/542, 5 May 1994.
48 *Ibid.*
49 Security Council, S/1994/716, 16 June 1994; and S/1994/893, 28 July 1994.
50 Abdumalik Abdullojonov became Acting Prime Minister in September 1992 and was formally elected to the post by the Supreme Soviet in late November 1992. He is a member of the Uzbek-speaking Khojent clan and had achieved political prominence after he supported Nabiev's presidential elections in 1991. Leading the Supreme Soviet from its temporary home in Khojent, he had difficulty in organising military security measures in the south and in establishing economic recovery programmes. He came into increasing conflict with the new Kulyabi political leader Imomali Rakhmonov. As a result of the Khojent-Kulyab conflict, which is as traditional in Tajik politics as the Republic is old, Abdullojonov later 'took' the post of Tajik Ambassador in Moscow, which he held until 1994 when he returned as a presidential candidate.
51 CSCE Mission to Tajikistan, 'Special Report: Moscow Meetings on U.N. sponsored Negotiations', by Olivier Roy, Vienna, 10 August 1994, p. 2, paragraphs 3 and 4.
52 *Ibid.*, p. 1.
53 'Letter dated 21 September 1994 from the Permanent Representative of the Islamic Republic of Iran to the United Nations, addressed to the Secretary General', Security Council, S/1994/1080, 21 September 1994. See also S/PRST/1994/56, 22 September 1994; S/1994/1091, 23 September 1994; and S/1994/1102, 27 September 1994.
54 Security Council, S/1994/1102, 27 September 1994.
55 CSCE Mission to Tajikistan, 'Political Report', Doc. 866/94, Vienna, 6 October 1994, p. 4.
56 CSCE Mission to Tajikistan, 'Special Report: Moscow Meetings on U.N. sponsored Negotiations', Vienna, 10 August 1994, p. 2.
57 See 'Letter dated 21 September 1994 from the Permanent Representative of the Islamic Republic of Iran to the United Nations, addressed to the Secretary General', Security Council, S/1994/1080, 21 September 1994; Security Council, S/PRST/1994/56, 22 September 1994; and S/1994/1102, 27 September 1994.
58 See Security Council, S/1994/542, 5 May 1994; and S/1994/893, 28 July 1994.
59 At these Inter-Tajik Talks, the armed opposition was represented by a small delegation that included the principal negotiator for the opposition, First Vice-President of the Islamic Revival Party, Mr Turajonzoda, and the coalition's Acting Head, Mr O. Latifi. The delegation of the Tajik government was again led by Mr A. Dostiev.
60 Security Council, S/RES/968, 16 December 1994.
61 Security Council, S/1994/1363, 30 November 1994.

62 CSCE Mission to Tajikistan, 'Political Report', Doc. 866/94, Vienna, 6 October 1994, p. 4.

63 See, for example, OSCE Mission to Tajikistan, 'Bi-weekly Activity Report, December 2–16, 1994', written by Janusz Wawrzyniuk, Mission Member, Vienna, 20 December 1994, p. 3. See also OSCE Mission to Tajikistan, 'Activity Report No. 7/95', 1–15 April 1995; and 'Activity Report No. 9/95', 1–15 May 1995.

64 OSCE Mission to Tajikistan, 'Activity Report No. 3/95', 1–14 February 1995, p. 3.

65 CSCE Mission to Tajikistan, 'Political Report', Doc. 866/94, Vienna, 6 October 1994, p. 4.

66 OSCE Mission to Tajikistan, 'Activity Report No.8/95', 16–30 April 1995; and 'Activity Report No. 9/95', 1–15 May 1994.

67 OSCE Mission to Tajikistan, 'Report on the visit of Director Kubis to Tajikistan', Vienna, 23 May 1995; and 'Activity Report No. 9/95', 1–15 May 1995.

68 Security Council, S/1996/212, 22 March 1996; S/1996/412, 7 June 1996.

69 Security Council, S/1995/105, 4 February 1995, p. 2.

70 *Ibid.*

71 Security Council, S/1996/412, 7 June 1996, p. 4 and Annex.

72 *Ibid.*, Annex II; Security Council, S/1996/212, 22 March 1996, Annex I.

73 CSCE Mission to Tajikistan, 'Spot Report: Meeting with Minister of Foreign Affairs Alimov', Doc. 905/94, Vienna, 14 October 1994.

74 OSCE Mission to Tajikistan, 'Report on Parliamentary Elections and Activities of the Mission', Doc. 355/95, Vienna, 2 March 1995, p. 4.

75 *Ibid.*, p. 3.

76 UNHCR, *Report on Tajikistan: January 1993-March 1996*, Geneva, May 1996, pp. 14–15.

77 Security Council, S/1995/105, 4 February 1995.

78 OSCE Mission to Tajikistan, 'Report on Inter-Tajik Talks', Vienna, 7 June 1995.

79 OSCE Mission to Tajikistan, 'Activity Report No.10/95', 16–31 May 1995.

Supplementary Bibliography

(Documents and works not cited in footnotes.)

I DOCUMENTS

AMNESTY INTERNATIONAL. AI Index: EUR 01/01/94, January 1993.
—— AI Index: IOR 52/03/93, November 1993. 'Statements to the CSCE Human Dimension Implementation Meeting, Warsaw, 27 September – 15 October, 1993'.
—— AI Index: EUR 01/02/94, June 1994.
CSCE/OSCE. Fourth Meeting of the Council, 'Decision of the Rome Council Meeting', Rome, December 1, 1993.
—— CSCE Mission to Tajikistan, 'Spot Report: Meetings with Foreign Minister Alimov', from Olivier Roy, Head of Mission, Vienna, 1 August 1994.

—— CSCE Mission to Tajikistan, 'Bi-weekly Report', by Olivier Roy, Vienna, 15 August 1994.

—— CSCE Permanent Committee, 'Journal No. 36', 6 October 1994.

—— CSCE Mission to Tajikistan, 'Spot Report: Appeal to UN to send Elections Observers', Doc. 903/94, Vienna, 14 October 1994.

—— CSCE Mission to Tajikistan, 'Spot Report: Head of State Rakhmonov states that CSCE will send observers', Doc. 904/94, by Friederike Adlung, Acting Head of Mission, Vienna, 14 October 1994.

—— The Secretary General, *CSCE Annual Report, 1994*, Vienna, 14 November 1994.

—— CSCE Mission to Tajikistan, 'Bi-weekly Activity Report, November 21 – December 1, 1994', from Gantcho Gantchev, Acting Head of Mission, 2 December 1994.

—— OSCE Mission to Tajikistan, 'XXI Session of the Supreme Council', Doc. 1139/94, written by Janusz Wawrzyniuk, Mission Member, on December 2, 1994, Vienna, 6 December 1994.

—— OSCE Mission to Tajikistan, 'Protection/Human Rights Issues', by Gantcho Gantchev, Acting Head of Mission, 11 December 1994.

—— OSCE Mission to Tajikistan, 15 December 1994, by Gantcho Gantchev, Acting Head-of-Mission.

—— OSCE Permanent Council, 'Journal No. 3', 12 January 1995.

—— OSCE Mission to Tajikistan, 'Activity Report No. 4/95', 15–28 February 1995.

—— OSCE Mission to Tajikistan, 'Parliamentary elections – report on the press-conference', 28 February 1995.

—— OSCE Mission to Tajikistan, 'Parliamentary Elections: alleged violation reports', Doc. 376/95, by Janusz Wawrzyniuk, Acting Head of Mission, Vienna, 7 March 1995.

—— OSCE Mission to Tajikistan, 'Activity Report No. 6/95', 16–31 March 1995.

—— OSCE Mission to Tajikistan, 'Cease-Fire extension', by Janusz Wawrzyniuk, Mission Member, 27 April 1995.

THE INTERNATIONAL FEDERATION OF RED CROSS AND RED CRESCENT SOCIETIES. *Emergency Appeal 1994: Refugees, Relief and Rehabilitation. Federation Operations Worldwide.*

INTERNATIONAL MONETARY FUND. *Tajikistan*, by Hans Gerhard and Kenneth Warwick, ed. Margaret Karsten, International Monetary Fund Publication Services, Washington, D. C., May 1992.

PERMANENT MISSION OF THE RUSSIAN FEDERATION. *Press Bulletin*, No. 301 (2736), Geneva, 8 November 1994.

UNITED NATIONS. Security Council, S/1994/1118, 29 September 1994.

—— Security Council, S/1994/1178, 13 October 1994.

—— Security Council, S/1994/1236, 2 November 1994. 'Letter dated 31 October 1994 from the Permanent Representative of the Russian Federation to the United Nations, addressed to the Secretary-General'.

UNITED STATES DEPARTMENT OF JUSTICE. 'Tajikistan', *Alert Series: Political Conditions in the Post-Soviet Era* [AL/TJK/93.001], INS Resource Information Centre, Washington, D. C., September 1993, pp. 1–25.

II WORKS

ALLISON, Roy. *Peacekeeping in the Soviet successor states*, Chaillot Paper No. 18, Institute for Security Studies, Western European Union, Paris, November 1994.

BARYLSKI, Robert V. 'The Russian Federation and Eurasia's Islamic Crescent', *Europe-Asia Studies*, Vol. 46, no. 2, 1994, pp. 389–416.

BELOKRENITSKY, Vyacheslav Ya. 'Russia and Greater Central Asia', *Asian Survey*, Vol. 34, no. 12, 1994, pp. 1093–108.

BLOOMFIELD, Lincoln P. 'The Premature Burial of Global Law and Order: Looking beyond the Three Cases from Hell', *The Washington Quarterly*, Vol. 17, no. 3, 1994, pp. 145–61.

BORCKE, Astrid von. 'Der tadschikische BÜrgerkrieg: Lokale Tragdie oder geopolitische Herausforderung?', *Berichte des Bundesinstituts fÜr ostwissenschaftliche und internationale Studien*, no. 19, Kln, 1 March 1995.

CARLSSON, Staffan. *The Challenge of Preventive Diplomacy: The experience of the CSCE*, Editorial Office, Norstedts Tryckeri AB, Ministry of Foreign Affairs, Stockholm, 1994.

CROW, Susanne. 'Russia Promotes the CIS as an International Organisation', *RFE/RL Research Report*, Vol. 3, no. 11, 18 March 1994, pp. 33–8.

JAHANGIRI, Guissou. 'Anatomie d'une crise: le poids des tensions entre regions au Tadjikistan', *Cahiers d'études sur la Méditerranée orientale et le monde turco-iranien (CEMOTI)*, no. 18, July-December 1994, pp. 37–70.

LABER, Jeri. 'Appendix: Correspondence Related to Tajikistan', 18 December 1992, in Human Rights Watch/Helsinki Watch, *Human Rights in Tajikistan*, Memorial, December 1993.

LUCAS, Michael R. 'Russia and the Commonwealth of Independent States: The Role of the CSCE', *Helsinki Monitor*, Vol. 5, no. 4, 1994, pp. 5–37.

MALIK, Iftikhar H. 'Pakistan's National Security and Regional Issues: Politics of Mutualities with the Muslim World', *Asian Survey*, Vol. 34, no. 12, 1994, pp. 1077–92.

MARTIN, Keith. 'China and Central Asia: Between Seduction and Suspicion', *RFE/RL Research Report*, Vol. 3, no. 25, 24 June 1994, pp. 26–36.

ROY, Olivier. 'L'Asie centrale et le national-soviétisme', *Cahiers internationaux de Sociologie*, Vol. 96, 1994, pp. 177–89.

SHERR, James. 'Russia: Geopolitics and Crime', *The World Today*, Vol. 51, no. 2, February 1995, pp. 32–6.

SNYDER, Jed C. 'Russian Security Interests on the Southern Periphery', *Jane's Intelligence Review*, December 1994.

THÖNI, Julien. *The Tajik Conflict: The Dialectic Between Internal Fragmentation and External Vulnerability, 1991–1994*, Occasional Paper No. 3, Programme for Strategic and International Security Studies (PSIS), Geneva, 1994.

VOGEL, Heinrich. 'Partnership with Russia: some lessons from Chechnya', *The World Today*, Vol. 51, no. 4, April 1995, pp. 64–7.

WALKER, Peter. 'Mission to the CIS', *International Federation of Red Cross and Red Crescent Societies*, Geneva, March 1992.

HUMANITARIAN DIMENSION

Chapter 12

The International Committee of the Red Cross and the Conflict in Tajikistan

Jean-Marc Bornet

For 130 years, ICRC delegates have been bringing aid to victims of war on every continent. The suffering of prisoners, of civilians caught up in fighting, of starving people, and of soldiers mutilated by weapons which are sometimes prohibited are sadly familiar to them. The ICRC's philosophy of humanitarian aid, as well as its mechanisms, have been tried and tested. Yet Tajikistan, tucked away in the heart of Central Asia, was and still is a challenge for the ICRC, as indeed are all the other States that have emerged from the former Soviet Union. It is a recent challenge, since the organization has only been active there since 1992; a challenge partly met by the humanitarian activities which it has been possible to carry out for the victims of the conflict and its aftermath; and, finally, a challenge for the future, in view of the tasks that the ICRC hopes to be able to undertake.

The ICRC, a pioneering institution in Tajikistan

In March 1992, the ICRC carried out its first mission to Tajikistan, to encourage the country to adopt the Geneva Conventions of 1949 and their Additional Protocols of 1977, the two pillars of the edifice of contemporary international humanitarian law.

In September 1992, when disturbances in the region of Kurgan-Tyube in southern Tajikistan intensified, the ICRC, deeply concerned by the turn of events, established contact with the parties involved to inform them of its specific characteristics, particularly its neutrality, and the services it could provide. That month, Rakhmon Nabiev was removed from power by opposition forces.

Subsequently the clashes redoubled in intensity. Wishing to strengthen its contacts in a country where it was practically unknown,

219

the ICRC participated, as an observer, in the meeting of the Supreme Soviet held in Khojent in November 1992, during the course of which Imomali Rakhmonov took over as Head of State.

At that time, the ICRC had a permanent though still limited presence in the country, linked to its regional delegation in Tashkent. In January 1993, it opened a delegation in Dushanbe. Until February of that year, the ICRC was the only humanitarian organization in Tajikistan, soon to be joined by the UNHCR, Mdecins sans frontires (MSF) -Belgium and MSF-Netherlands.

In July 1993, after several missions in the region, the ICRC established a temporary office in Khorog in Gorny Badakhshan, which primarily allowed it to help victims of the skirmishes which took place in August 1993. At the time, it was the only humanitarian organization able to cross the line separating government forces from the defence forces of Gorny Badakhshan.

A case of application of humanitarian law

It should be remembered that the ICRC was at the origins of international humanitarian law, which contains rules relating to the conduct of hostilities and the protection of people who are not, or no longer, participating in the hostilities (the wounded, the shipwrecked, prisoners of war, the civilian population). In fact, as early as 1863 Henry Dunant, the founder of the Red Cross, had called not only for the creation of relief societies which could assist the medical services of armed forces on the battlefield – the forerunners of the National Red Cross and Red Crescent Societies – but also for 'some international principle, sanctioned by a Convention inviolate in character' which would provide protection for war victims and the medical personnel attending them.

The ICRC has contributed to the development and interpretation of this law over the years. The international community has also entrusted the ICRC with the responsibility of ensuring that the law is observed. On the international level the ICRC is often faced with the sensitive task of categorizing the situations in the countries where it operates, in order to determine which part of the law applies.

On 13 January 1993, Tajikistan indicated by a declaration of succession that it considered itself bound by the Geneva Conventions of 1949 and the Additional Protocols of 1977. The applicability of Article 3 (which is common to the four Conventions) to the conflict which was raging in Tajikistan was thus confirmed. This provision has the merit of containing the most fundamental rules of humanity and provides the legal basis for the activities of the ICRC or any other impartial humanitarian body, since it recognizes their right to offer their services to the parties in conflict.

At the heart of the ICRC's mandate: the protection of those who are not, or are no longer, involved in the hostilities

From the first hours of the conflict, the ICRC was concerned by the plight of those who had laid down their arms and were in the hands of the adverse party, and of civilians living in a hostile environment. However, it was chiefly its food and medical assistance activities which made the organization known and won it the trust of the authorities and the population. This assistance responded to immediate needs, but it also allowed the ICRC, through its contacts with the population in zones of conflict, to identify other humanitarian problems and to alert the regional authorities, or to contact the authoritites in Dushanbe.

It should be remembered that all the ICRC's activities are closely interlinked. When the ICRC, while distributing family parcels to displaced persons, hears allegations of summary executions, ill-treatment or harassment, it tries to obtain the agreement of the authorities to put an end to such abuses. When it visits detainees, it can bring them supplies, if it observes needs which cannot be met by the detaining authorities. The aid which the ICRC brings to an individual is comprehensive, because it is not enough merely to feed someone in order to restore his dignity, or to protect him from ill-treatment if he is dying of hunger or tormented with worry about the fate of his family.

For example, in Tajikistan the ICRC has been particularly concerned about the plight of people from the Garm Valley and the Pamir Mountains who went back more or less of their own accord to their villages in southern Tajikistan. When displaced persons were returned to their homes on a massive scale without there being appropriate structures to receive them, as was the case in March 1993 for 8,000 people brought back to Kabodyon, the ICRC approached the authorities asking them to take action. It also asked them to find a solution for homeless families and to find out what had happened to people reported missing by their relatives. These are only a few examples of a basic responsibility of the ICRC, which has often managed to persuade the civilian and military authorities to elucidate certain cases or take the necessary measures.

The neutrality which is not only proclaimed but practised by ICRC delegates has played a decisive role in this regard and allowed the ICRC to carry out its humanitarian activities on both sides of the conflict. Its independence, as a private Swiss association in no way linked to any government, and its impartiality towards victims have often helped it to overcome the resistance that always arises when it comes to authorizing a humanitarian operation in favour of an adversary.

Unfortunately, at the time of writing, the ICRC has not yet obtained general access, in accordance with its customary working procedures, to people arrested as a result of the events in Tajikistan. These working procedures are the same in all countries where the ICRC operates: it must have access to all detainees covered by its mandate and be allowed to register them; it must be authorized to visit all places of detention and repeat its visits; and finally it must be allowed to talk to the prisoners in private.

In Tajikistan, ever since January 1993 the delegation has been asking the Ministry of the Interior (MVD) and the Committee of National Security (KNB) for permission to visit detainees arrested in connection with the conflict. The first visits had to be interrupted because of an obstacle arising from national legislation: the ICRC could have general access to convicted detainees, but not to those in preventive detention, for whom individual authorization had to be sought from the examining magistrate.

The ICRC is currently discussing the matter with the highest State authorities. It hopes that a solution can be found and that it will be permitted to visit detainees in Tajikistan, as it does in a great many other countries with similar legislation: the Russian Federation (detainees held in connection with the conflict between the Ossetians and the Ingush and with the clashes at the White House in October 1993), Armenia and Azerbaijan (the Nagorny Karabakh conflict), Georgia (the Abkhaz conflict), Moldova, etc.

Such visits have a purely humanitarian goal, that is, to monitor the treatment and living conditions of prisoners. They do not confer any legal status whatsoever on the arrested persons. In fact, because of the specific nature of the ICRC, whose long-standing activities in the field of detention have been recognized by the international community for many years, the Supreme Soviet should be able to make an exception to the legislation. For the record, the first ICRC visits to security detainees date back to 1917, in Hungary.

The ICRC intends to pursue its contacts in Dushanbe, in order to emphasize the value of an objective assessment, by an outside entity well-known for its independence, of the situation of people arrested in connection with the conflict. This form of support provided to the authorities would be offered, as usual, with the greatest discretion. Indeed, the ICRC's aim is not to give a favourable or unfavourable opinion of the detaining authorities' behaviour, but to help them assume their responsibilities in a sensitive area.

Emergency and development

In present-day conflicts the civilian population is always the worst affected, because of the indiscriminate character of the fighting and the use of sophisticated weaponry. The ICRC therefore provides emergency food and medical aid intended to meet the most pressing needs of civilians not involved in the hostilities. This aid is temporary, to allow people affected by the conflict to get through a difficult time. Such programmes are aimed in particular at people living in an environment that makes their safety precarious.

In Tajikistan, the ICRC has provided significant amounts of relief supplies for displaced persons, particularly between December 1992 and May 1993, in the Garm Valley, in Dushanbe and in the south of the country. It has also supplied food to the community kitchen of a transit centre for displaced persons in Dushanbe. Over this period, ICRC aid amounted to 2,100 tonnes for 860,000 beneficiaries. The ICRC's activities in Badakhshan started later and have been fairly modest, chiefly because the tasks have been shared with the Federation (the situation in Badakhshan was categorized as non-conflictual) and because of the presence of the Aga Khan Foundation.

As an illustration, during the period December 1992 to March 1993 the ICRC distributed family parcels, clothes, shoes, blankets and plastic sheeting to 35,000 displaced people living in centres in Dushanbe. Some 30,000 other people who had been taken in by their relatives also benefited from ICRC food aid, distributed with the help of the National Society. Another example: in the same period, the ICRC gave wheat and family parcels to over 270,000 displaced people living near the Afghan border, mainly in the Kumsangir region. Finally, in November 1993, in Khatlon Oblast, the ICRC supplemented a UNHCR housing reconstruction programme by distributing plastic sheeting which allowed people to make roofs to protect themselves from the elements.

In carrying out such projects, the ICRC has been faced with several challenges: first of all, the practical difficulties of transporting relief supplies, which were sent directly from Kiev. From a logistical point of view, setting up large-scale operations in an unknown cultural context has not been an easy task.

It then became rapidly apparent that the nutritional content of the family parcels might endanger the displaced people they were intended to help. Certain foodstuffs in the parcels had considerable economic value in the Tajik context, because of the impossibility of finding them on the local market. Moreover, how could the ICRC make the long-time residents of a region understand that it was concerned with displaced people, who were victims of the conflict, rather than the residents themselves, who might be suffering hardship just as severe? This prompted the ICRC to distribute wheat to the entire population of the villages in southern Tajikistan where it was providing aid, with displaced persons receiving additional basic necessities.

Finally, emergency is a relative concept. In Africa, providing emergency food aid means saving human lives. In the Tajik context, as in all the newly independent States, emergency is not defined in such drastic terms. Standards of living in the former USSR were higher before the conflict; and local solidarity had some positive effects. For example, the displaced persons who returned to the south of Tajikistan were sometimes rehoused with families, which made it more difficult to identify them. All things considered, the ICRC was faced with a dilemma: it had either to approach the Tajik problem on the basis of principles developed through its experience in the Third World, or to raise its criteria for intervention. It opted for the second solution.

On the medical front, the ICRC provided medical aid to some hospitals treating war victims, especially the wounded. It also established a mobile clinic in southern Tajikistan, which allowed people who for security reasons were afraid of going to State medical structures for help to have access to the treatment their condition required. At the height of the conflict, it approached the authorities with the request that medical staff who were natives of regions considered hostile and who were working in government-controlled organizations be protected or even, in case of danger, evacuated. In all the ICRC's fields of activity, the protection of individuals remains a central concern.

The ICRC met with the same kind of challenge on the medical front as on the food front in Tajikistan: how could it explain to doctors in hospitals lacking even basic supplies that the ICRC's aid was primarily intended for the war-wounded, and thus limited? It is only in siege conditions or in regions where, because of the conflict, the ICRC is the only organization to have access, that it distributes basic medicines for emergencies not connected with the conflict. It will not consider doing this where the help of other humanitarian organizations, such as MSF, can be enlisted. Yet the needs are immense because of the upheaval caused by the dissolution of the Soviet Union, particularly the collapse of the economy and the disruption of commercial exchanges. But how can the ICRC alone cope with so many needs, which are currently attributable not to the aftermath of the conflict but to the country's state of development?

In Tajikistan, the ICRC encountered a paradox: the hospitals had no shortage of doctors, but the doctors had no resources. The private medical sector was non-existent. It was a question of understanding the complicated administrative procedures and of overcoming difficulties of communication. Moreover, any duplication of the efforts of MSF had to be avoided. The medical activities of the ICRC during the emergency phase certainly contributed to its reputation in the country. They have now been more or less put on hold, as the situation in the country has stabilized.

Teaching through action

In order to act, one has to be known and, in a conflict situation, respected. It is important that the red cross should be a familiar sign to the soldiers manning every roadblock, whether they are official armed forces, independent militias such as those operating in southern Tajikistan, or opposition forces. The red cross must be a symbol of neutrality and impartiality; it is not only access to the wounded which depends on this, but the safety, or even the lives, of ICRC delegates.

For soldiers to be expected to act in accordance with the rules of international humanitarian law, they do not have to be 'taught' the law, but they must be made aware of the fact that respect for humanitarian standards and self-restraint in the conduct of hostilities are in no way incompatible with military requirements. Terror is a means of warfare which is successful only in the short term, and which brings infamy on those who practise it. In the long term, it destroys any possibility of reconciliation. As for weapons which cause excessive suffering, which seventeen States pledged to give up as early as 1868 when they signed the St Petersburg Declaration, their use should be unthinkable in contemporary conflicts.

These messages, which the ICRC spreads on all continents, were brought to Tajikistan by its delegates. Since the beginning of the operation they have used every available opportunity to publicize the nature, the aims and the working principles of the ICRC, both in official circles – in this respect the ICRC's presence at the meeting of the Supreme Soviet in Khojent in November 1992 played a major role – and among private individuals. Television was a favoured medium at the height of the conflict, and ICRC publications in Russian were widely distributed.

In 1993 the ICRC made a major effort in terms of human and financial resources to have its brochures, leaflets and posters printed in Russian for use in all the newly independent States.

The challenge is a considerable one, because the content, if not the very existence, of international humanitarian law is largely unknown throughout the former Soviet Union. There is great interest in the subject, however, as the ICRC had the opportunity to see at a symposium for senior military officers, held in St Petersburg in December 1993. Thirty-two states took part, among them Tajikistan.

In 1993 the ICRC concentrated its efforts on making itself known in Tajikistan. In 1994 the focus should shift to projects designed to disseminate international humanitarian law among the armed forces.

Growing cooperation with the Red Crescent in Tajikistan

The ICRC is part of the International Red Cross and Red Crescent Movement, to which the Federation and the recognized National Societies of 161 countries also belong. Originally the National Societies were created to assist military medical services; after the First World War they took on new tasks which could also be carried out in peacetime, such as helping the elderly and the disabled, training medical staff, first aid, blood transfusion and many other activities.

The Alliance of Red Cross and Red Crescent Societies of the USSR was one of these Societies, which was dissolved at the same time as the Soviet 'empire'. Its former branches, such as the Tajik Red Crescent, have nevertheless continued to offer services to the most needy members of society, notably the help given by nurses to elderly people living alone. Most of these Societies, which in the Soviet era were closely tied to the government health services, are now going through a period of transition.

In order to become full members of the Movement, in which they already participate *de facto*, these Societies have to fulfil a number of conditions set by the International Conference of the Red Cross in 1948. The ICRC is responsible for seeing that the candidate National Societies conform to these conditions.

This is why it is closely following the activities of the Tajik Red Crescent, which it provides with support in three main areas: staff training, achieving greater autonomy *vis à vis* the public authorities, and strengthening operational capacity. The ICRC is currently helping the Society learn how to conduct a tracing operation, to restore links between family members separated by the conflict. It has also made representations to the authorities, urging them to respect the independence of the Red Crescent Society. Finally, it has involved the Red Crescent in some aid programmes in Dushanbe and Kurgan-Tyube, a form of cooperation which has just resumed after a break of several months.

While the ICRC is able to give limited support to the Society in certain areas, it also has the privilege of enjoying the support of a local partner whose knowledge of the cultural background is an asset. When the ICRC took its first steps in Tajikistan, the support of the Tajik Red Crescent was most valuable, especially in contacts with the authorities. In 1994 this cooperation was strengthened, in close liaison with the International Federation of Red Cross and Red Crescent Societies, which over the last few months had been present in regions of the country unaffected by the conflict, working out of its delegation in Almaty.

Towards a reorientation of the ICRC's work in Tajikistan

The presence of the ICRC in Tajikistan has been through several phases. The first, the emergency phase, consisted in large-scale food distributions to people fleeing the fighting, combined with action aimed at ensuring that the physical and mental integrity of those not involved in the hostilities was respected.

During the second phase, the ICRC provided material aid to displaced persons returning to their places of origin in a state of utter destitution, in cooperation with UNHCR, which concentrated its assistance on the Tajik refugees returning from camps in Afghanistan. Here again the safety of those returning home was at the heart of the ICRC's concerns.

Finally, the third and current phase, which could be described as 'post-emergency'. Today, Tajikistan needs development aid above all, and other organizations have already taken over, or are in the process of doing so: PAM, PNUD, the Federation, UNHCR, UNICEF, the Aga Khan Foundation. The ICRC is therefore planning to scale down its activities in Tajikistan, especially as far as food and medical aid are concerned.

The effects of the conflict are still being felt, however, and access to people detained in the course of the events remains a priority for the ICRC, along with the protection of the civilian population and the dissemination of international humanitarian law.

These objectives pose an enormous challenge: it is easier to distribute aid than to intercede for people affected by the conflict or to inform combatants about the rules of conduct. This relationship between assistance and protection of individuals is a familiar debate for the ICRC, which has always favoured protection, while knowing that it is often inseparable from aid.

It should not, however, be forgotten that beyond the words there are human beings, such as the children who have returned to Tajikistan from Afghanistan and whom ICRC delegates are trying to put back in touch with their parents, or the women who have gone back to their villages and for whom the ICRC has provided a roof, or the men reported missing to whom the ICRC is attracting the authorities' attention. May the Committee's work contribute to promoting a spirit of harmony and tolerance for future generations: this is our dearest wish.

Chapter 13

The Human Rights Situation in Tajikistan (1992–1993)

Ian Gorvin

Amnesty International has described the situation in Tajikistan in the period since the start of factional violence in May 1992 as a human rights disaster. Furthermore, this has been a disaster which has been largely ignored by the rest of the world. Appalling human rights abuses by the parties involved have been alleged throughout the armed conflict in Tajikistan, and are continuing. However, information about the true extent of those abuses remains far from complete.

Amnesty International takes no position on the political objectives of the parties to the conflict in Tajikistan. The organisation is working solely to oppose human rights violations, including those resulting from the conflict, which fall within its mandate. In two reports published in 1993 Amnesty International has detailed a wide range of human rights violations in Tajikistan. These fall broadly into three categories:

- Firstly, extrajudicial executions, 'disappearances' and torture on a large scale perpetrated by armed forces either subordinate to, or acting with the complicity or tacit approval of the current government.
- Secondly, the arrest and prosecution of prisoners of conscience, the torture of political prisoners in pre-trial detention, and the imposition of judicial death sentences on people including political prisoners sentenced after possibly unfair trials.
- Thirdly, summary and arbitrary executions by forces apparently subordinate to the self-proclaimed 'government-in-exile' of Tajikistan, based since early 1993 in northern Afghanistan.

In our first report on Tajikistan, published in May 1993 under the title *Hidden Terror: Political Killings, 'Disappearances' and Torture since December 1992*, Amnesty International focused on events which took place mostly in Dushanbe in the weeks immediately after forces loyal to the government elected in Khojent in November took control of the capital. We noted that other human rights abuses as grave as those detailed in the report had been alleged by all sides during other periods of the conflict and in other locations, but at the time of writing it was largely impossible for Amnesty International to obtain verification of those other alleged abuses, or to identify and target the perpetrators. We stressed that the accountability of the current government of Tajikistan for extrajudicial executions and other violations of human rights does not diminish because similar acts are committed by opposition groups.

Amnesty International received what we regard as reliable and consistent reports from a number of sources that in and around Dushanbe, in the period from 10 December to approximately the end of February, scores, possibly hundreds of people, most of them unarmed civilians, had been extrajudicially executed either by government law-enforcement personnel or by pro-government para-military forces, or had 'disappeared' after being taken into custody by such forces. The victims were reported to be mainly people originating from the Garm district or from Gorny Badakhshan who had been targeted because these areas were believed to be centres of opposition support. Journalists identified with the opposition were also targeted for summary execution, or 'disappeared'.

These political killings and 'disappearances' were reported to have followed checks of identity papers during vehicle searches at roadblocks throughout Dushanbe, identity checks at the airport, or house-to-house searches. Eyewitnesses reported incidents in which men in military uniform boarded buses in Dushanbe and removed people they identified either by their appearance or by their personal documents as Pamiris, then shot them on the spot. In one reported case a family of seven people, including an eighty-year-old woman and a child of four, were massacred in their apartment. In other cases, people were detained on the street, in their homes, at their workplaces or at the airport and placed under arrest, and their bodies were found later in the street or in the morgue. Others detained in this way simply 'disappeared', leaving their families suffering the agony of not knowing what has happened to them. Amnesty International has obtained from unofficial sources the names of almost 300 people who allegedly were extrajudicially executed by pro-government forces or 'disappeared' in and around Dushanbe in this period. Some sources put the number of victims at around 2,000 people.

Amnesty International identified the perpetrators of the political killings and 'disappearances' in Dushanbe as forces of the Interior Ministry or of the People's Front of Tajikistan. This paramilitary group drew its members mainly from Kulyab Province in the south of the country, and took a leading role in the assault on Dushanbe in December.

The government consistently denied that its own security forces or agents of the People's Front were responsible for the killings and 'disappearances' in Dushanbe in the period after it came to power. Reacting to Amnesty International's report, the Interior Ministry published a statement denouncing Amnesty International as an organisation whose main aim was 'the publication and dissemination of slanderous material'. The government blamed criminal gangs, and pledged to take action against them. However, the US State Department country report on Tajikistan for 1992 commented that 'well-placed individuals, including some in the Tajikistan government' had stated that forces responsible for these killings and 'disappearances' were acting with the tacit support of senior government officials. A number of factors appear to support the view that these forces were acting at least with the knowledge and complicity of officials, including law-enforcement personnel. For example, eye-witnesses report that these forces were equipped with military hardware including armoured personnel-carriers, and were openly operating roadblocks in Dushanbe and conducting identity checks in places such as the airport. And take for example the following case of a young Pamiri man who recounted his story to a BBC journalist visiting Gorny Badakhshan in April. Three months earlier this young Pamiri had survived summary execution by forces whom he described as being from the People's Front. He recounted how armed men had come to his family's apartment in Dushanbe, beaten him and his family with rifle butts, and taken him and his two older brothers outside at gunpoint. They were bundled into a car, driven to the riverbank and shot. The youngest brother survived because he fell, wounded, under the bodies of the others who were shot dead. Significantly, he reported that the car in which they were taken to the river was twice stopped at roadblocks being operated by Interior Ministry personnel, who did nothing to intervene, ignoring the fact that the three passengers were clearly injured and bleeding from the beating they had just received. He claims that the operators of the roadblocks even joked with his captors about where the brothers were being taken, and what lay in store for them.

Officially, the People's Front no longer exists. Shortly before his death in March, Sangak Safarov announced that it was being disbanded and urged its members to enlist in the government security forces. However, Amnesty International has received persistent reports since then that armed groups of Kulyabis, described as 'pro-government', continue to be active in Dushanbe and in southern Tajikistan, and carry out human rights abuses with impunity. In the report by the CSCE observer mission in Tajikistan, for the period up to October 1993, the mission questioned the seriousness of the government's stated commitment to halt human rights abuses by so-called 'unidentified' groups. Although after February fewer incidents of extrajudicial execution and 'disappearance' came to our attention, Amnesty International received allegations that Kulyabi forces continued to be responsible for politically or ethnically motivated killings, 'disappearances' and rape in Dushanbe and in southern rural areas, where victims included refugees returning to their home areas. There have even been allegations of the maintenance by these Kulyabi forces of unofficial prison camps in which some of the 'disappeared' may be held.

Not only does the government seem unwilling or unable to bring these paramilitary forces under control, but there have even been allegations that the organisers of some of these forces simultaneously hold high office in the government security forces or in provincial government. Such people are alleged to be responsible, for example, for the 'disappearance' of the Shoyev brothers, ethnic Garmis who went into exile in Moscow in January. In June Saidsho Shoyev, who is a Member of Parliament, accepted an invitation to attend the forth-coming session of Parliament from Prime Minister Abdullojonov, who personally undertook to guarantee his safety. Saidsho Shoyev travelled to Dushanbe accompanied by his brother Siyarsho, who was also in exile. In late July the brothers were seized from a street in the centre of Dushanbe by armed men, bundled into a car and driven away. They have not been seen since. Unofficial sources report that from its number plates the car was identifiable as belonging to the Ministry of Defence.

In the second Amnesty International report, published in October 1993 under the title *Human Rights Violations against Opposition Activists*, we featured the cases of a number of people previously active in the opposition parties and movements who are now in detention in Tajikistan.

One of these is the poet Bozor Sobir, who is regarded by Amnesty International as a prisoner of conscience. He was detained without a warrant on 26 March at Dushanbe airport, and was charged on 5 April with 'incitement to illegal deprivation of freedom' and 'attempting to inflame inter-ethnic discord'. The first charge relates to an incident in April 1992 when Sobir, addressing opposition demonstrators in Dushanbe, criticised a group of parliamentary deputies who were subsequently taken hostage. The second charge relates to Sobir's writing, especially a poem entitled 'Mixing Blood with Flour', which the authorities maintain is anti-Russian. However, Amnesty International and other human rights groups take the view that the poem is not an attack on the Russian people but on Russia as an imperialist power and on the effect of that imperialism on Tajikistan. Amnesty International believes that the criminal charges against Sobir are without reasonable foundation. Bozor Sobir was put on trial in the Supreme Court in Dushanbe. Possibly as a result of international pressure on his behalf, Imomali Rakhmonov publicly called on the court not to sentence him to imprisonment.

Amnesty International also learned of the cases of two probable prisoners of conscience who were sentenced in March to prison terms, following separate trials on illegal firearms possession charges. There are allegations that the charges were fabricated to punish these men for their opposition political activities. Democratic Party activist Dzhumaboy Niyazov was sentenced to seven years' imprisonment by the city court in Khojent for illegal possession of cartridges for an automatic weapon, and Rastokhez activist Nuriddin Sadiriddinov was sentenced by the district people's court in Asht, Leninabad Province, to ten years' imprisonment for illegal possession of a pistol and bullets. In both cases sources claimed that the firearms and ammunition had been planted during police searches of their homes.

A number of similar cases have been reported to Amnesty International, all from Leninabad Province, but details remain scarce.

Throughout 1993 Amnesty International continued to call on the authorities to guarantee the physical safety of the political prisoners Mirbobo Mirrakhimov, Akhmadsho Kamilov, Khayriddin Kasymov and Khurshed Nazarov, who had reportedly been severely and persistently tortured in pre-trial detention in Dushanbe. They are all former state broadcasting executives or television journalists who were arrested in January in neighbouring Central Asian countries after fleeing Tajikistan, and handed over to Tajik law enforcement agents. They were charged with calling for the overthrow of the government. Amnesty International first received allegations about the torture of these men shortly after their arrest. All were reported to have suffered beatings during interrogation, as a result of which Khayriddin Kasymov was reported to have suffered a broken nose and had several teeth knocked out. It was also alleged that Akhmadsho Kamilov was not allowed by his interrogators to sleep or to sit for long periods. In August Amnesty International received disturbing new information which suggested that the torture of these men had continued. A delegation from the Russian human rights group Memorial and the US-based human rights monitoring group Helsinki Watch, which visited Tajikistan in May and June 1993, reports that they sought official permission for a meeting with the four prisoners. The investigator in charge of the case, an officer from the Committee for National Security, was prepared to give permission only for the monitors to see these men but not to speak to them. He initially suggested that they would be able to see them at a distance of fifteen metres, but when the delegates refused he attempted to negotiate with them about the distance, finally offering to have the men walk past the delegates at a distance of five metres. He categorically refused a request that the prisoners should be asked to lift their shirts so that a doctor in the delegation could observe the condition of their bodies. The human rights monitors refused to agree to the conditions offered by the investigator, and so no meeting with the prisoners took place. The monitors concluded that the behaviour of the authorities gave great cause to suspect that the prisoners had been severely beaten.

After Amnesty International first publicised its concerns in this case in its May report on Tajikistan, the press centre of the Ministry of Internal Affairs reacted by accusing the organisation of 'shedding crocodile tears about the fact that such-and-such a political prisoner is spending a sleepless night in prison and so-and-so has had his nose broken'. The statement from the Interior Ministry observed that 'prisons are for keeping criminals, and not sanatoria for improving health'.

As an organisation committed to the worldwide abolition of capital punishment, Amnesty International has consistently called on the authorities in Tajikistan to abolish the death penalty, which currently remains in force for eighteen offences in peacetime. Amnesty International knows of six death sentences passed in Tajikistan in 1993. One of those sentenced to death was political prisoner Adzhik Aliyev, an activist of the Islamic Renaissance Party, who was convicted in August for crimes including treason, terrorism and murder, following a possibly unfair trial. It has been reported that the main evidence against Aliyev was a confession which his lawyers allege was made under duress following his arrest in January 1993. It has also been reported that witnesses at the trial in August failed to place Aliyev at the scene of crimes for which he was eventually convicted. Furthermore, Amnesty International was concerned that for around four months of his pre-trial detention Aliyev was not represented by a lawyer, and that this absence of legal representation may have jeopardised the fairness of the investigation of his case and consequently his trial. Adzhik Aliyev remains on death row at the time of writing while his lawyers seek a judicial review of his case.

In a second political case, in late November death sentences were passed on two men accused of organising the assassination in August 1992 of Tajikistan's Procurator-General, Nurullo Khuvaydullayev. Concerns were also expressed by unofficial sources in Tajikistan about the evidence on which at least one of these men, Rakhimbek Nurullobekov, was convicted.

In its October report on Tajikistan Amnesty International also addressed the issue of recent human rights abuses by opposition forces. Specifically, we reported that in June, forces apparently subordinate to the opposition 'government-in-exile' and based in the Kalai-Khumb district of Gorny Badakhshan were alleged to have summarily executed nine government soldiers whom they had taken prisoner. We also reported that in July up to 200 civilian residents of the village of Sarigor in Khatlon Province may have been deliberately killed by opposition forces based in Afghanistan who entered the village after overrunning the nearby 12th Border Post.

In its reports and in individual campaigns undertaken by Amnesty International members worldwide, the organisation has made a number of recommendations to the authorities in Tajikistan. We have called on the government to undertake a full and impartial investigation of all reports of extrajudicial executions and 'disappearances' and to bring those responsible to justice. We called for the immediate and unconditional release of Bozor Sobir, and for judicial review of the cases of Dzhumaboy Niyazov and Nuriddin Sadiriddinov. We also called on the government to ensure that Mirbobo Mirrakhimov, Akhmadsho Kamilov, Khayriddin Kasymov and Khurshed Nazarov were not subjected to torture or any other form of ill-treatment. We called for judicial review of the case of Adzhik Aliyev, and for commutation of all pending death sentences and complete abolition of the death penalty.

Also, Amnesty International has written to the leaders of the Democratic and Islamic Renaissance Parties, as representatives of the self-proclaimed 'Government-in-Exile of the Republic of Tajikistan', expressing concern about the reported summary executions of captured government soldiers and civilian residents of Sarigor. Amnesty International is calling on them to ensure that all armed forces subordinate to or acting with the approval of the 'government-in-exile' respect the Geneva Conventions and other international human rights and humanitarian standards.

Selected Bibliography

AKINER, Shirin. *Central Asia: New Arc of Crisis?*, Whitehall Papers, Royal United Services Institute for Defence Studies, London, 1993.

—— *Islamic Peoples of the Soviet Union: An historical and statistical handbook*, 2nd Edition, KPI Ltd., London, 1986.

ALLWORTH, Edward A. (ed.). *Central Asia: 120 Years of Russian Rule*, Duke University Press, Durham, N. C., 1989.

—— *The Modern Uzbeks from the Fourteenth Century to the Present*, Hoover Institution Press, Stanford, 1990.

Asie Centrale: Aux confins des empires, réveil et tumulte. Autrement, no. 64, October 1992.

ATKIN, Muriel. *The Subtlest Battle: Islam in Soviet Tadjikistan*, University Press of America, 1989.

BARRY, Françoise. 'Les missions de la CEI: un bilan', *Le Courrier des pays de l'Est*, no. 374, November 1992, pp. 55–63.

BAZIN, Louis. 'Les peuples turcophones en Eurasie: un cas majeur d'expansion ethnolinguistique', *Hérodote*, July-September 1986, pp. 75–108.

BENNIGSEN, Alexandre. 'Mullahs, Mujahidin and Soviet Muslims', *Problems of Communism*, November-December 1984, pp. 28–44.

BENNIGSEN, Alexandre and LEMERCIER-QUELQUEJAY, Chantal. *Le mouvement national chez les musulmans de Russie avant 1920*, Mouton, Paris and La Haye, 1960–64.

—— *Les musulmans oubliés, L'Islam en URSS aujourd'hui*, Fraçnois Maspero, Paris, 1981.

—— 'La guerre d'Afghanistan et l'Asie centrale soviétique', *Politique étrangère*, no. 3, 1984, pp. 623–4.

—— *Le soufi et le commissaire. Les confréries musulmanes en URSS*, Seuil, Paris, 1986.

CAGNAT, René and JAN, Michel. *Le Milieu des empires. Entre URSS, Chine et Islam, le destin de l'Asie centrale*, Robert Laffont, Paris, 1990.

CANFIELD, Robert L. (ed.). *Turko-Persia in Historical Perspective*, Cambridge University Press, Cambridge, 1991.

CANFIELD, Robert L. 'Restructuring in Greater Central Asia: Changing Political Configurations', *Asian Survey*, Vol. 32, no. 10, October 1992, pp. 875–901.

CARANTINI, R. *Dictionnaire des nationalités et des minorités en URSS*, Larousse, Paris, 1990.

CARRERE d'ENCAUSSE, Hélène. 'La politique culturelle du pouvoir tsariste au Turkestan (1867–1917)', *Cahiers du monde russe et soviétique*, July-September 1962, pp. 374–407.

—— *Réformes et révolution chez les musulmans de l'Empire russe*, 2nd Edition, Presses de la Fondation national des sciences politiques, Paris, 1981.

—— *La gloire des nations ou la fin de l'Empire soviétique*, 2nd Edition, Fayard, Paris, 1991.

CAVANAUGH, Cassandra. 'Uzbekistan Looks South and East for Models', *RFE/RL Research Report*, 9 October 1992, pp. 11–13.

Cela s'appelait l'URSS et après ... Hérodote, no. 64, January-March 1992.

CENTLIVRES, Pierre and CENTLIVRES-DEMONT, Micheline. *Et si on parlait de l'Afghanistan*, Editions des EHESS, Paris, 1989.

Central Asia. Current History, Vol. 93, no. 582, April 1994.

CHOUKOUROV, Charif and Roustam. *Peuples d'Asie centrale*, Syros, Paris, 1994.

CRAIG HARRIS, Lillian. 'Xinjiang, Central Asia and the Implications for China's Policy in the Islamic World', *The China Quarterly*, March 1993, pp. 111–29.

CRITCHLOW, James. 'Will There Be a Turkestan?', *RFE/RL Research Report*, Vol. 1, no. 28, 10 July 1992, pp. 47–50.

DANNREUTHER, Roland. *Creating New States in Central Asia*, Adelphi Papers, no. 288, London, March 1994.

DASTARAC, A. and LEVENT, M. 'Nouvelle donne stratégique au Pakistan: Islamabad regarde vers l'Asie centrale', *Le Monde Diplomatique*, December 1991.

Des ethnies aux nations en Asie centrale. Revue du monde musulman et de la Méditerranée, no. 59–60, 1991–92.

DJALILI, Mohammad-Reza. 'L'Iran face au Caucase et à l'Asie centrale', *Le Trimestre du monde*, 4th Quarter, 1992, pp. 181–90.

DOR, Rémy, (ed.). *L'Asie centrale et ses voisins*, INALCO, Paris, 1990.

ENCYCLOPAEDIA IRANICA. Vol. V, Part 2, s.v. 'Central Asia', Mazda Publishers, Costa Mesa, California, 1990.

FERRO, Marc. 'Des républiques à la dérive', *Le Monde Diplomatique*, May 1990.

—— (ed.). *L'état de toutes les Russies*, La Découverte/IMESCO, Paris, 1993.

FIERMAN, William (ed.). *Soviet Central Asia: The Failed Transformation*, Westview Press, Boulder, Col., 1991.

FOURNIAU, Vincent. *Histoire de l'Asie centrale*, 'Que sais-je?', PUF, Paris, 1994.

FRANK, Andre Gunder. *The Centrality of Central Asia*, Comparative Asian Studies 8, University Press, Amsterdam, 1992.

FULLER, Graham E. *The 'Center of the Universe': The Geopolitics of Iran*, Westview Press, Boulder, Col., 1991.

—— 'The Emergence of Central Asia', *Foreign Policy*, Spring 1990, pp. 49–67.

GLADNEY, Dru C. *Muslim Chinese: Ethnic Nationalism in the People's Republic*, Harvard University Press, Cambridge, Mass., 1991.

Selected Bibliography

GLEASON, Gregory. 'The Struggle for Control over Water in Central Asia: Republican Sovereignty and Collective Action', *Report on the USSR*, June 1991, pp. 11–14.

—— 'Independent Muslim Republics in Central Asia: Legacy of the Past, Shape of the Future', *Journal of the Institute of Muslim Minority Affairs*, July 1992, pp. 355–75.

GOBLE, Paul A. 'Russia and its Neighbours', *Foreign Policy*, Spring 1993, pp. 79–88.

GOTZ, Thomas. 'Letter from Eurasia: the Russian Hands', *Foreign Policy*, no. 92, Autumn 1993, pp. 92–116.

GRESH, Alain. 'Lendemains indécis en Asie centrale', *Le Monde Diplomatique*, January 1992.

—— 'Les Républiques d'Asie centrale s'engagent sur des chemins divergents', *Le Monde Diplomatique*, December 1992.

GROUSSET, René. *L'Empire des steppes*, Payot, Paris, 1980.

HARRISSON, Selig S. 'L'Afghanistan s'installe dans la fragmentation', *Le Monde Diplomatique*, January 1992.

HAUNER, Milan. 'Soviet Eurasian Empire and the Indo-Persian Corridor', *Problems of Communism*, January–February 1987, pp. 25–35.

—— 'From Soviet Union to Central Eurasia', *The Eurasian Report*, Vol. 2, no. 1, 1992.

HETMANEK, Allen. 'Islamic Revolution and Jihad come to the former Soviet Central Asia: the case of Tadjikistan', *Central Asian Survey*, Vol. 12, no. 3, 1993, pp. 365–78.

HOPKIRK, Peter. *The Great Game: on Secret Service in High Asia*, Oxford University Press, Oxford, 1991.

HYMAN, Anthony. 'Moving out of Moscow's orbit: the outlook for Central Asia', *International Affairs*, 69, 2, 1993, pp. 289–304.

JAHANGIRI, Guissou. 'Le Tadjikistan, éléments pour la construction d'une nation', *Le Trimestre du monde*, 4th Quarter 1992, pp. 154–66.

KAHN, Michèle. 'Les Russes dans les ex-républiques soviétiques', *Le Courrier des pays de l'Est*, no. 376, January–February 1993, pp. 3–20.

KARPAT, Kemal. 'The old and new Central Asia', *Central Asian Survey*, Vol. 12, no. 4, 1993, pp. 415–25.

KOLSTO, Pal. 'The New Russian Diaspora: Minority Protection in the Soviet Successor States', *Journal of Peace Research*, Vol. 30, no. 2, 1993, pp. 197–217.

—— *L'Asie centrale*. Cahiers du monde russe et soviétique, January–March 1991.

—— *L'émergence du monde turco-persan*. Cahiers d'études sur la Méditerranée orientale et le monde turco-iranien, no. 14, 1992.

LOMME, Roland. 'Géopolitique des frontières de la Communauté des Etats Indépendents', *Relations internationales et stratégiques*, no. 5, Spring 1992, pp. 117–35.

LOUGH, John. 'The Place of the 'Near Abroad' in Russian Foreign Policy', *RFE/RL Research Report*, 12 March 1993, pp. 21–9.

MALASHENKO, Alexei, 'L'islam comme ferment des nationalismes en Russie', *Le Monde Diplomatique*, May 1992.

MALIK, Hafeez (ed.). *Central Asia: Its Strategic Importance and Future Prospects*, St. Martin's Press, New York, 1994.

MALTOR, Isabelle and OUYANG Dongfang. 'Chine: nouvelle donne régionale pour le Xinjiang', *Le Monde Diplomatique*, November 1993.

McCAGG, William O., Jr. and SILVER, Brian D. (eds.). *Soviet Asian Ethnic Frontiers*, Pergamon Press, New York, 1979.

MENON, Rajan and BARKEY, Henri J. 'The Transformation of Central Asia: Implications for Regional and International Security', *Survival*, Vol. 34, no. 4, Winter 1992–93, pp. 68–89.

MESBAHI, Mohiaddin. 'Russian Foreign Policy and Security in Central Asia and the Caucasus', *Central Asian Survey*, Vol. 12, no. 2, 1993, pp. 181–215.

MIRSKY, I. George. 'Central Asia's Emergence', *Current History*, October 1992, pp. 334–8.

NOLDE, Boris. *La formation de l'Empire russe. Etudes, notes et documents* (2 vols), Institut d'études slaves, Paris, 1952 and 1953.

OLCOTT, Martha Brill. 'Central Asia on its own', *Journal of Democracy*, Vol. 4, no. 1, January 1993, pp. 92–103.

—— 'Central Asia's Catapult to Independence', *Foreign Affairs*, Summer 1992, pp. 108–30.

—— 'Central Asia's Post-Empire Politics', *Orbis*, Spring 1992, pp. 253–68.

—— 'Soviet Central Asia: Does Moscow Fear Iranian Influence?', in ESPOSITO, John L. (ed.), *The Iranian Revolution and Its Global Impact*, Florida International University Press, Miami, 1990, pp. 203–30.

PANICO, Christopher J. 'Uzbekistan's Southern Diplomacy', *RFE/RL Research Report*, 26 March 1993, pp. 39–45.

PIPES, Richard. *The Formation of the Soviet Union: Communism and Nationalism 1917–1923*, Harvard University Press, Cambridge, Mass., 1954.

POLIAKOV, Sergei. *Everyday Islam: Religion and Tradition in Soviet Central Asia*, M. E. Sharpe, Armonk, N. Y., 1992.

POUJOL, Catherine. 'La Russie, l'islam et les Etats d'Asie centrale', *Les Cahiers de l'Orient*, 2nd Quarter 1993, pp. 112–21.

RO'I, Yaacov. 'Central Asian Riots and Disturbances, 1989–1990: Causes and Context', *Central Asian Survey*, Vol. 10, no. 3, 1991, pp. 21–54.

—— 'The Islamic Influence on Nationalism in Soviet Central Asia', *Problems of Communism*, July-August 1990, pp. 49–64.

—— 'The Soviet and Russian Context of the Development of Nationalism in Soviet Central Asia', *Cahiers du monde russe et soviétique*, Vol. 32, no. 1, January-March 1991, pp. 123–42.

ROY, Olivier. 'Frontières et ethnies en Asie centrale', *Hérodote*, no. 64, January-March 1992, pp. 169–82.

—— 'Géopolitique de l'Asie centrale', *Cahiers du monde russe et soviétique*, Vol. 32, no. 1, January-March 1991, pp. 143–52.

RUBIN, R. Barnett. 'The Fragmentation of Tadjikistan', *Survival*, Vol. 35, no. 4, Winter 1993–94, pp. 71–91.

RUMER, Boris Z. 'The Gathering Storm in Central Asia', *Orbis*, Winter 1993, pp. 89–105.

RUPERT, James. 'Nouvelles donnes en Afghanistan', *Le Monde Diplomatique*, June 1992.

SELLIER, Jean and SELLIER, André. *Atlas des peuples d'Orient. Moyen-Orient, Caucase, Asie centrale*, La Découverte, Paris, 1993.

SHASHENKOV, Maxim. *Security Issues for the Ex-Soviet Central Asian Republics*, Brassey's (for the Centre for Defence Studies), London, 1992.

SMITH, Graham (ed.). *The Nationalities Question in the Soviet Union*, Longman, London and New York, 1990.

TADJBAKHSH, Shahrbanou. 'The Bloody Path of Change: the Case of Post-Soviet Tadjikistan', *The Harriman Institute Forum*, Vol. 6, no. 11, July 1993, pp. 1–10.

VAMBERY, Arminius. *Voyages d'un faux derviche dans l'Asie centrale. De Téhéran à Khiva, Bokhara et Samarcand par le désert turkoman*, Editions Yoz-Feng, Paris, 1987 (reproduction of the original edition of 1873).

WAKIL, Abdul. 'Iran's relations with Afghanistan after Islamic revolution', *Orient*, 32, 1, 1991, pp. 97–115.

MAPS

Tajikistan

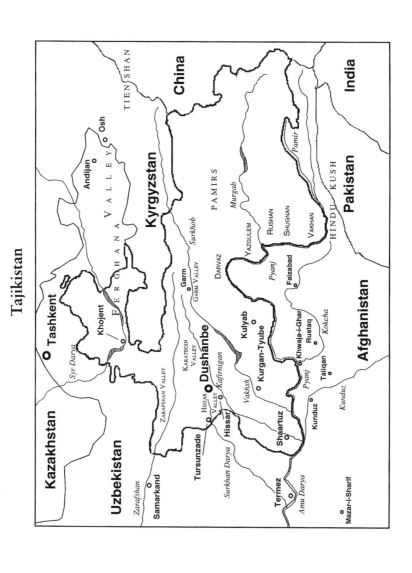

Tajikistan: Administrative Divisions

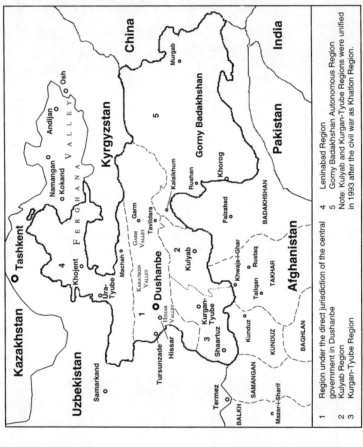

1   Region under the direct jurisdiction of the central
    government in Dushanbe
2   Kulyab Region
3   Kurgan-Tyube Region
4   Leninabad Region
5   Gorny Badakhshan Autonomous Region
    Note: Kulyab and Kurgan-Tyube Regions were unified
    in 1993 after the civil war as Khatlon Region.

Regional Groups or Clans

Drug Trade

Concentration of Tajik opposition fighters and Afghan mujahidin

Established route for drug trafficking, from Afghanistan through Badakhshan to Osh in Kyrgyzstan, then on to Kazakhstan and the other republics

New route for drug trafficking, across central Tajikistan to Kyrgyz districts of Leilek and Batken, then to Osh